Additional Praise From Reengineering Professionals in Many Industries!

"A road map to successful process reengineering."
> —W. T. Johnson, Vice-President Finance
> Grace Logistics Services, Inc.

"Finally, a practical easy-to-understand reengineering guide, rather than a rigid set of rules. The Rapid Re methodology considerably shortens the implementation cycle time, producing faster results."
> —Tony Coalson, Director, Corporate Enterprise Group
> Murata Electronics North America, Inc.

"At last, reengineering is no longer a buzzword. All you need is within these pages."
> —Dr. Marion Bamberger, Market Strategy Manager
> Glaxo Research and Development Limited (United Kingdom)

"A radical and thought-provoking 'journey' for executives willing to see beyond conventional myopia and into value-added business visions and results."
> —Larry Karas, Environmental Supervisor, Advanced Technology
> Group, Hoechst Celanese Corporation

"A valuable bookshelf reference for executives. It provides both a reengineering orientation and a process geared for successful implementation."
> —Bill Quinn, General Manager and Vice-President Professional &
> Printing Imaging, Eastman Kodak & Co., Latin American Region

"A complete guide to the reengineering process from beginning to end—including an example to clearly illustrate each step."
> —Bonnie L. Boccitto, Senior Vice-President
> Prudential Reinsurance Company

"The one basic tool to survive the reengineering process. A must for executive management."
> —Dr. Alex Giaquinto, Vice-President Worldwide
> Regulatory Affairs, Schering-Plough Corporation

"An unpretentious, definitive reengineering guide punctuated with meaningful examples. I found myself frequently referring to it as our reengineering effort took shape."
—Dean Poi, Assistant Vice-President, Life Administration
Provident Life and Accident Insurance Company

"Reengineering at work. An innovative and insightful guide."
—William J. Rauscher, Director, Information Management
Harris Corporation

"*The Reengineering Handbook* is a realistic, value-based business process evaluation tool that's a must for anyone considering reengineering. It's a clear, no-nonsense *Handbook* of what should be done and what shouldn't!"
—Alfred J. Discepolo, Senior Vice-President
Blue Cross/Blue Shield Maryland; Chief Operating Officer
Columbia Medical Plan

"This easy-to-understand book addresses the uncertainties everybody faces when considering and implementing a reengineering program. Following the methodology in the book will make a reengineering program easier, faster, and more successful."
—Dr. John H. Nicholson, Senior Vice-President, Availl, Inc.

"Right on target. An accurate and specific treatise by true practitioners of business process reengineering. Tired of listening to conflicting generalities from industry gurus? Read this book."
—Len Bergstrom, President, Real Decisions
a Gartner Group Company

"A practical and realistic guide. The Rapid Re methodology, outlined and detailed, is the first of its kind and will become the standard platform for reengineering in the 90s."
—Gus P. Nuzzolese, Senior Vice-President, Sutton & Edwards

"This book is a must for those executives who are reengineering their organizations."
—Dr. Donald A. Deieso, President and CEO, Metcalf & Eddy, Inc.

THE
REENGINEERING
HANDBOOK

A STEP-BY-STEP GUIDE TO BUSINESS TRANSFORMATION

RAYMOND L. MANGANELLI
MARK M. KLEIN

American Management Association

New York • Atlanta • Boston • Chicago • Kansas City • San Francisco • Washington, D.C.
Brussels • Mexico City • Tokyo • Toronto

This publication is designed to provide accurate and authoritative information in regard to the subject matter covered. It is sold with the
understanding that the publisher is not engaged in rendering legal,
accounting, or other professional service. If legal advice or other expert assistance is required, the services of a competent professional
person should be sought.

Portions of Chapter 10 are reprinted from Information Strategy:
The Executive's Journal (New York: Auerbach Publications),
© 1994 Warren, Gorham & Lamont. Used with permission.

Library of Congress Cataloging-in-Publication Data

Manganelli, Raymond L.
       The reengineering handbook : a step-by-step guide to business
    transformation / Raymond L. Manganelli and Mark M. Klein.
          p.   cm.
    Includes bibliographical references and index.
    ISBN 0-8144-0236-4
    1. Organizational change—Management.   2. Corporate
    reorganizations.   I. Klein, Mark M.   II. Title.
    HD58.8.M257   1994
    658.4'063—dc20   94-26609
                                                          CIP

Printing number

10   9   8   7   6   5   4   3   2

To
Cathy Manganelli
and
Sheila Paris Klein,
who have encouraged, inspired,
and shared in all of our best work

Contents

Preface

Reengineering, the preeminent business performance improvement technique for the '90s, has achieved a startlingly rapid ascendancy. A reengineering survey conducted by Gateway Management Consulting in 1993 shows that 88 percent of senior executives regard reengineering as their initiative of choice for achieving strategic business goals, as opposed to outsourcing, downsizing, restructuring, or automation.

Why reengineering? The rate of change in the business world has accelerated to the point that initiatives capable of achieving incremental performance improvements cannot keep up. Breakthrough, discontinuous performance gains are the only way to equal or exceed the rate of change going on in the world around us. Reengineering, the rapid, radical redesign of business processes to achieve *breakthrough* performance enhancement, has achieved such performance gains in companies as diverse as GM Saturn, PepsiCo, U.S. Sprint, Conoco and Connecticut Mutual Life Insurance. In its simplest form reengineering changes the business process to fix the fit between the work, the worker, the organization, and its culture to maximize business profitability.

How can it be done? Performance breakthrough achieved through the redesign of work processes can indeed be found by reviewing the history of business, but the achievement of such breakthroughs has been both haphazard and extremely rare. Reengineering, when guided by a formal methodology, puts the achievement of breakthrough performance enhancement on a systematic agenda.

This *Handbook* uses the five-stage Rapid Re™ methodology as its guide. The Rapid Re methodology will guide the reengineering team to Prepare itself, Identify processes to reengineer, En Vision a performance breakthrough, design a Solution capable of achieving that Vision, and Transform the work to implement that Solution. The Rapid Re methodology is designed to be used by businesspeople working with ordinary business tools they already know.

This *Handbook* is a how-to guide for all of the players in a reengineering project from the executives who want to find out quickly if reengineering is right for them, to project leaders who must map out the plan for success, through corporate trainers who must equip the team members for action. Designed to be read by different readers in different ways, the handbook is organized into four sections: Framework for a summary introduction, Methodology for a discussion of each reengineering stage and task, Resources for tools and rules of thumb, and Appendixes for real world examples and reference materials. The entire *Handbook* is organized as stand-alone sections so that readers who have already read the Framework section can read only the subjects that interest them. In short, the *Handbook* is designed to be a long-term reference for success—on your shelf when you need it—and in the hands of you and your staff when you need to reengineer.

Acknowledgments

We acknowledge with much gratitude those who helped make this book possible:

From Gateway:
Cathy Fitzpatrick, Steve Raspa, Jim Bonine, John Girvin, Maureen Cross, and Leslie Kern.

From the American Management Association:
Tony Vlamis, Ed Selig, Kathy Hoes, and Martha Peak.

From our readers, reviewers, and friends:
Bill Johnson (Grace Logistics Services), Dr. Alex Giaquinto (Schering Plough), and Bill Duncan (McDonnell Douglas).

And to all of our clients, colleagues, and comrades, who have the courage, the vision, and the perseverance to embrace change and to achieve breakthrough performance through reengineering.

Uses of This Book

As a consequence of reengineering's rapid climb to widespread acceptance, large numbers of people need to be trained and equipped to reengineer their companies. This *Reengineering Handbook* is just one facet of a series of AMA training programs and reference resources designed to systematically equip organizations and individuals with reengineering knowledge and skills.

The *Handbook* provides how-to guidance for every phase of a reengineering project's life, and for all of its participants from executive project sponsors through corporate trainers. The *Reengineering Handbook* is designed to flexibly support the needs of these various readers, including:

- ❏ Senior executives and others who need to be quickly introduced to the key elements of reengineering
- ❏ Reengineering practitioners, who are provided with detailed discussions of all reengineering activities supported by a completely worked-out example
- ❏ Project leaders, for whom a complete methodology is provided to guide them as they plan and manage reengineering projects
- ❏ Anyone wishing to quickly find and refresh their understanding of any reengineering facet, this handbook is designed to be a quick reference
- ❏ Corporate training leaders using this *Handbook* alone or in conjunction with materials from the AMA's three-day Reengineering Seminars and the AMA's Reengineering Videos and for educators in academia, a worked reengineering problem is provided so they may illustrate key course points using the problem as the example

This *Handbook* is designed to provide readers with as much or as little information as they require and to put the right information at their fingertips quickly. A few simple instructions should help to get you get started.

> First, everyone should *read all* of the Framework section. For many readers that introduction to reengineering will be all the detail they require.
>
> Then, refer to Figure P-1 for a road map of which *Handbook* resources might best meet the needs of you or your coworkers.
>
> Note: After reading the Framework section you will find that any other section can be read on its own on a stand-alone basis. You will be able to find what you need and read only that relevant material.

Throughout the Methodology section, we illustrate the work of each stage and task using the reengineering of The ABC Toy Company (not a single company, but a composite of companies that we have worked with) as an example. In order to get the best understanding of the worked example, a reader may wish to follow it through the whole Methodology section beginning in Chapter 2. But, that is usually not necessary because each of the chapters on stages of the Methodology (Preparation, Identification, Vision, Solution, and Transformation) begins with a recap of the key points of the methodology and the progress of the example up to that point. Each chapter's Recap section will be sufficient background for most readers.

For emphasis, the ABC Toy Company Example text is indented whenever it occurs as follows:

> The ABC TOY Company is a manufacturer of blow-molded and injection-molded plastic figures of cartoon and comic book characters. It sells these figures through a direct sales force to national and regional toy and variety store chains. The business is highly seasonal. Every February, there is a toy fair in New York City at which the toy manufacturers present their new lines to the buyers. Thereafter, customers place opening orders. . . .

A quick lookup matrix of handbook resources in the Framework, Methodology, Resources, and Appendixes sections is presented in Figure P-1.

The major sections of the *Handbook*—Framework, Methodology, Re-

Figure P-1. Quick lookup matrix of handbook resources.

Reader	Framework	Methodology	Resources	Appendixes
Executives	Read for concise summary of key points.			Case Study examples in major industries
Project Team Leaders	Read as necessary introduction to balance of *Handbook*.	Read all of Methodology as planning guide. • Introduction • Preparation • Identification • Vision • Solution • Transformation	Selecting reengineering tools Ten precepts for success Why reengineering projects fail	Case Study examples Summary Outline of methodology for quick reference Related Readings on Reengineering BPR project examples Comparison of BPR approaches
Practitioners	Read as necessary introduction to balance of *Handbook*.	Read Introduction, then go to any Stage or Task and read about that topic only. **Business Roles** • Preparation • Identification • Vision • Solution (Social) **Developer Roles** • Solution (Technical) • Transformation	Selecting reengineering tools Ten precepts for success	Glossary BPR project examples
Trainers	Read as necessary introduction to balance of *Handbook*.	Read Introduction, then refer to worked example to illustrate Methodology.		Glossary BPR project examples
Quick Reference Readers	Read as necessary introduction to balance of *Handbook*.	Go to any Stage or Task and read about that topic only.	Ten precepts for success Why reengineering projects fail Case Study examples by major industry	Summary outline of methodology to look up any task. Related Readings on Reengineering Glossary

sources, and Appendixes—each add another layer of detail to the discussion of reengineering:

❑ The Framework section gives all readers a necessary foundation in reengineering: the history of breakthrough thinking, what reengineering is and is not, why a reengineering methodology is necessary. Finally, the Framework section introduces the Rapid Re methodology for ensuring reengineering project success.

❑ The Methodology section details the life of a reengineering project from Preparation where the team and its charter are formed, through Identification of the business process to be reengineered, to implementation where a new Vision of the improved process is seen, a Solution reflecting that Vision is designed, and the business process Transformed to meet that Vision.

❑ The Resources section describes reengineering resources the team might use, from reengineering project tools to precepts for success.

❑ The Appendixes present examples of successful reengineering projects across major industries and a comparative review of reengineering methods plus supporting reference materials including a Summary Methodology Outline, a Glossary, and a bibliography of related readings.

In summary, to use this *Handbook,* first read the Framework section, then any other part of the *Handbook* may be read on its own.

Section I

Framework

1

The Business Process Reengineering Framework

A Historical Perspective

"Is breakthrough thinking new?" This question is the most frequently asked about business process reengineering (BPR). In order to answer this question, it is useful to move back in time to 1898 and the Spanish-American War. During the Spanish-American War, the U.S. Navy fired, in total, 9,500 shells. Only 121 of these shells—1.3 percent—hit anything at all. While this batting average by today's standards appears to be disastrous, in 1898 it represented world-class performance; the United States did indeed win the Spanish-American War.

In 1899, in a further display of its then prevailing leadership in naval gunnery accuracy, the U.S. Navy held an exhibition target practice to benchmark its performance. In a total of twenty-five minutes of firing at a target ship at a distance of approximately one mile, exactly two hits were registered and those were to the sails of the target ship. Yet by 1902 (Figure 1-1), the U.S. Navy could hit a similar target ship every time it fired; half the shells could hit a square fifty inches on each side.

What could possibly have caused such remarkable breakthrough performance results in so short a time? To answer this question, we need to examine the story of a young naval artillery officer named William Sowden Sims. Most people have never heard of William Sowden Sims. And yet it could be said that he changed the world. He did it through a process that we now call *reengineering*. A century ago, aiming a gun on

Figure 1-1.   1902.

the high seas was a haphazard affair. The gun, the target, and the seas all around were in constant motion. The traditional heroes in naval combat were ship navigators who maneuvered the ships in and out of position, giving the gunners a chance to go about their clumsy business. But, while on maneuvers on the China Seas, Sims noted some of the breakthroughs in accuracy that British gunners had begun to accomplish with only slight adjustments to the way they targeted and fired. Sims began to wonder what would happen if these innovations were developed further and put to use aboard American ships. The process elements for naval artillery were fairly simple a century ago: There was a gun, a crank to elevate the gun to the appropriate trajectory to fire a shell the normal range of one mile, and a telescope mounted on the barrel of the gun in order to keep the target in sight until just before the firing recoil. Sims discovered a very simple way to dramatically improve the gun's aim, a way that would compensate for the height and timing of the ship's roll.

First Sims suggested adjusting the gear ratios so that the gunner could easily raise and lower the gun to follow a target throughout the ship's roll. Second he advocated moving the gun sight from the barrel so that the gunner would not be affected by the gun's recoil. This innovation allowed the gunner to maintain sight of the target throughout the act of firing. The result: continuous aim firing.

According to calculations performed by Sims in his extensive notes, he predicted that his modifications to the process had the potential to increase accuracy by over 3,000 percent, without additional cost, without the use of additional technology, and without the need for additional manpower. Excited about the opportunity of bringing such a process performance breakthrough to the navy, Sims wrote a letter to his superiors.

In the minds of his superiors, William Sims was an "irritant"; his letter went without response. Sims, however, did not stop at one or two letters to the navy's chief officers. Over the course of two years, he sent over a dozen letters, each one imploring them to listen to what he believed to be groundbreaking ideas for change, ideas that could radically alter and improve the performance of the navy's artillery. But his suggestions were largely ignored. And no wonder—the navy had just come off one of the largest victories in its history.

To understand why Sims's first dozen letters fell on deaf ears, it is useful to examine the organizational structure of the navy in 1902 (Figure 1-2). Navigators dominated the line command of the navy because navigation was the key to victory. Since for many years, navigators had to compensate for the inaccuracy of the artillery, navigation was cele-

Figure 1-2. The organization.

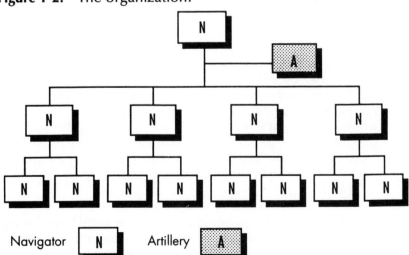

Navigator   N   Artillery   A

brated as the differentiating skill that would ensure victory. Navigators occupied the most important positions in the navy.

Sims's letters were rejected for several reasons:

- ❑ If it could be done, someone would be doing it already.
- ❑ If it could be done, a navigator would have thought of it.
- ❑ If it is done, what would be the impact on the navy's organizational structure?

Sims persevered. He never lost sight of his goal. He sent his thirteenth letter to the then commander-in-chief, President Theodore Roosevelt. Upon reading Sims's letter proposal, Theodore Roosevelt was amazed. Roosevelt had become a national hero during the Spanish-American War. He understood military issues, and he understood the powerful potential of Sims's idea if this breakthrough change were pursued vigorously.

Roosevelt took action. He immediately responded to Sims's letter, and he ordered the distribution of Sims's report to every officer in the U.S. Navy. The consequent breakthroughs in productivity were enormous, equaling Sims's predicted 3,000 percent!

Eventually, Sims redirected the course of navy training and retooling, rose to the rank of admiral, and served as president of the Naval War College. What began as an attempt to change the way navy guns were fired ultimately changed the navy itself. Never again was the platform and navigation as important as the weapons it carried. Continuous aim firing changed the entire organizational fabric of the U.S. Navy and, in turn, every other navy in the world.

The lessons that we can learn from the Sims story include the following:

- ❑ *Reengineering and breakthrough innovation are not new.* What is new is the willingness of many senior corporate executives to apply these techniques to their businesses.
- ❑ *Breakthroughs occur through "vision."* Sims was able to break through the boundaries of conventional thinking that had limited performance for previous decades and was able to "see" the potential for radical improvement where others had only "looked."
- ❑ *Organizational intractability is always the number one obstacle.* The world is filled with navigators who seek to bury breakthrough ideas under a mountain composed of the not-invented-here syndrome, self-interest, and parochial concerns.

❏ *Senior management sponsorship is essential.* Only a Teddy Roosevelt-like senior-level executive can empower a reengineering team to implement the technical and organizational changes required to achieve breakthrough performance.

❏ *The change agent is usually an outsider or a "contrarian."* Often, the best ideas for change issue from a member of the organization who is not part of its legacy power structure.

❏ *Benchmarking has its limits.* Even when you are a world-class performer, there may still be opportunities for 3,000 percent improvement in the process.

❏ *Ambition can be as powerful a motivator as pain and fear.* Organizations should not look to reengineer only when they are in trouble; performance breakthroughs can also be achieved by a thriving organization that wants to stay on top.

❏ *Perseverance is the greatest virtue.* Breakthrough ideas are not always adopted the first time they are proposed. (Sims wrote thirteen times!)

❏ Three thousand percent improvement is possible. Reengineering performance goals are not incremental goals: They seek breakthrough performance outcomes that can be stated as "better than our organization has ever done or ever thought it could do."

Getting to Know About Reengineering

The story of William Sowden Sims is a wonderful illustration of the potential and precedent for achieving breakthrough performance enhancements through work process revision. Today, we would call Sims's improvement to the naval gunnery process reengineering. Although the act of achieving breakthrough performance enhancement through process redesign is not new, reengineering, the systematic method for achieving those enhancements, is new and needs concise definition. In the following discussion we:

❏ Establish reengineering's definition.
❏ Examine the backdrop of trends against which reengineering is performed.
❏ Compare reengineering to other improvement programs.

Reengineering Definitions

Reengineering is the rapid and radical redesign of strategic, value-added business processes—and the systems, policies, and organizational structures that support them—to optimize the work flows and productivity in an organization. Let us begin the examination of this definition by looking at the definition of a process.

A process (Figure 1-3) is an interrelated series of activities that convert business inputs into business outputs. Processes are composed of three primary types of activities: value-adding activities (activities important to the customer); hand-off activities (activities that move work flow across boundaries that are primarily functional, departmental, or organizational); and control activities (activities that, for the most part, are created to control the handoffs across the boundaries previously described).

Figure 1-4 illustrates how a process winds its way—inefficiently and ineffectively—through the many boundaries and controls of most existing corporate organizations. Every boundary creates a handoff and usually two controls: one control for the person handing off and the second control for the person receiving. Therefore, the more serpentine the process flow within an organization—that is, the more boundaries that a process must traverse as it winds its way through a corporation—the more nonvalue-adding activities are present within a process.

Our definition of reengineering differentiates between process types. Through rapid and radical redesign we seek to change not all processes within an organization but only those that are *both* strategic and value-added.

The kinds of process classifications in an organization are shown in Figure 1-5. Strategic processes are those that are of essential importance to a company's business objectives, goals, positioning, and stated strategy; strategic processes are integral to how a company defines itself.

Figure 1-3. What is a process?

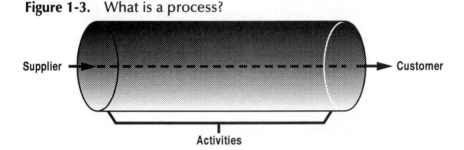

A process is an interrelated series of activities that convert business inputs into business outputs (by changing the state of relevant business entities).

Figure 1-4. Process flow—where processes fit into your current organization.

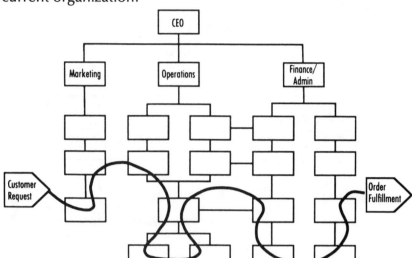

Value-added processes are processes that are essential to a customer's wants and needs and that a customer is willing to pay for; they deliver or produce something that he or she cares about as part of the product or service offered.

Figure 1-6 shows where we look to identify processes to reengineer. The primary targets of business process reengineering (BPR) are processes that are both strategic and value-added. If most corporate business units can be functionally decomposed into twelve to twenty-four processes, usually no more than a half dozen are both strategic and value-added. To achieve maximum return on our investment in reengineering, it is both logical and prudent to begin by focusing on the most important processes in the corporation.

In BPR, we look not only at the strategic, value-added business processes but also at all of the systems, policies, and organizational structures that support these processes:

❑ Systems supporting process activities range from data processing and management information systems (MISs) on the one hand to social and cultural systems on the other hand.
❑ Policies supporting process activities normally embody the written rules and regulations that prescribe conduct and behavior with regard to how the work is done.

Figure 1-5. Strategic value-added processes—are all processes in an organization of equal importance?

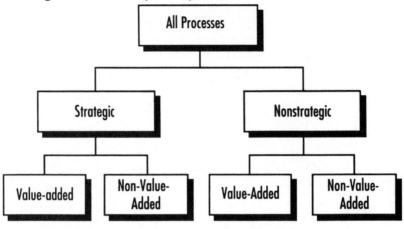

Figure 1-6. Selecting processes—how do we decide which processes to reengineer?

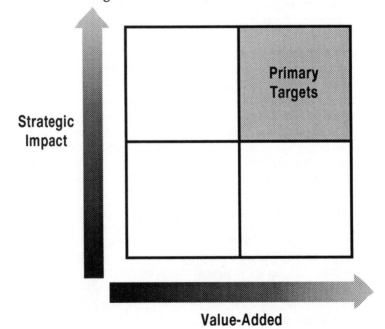

❏ Organizational structures supporting process activities are the work groups, departments, functional areas, divisions, units, and other containers into which workers are divided as they attempt to pursue their work.

A process cannot be changed unless all the supporting elements are changed as well. Therefore an essential early step of a reengineering effort is to clearly identify and quantify all of the resources in a corporation that are dedicated to each specific process.

Our definition of reengineering expects to produce the optimization of work flow and productivity in an organization. This optimization is measured in terms of business outcomes: by increases in profitability; in market share; in revenue; and in return on investment, equity, or assets. Conversely, reengineering can be measured by reduction in cost, whether it be total cost or unit cost.

A most important element of BPR is the deliberate and explicit mapping of these business outcomes, which senior executives sponsoring the program care about, with process outcomes, which the reengineering team is looking to optimize. Without establishing this explicit, quantifiable link between business and process outcomes, reengineering programs are doomed to fail. Process outcomes—measured in speed, accuracy, and cycle-time reduction—are not ends in themselves; they are merely means to the end of improved business performance as measured by the normal financial parameters used to measure corporations. (It is important to note here that in government and nonprofit organizations, business outcomes are measured not in revenue and profit terms but in terms of such parameters as the number of customers served by a program or the number of cases successfully disposed of.)

Using BPR, we expect to achieve these breakthrough business performance goals—levels of performance we have never been able to achieve and never thought we could—by identifying our strategic, value-added processes and applying to them a rapid and radical redesign:

❏ Reengineering must be done *rapidly* because senior executives require results in shorter time frames than ever before: Reengineering programs inevitably fail if they take too long to produce any results.

❏ Reengineering programs need to be *radical*—that is, results must be notable and even perhaps remarkable—because the process is difficult and will never get the requisite executive sponsorship and sanctioning without the promise of more than simply incremental results.

❑ Reengineering mandates a *redesign* of processes focused on identifying and enhancing the value-added activities in a process and attempting to eliminate everything else.

So we can see that in order to fulfill all the elements of our definition of business process reengineering, we need to identify:

❑ The breakthrough business results that are the objective and goal of our reengineering effort
❑ The business processes—usually twelve to twenty-four in total—that represent all of the activities that we perform in producing the product or service in our business
❑ The strategic value-added business processes—that is, the subset of all processes that are important both to our corporate strategy and to our customers
❑ The supporting elements—that is, the systems, policies, and organizational structures that exist in order to enable our strategic, value-added business processes
❑ A definition of "rapid" (our customized definition of what a suitable time frame is to us) and "radical" (our customized definition of what breakthrough change means to us) "redesign"

The activities that we defined previously as reengineering must be performed against a backdrop of senior management attitudes and business realities that govern and affect how reengineering projects may be successfully delivered. In the next sections we review this backdrop of trends and compare the differing way that reengineering and other productivity improvement programs respond to those trends.

Reengineering Trends

Drawing on extensive surveys of senior executives conducted in 1992, 1993, and 1994 (Corporate Reengineering Survey, Gateway, 1993 and 1994; Corporate Strategic Initiatives Survey, Gateway, 1992) we have identified a number of important trends occurring in today's business environment regarding reengineering:

❑ Reengineering is the number one initiative taken by senior executives to achieve their strategic goals (Figure 1-7).
❑ Competition, profitability, and market share are the issues cited most frequently by senior executives for turning to business process reengineering (Figure 1-8).

Figure 1-7. Initiatives taken by senior executives for achieving strategic goals.

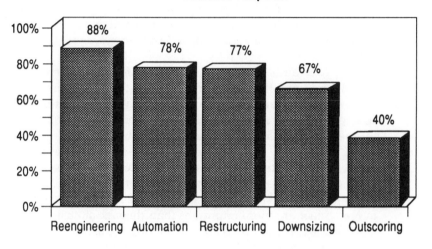

Database Response

Figure 1-8. Reasons cited by senior executives for BPR.

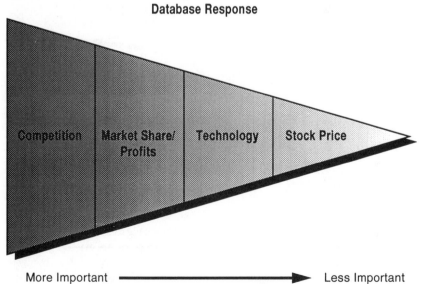

Database Response

❏ The majority of executives expect to see business process reengineering results in one year or less (Figure 1-9).

❏ Almost half of the executives will turn to a reengineering program if it can affect at least 10 percent of their revenue or expenses; almost 90 percent of executives will turn to reengineering if it will affect 25 percent of revenue or expenses (Figure 1-10).

❏ Almost two-thirds of all reengineering efforts are interdepartmental and cross-functional (Figure 1-11); the consensus is that understanding markets and customers is the most critical process to reengineer for most senior executives (Figure 1-12).

❏ Business goals, such as increasing profitability, increasing customer satisfaction, decreasing costs, and increasing revenue, are more important to executives in reengineering than process goals such as increasing accuracy and speed (Figure 1-13).

❏ The organizational impact of reengineering and the time it takes to reengineer are more important than the risk or cost of reengineering when executives are considering sponsoring a reengineering project (Figure 1-14).

Figure 1-9. Timeframe in which executives need to see results.
Database Response

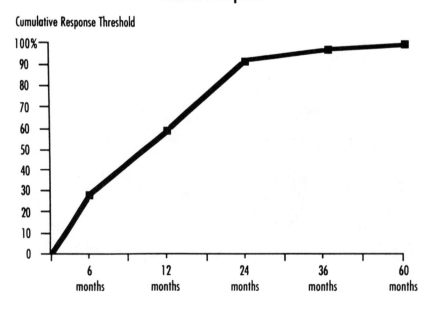

Figure 1-10. Percentage of revenues or expenses needed to be impacted.

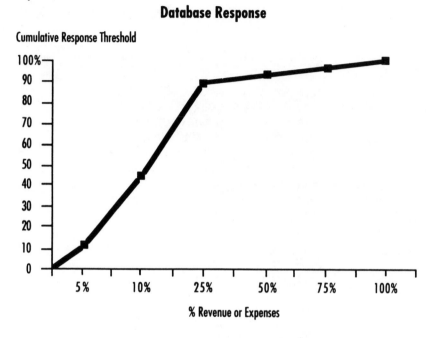

Database Response

Cumulative Response Threshold

% Revenue or Expenses

Figure 1-11. Focus of BPR improvement efforts.

Database Response

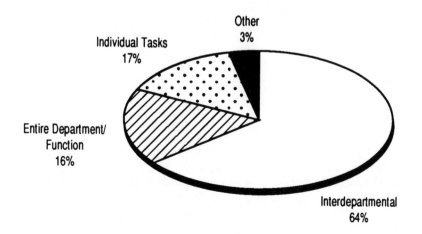

Figure 1-12. Critical processes to business strategy and customers.

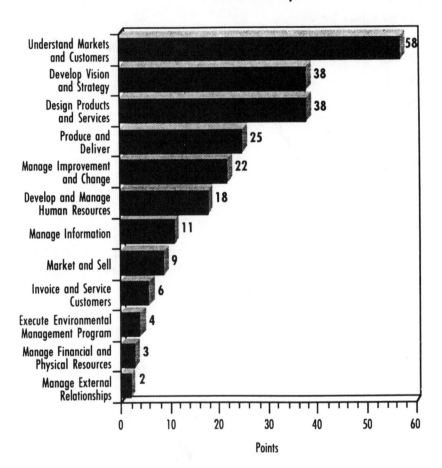

Database Response

Reengineering responds to evolving trends in the business environment where more traditional incremental improvement programs fail.
In many cases, only reengineering promises sufficiently rapid and radical change to keep up with the changing business environment.

Figure 1-13. Goals important to organizations.

Figure 1-14. Obstacles to reengineering.

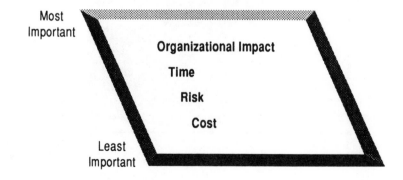

Reengineering vs. Incremental Improvement Programs

Reengineering is about radical change. And if there is one thing that most of us know from experiences with our own organizations, it is that they do anything and everything possible to avoid radical change. Continuous incremental improvement—in direct contrast to BPR—is more in line with how organizations naturally deal with change (Figure 1-15). Continuous improvement places emphasis on small, incremental changes; the object is to improve on what an organization is already doing.

These incremental changes to improve business performance typically take one of several forms, e.g., quality, automation, reorganization, downsizing, rightsizing. But what happens when you apply continuous improvement techniques in a business world where the rate of change is no longer continuous? You wind up with a landscape littered with failed improvement programs. The failure of so many continuous incremental improvement programs is not the failure of the good people trying to make these programs work. The failure results instead from a

Figure 1-15. Reengineering vs. other programs.

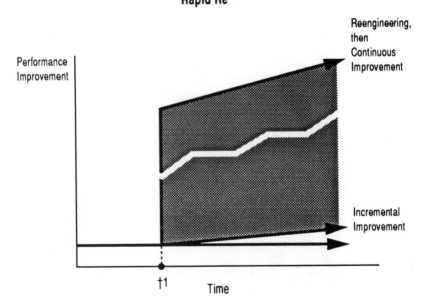

Rapid Re™

world that suddenly demands breakthroughs in place of incremental changes.

BPR differs from continuous incremental improvement programs in several important ways. (Figure 1-16). BPR is:

❏ Not just automation, although it often uses technology in creative and innovative ways.
❏ Not just reorganization, although it almost always requires organizational change.
❏ Not just downsizing, although it usually improves productivity.
❏ Not just quality, although it is almost always focused on customer satisfaction and the processes that support it.

BPR is a balanced approach that may contain elements of these more traditional improvement programs with which it is often confused (Figure 1-17). But BPR is also much more.

First, BPR seeks *breakthroughs* in important measures of performance rather than incremental improvements. Second, BPR pursues multifaceted improvement goals, including quality, cost, flexibility, speed, accuracy, and customer satisfaction, *concurrently*, whereas the other programs focus on fewer goals or trade off among them.

In order to accomplish these results, BPR adopts a *process perspective* of the business, where the other programs retain functional or organizational perspectives. (TQM—total quality management—does examine the processes, but to incrementally improve them, not to reengineer

Figure 1-16. Reengineering vs. other programs.

	Reengineering	Rightsizing	Restructuring	TQM	Automation
Assumptions Questioned	Fundamental	Staffing	Reporting Relationships	Customer Wants and Needs	Technology Applications
Scope of Change	Radical	Staffing, Job Responsibilities	Organization	Bottom-up	Systems
Orientation	Processes	Functional	Functional	Processes	Procedures
Improvement Goals	Dramatic	Incremental	Incremental	Incremental	Incremental

Figure 1-17.   Reengineering vs. other programs.

them.) It also involves a willingness to rethink how work should be done, even to totally discard current practices if that should prove necessary. Finally, BPR takes a *holistic* approach to business improvement, encompassing both the technical aspects of processes (technology, standards, procedures, systems, and controls) and the social aspects (organization, staffing, policies, jobs, career paths, and incentives). In other words, *business process reengineering leverages technology and empowers people.*

Although the definition and benefits of BPR are clear, that does not mean that the way to achieve those benefits is obvious. Influenced by the need for radical redesign, the need to rethink the entire business process, we might feel that the best way to do this would be to start fresh with a clean piece of paper. But we will see in the following section that this intuitively appealing approach of starting with a clean sheet of paper is the wrong way to do reengineering. Just as we would not begin a trip into unfamiliar territory without a road map, we should not begin a reengineering project without a methodology to show us the way.

Methodology vs. a Clean Sheet of Paper

Mozart, it is said, wrote his musical compositions only once, and on a clean sheet of paper, without any subsequent changes. Michaelangelo, before him, contended that he was able to visualize a completed statue within the uncut block of marble. The works of these two masters were considered breakthroughs in their respective fields. We marvel at their creations to this very day. Although few of us see ourselves as Mozarts or Michaelangelos, we all have the creative urge. We take exceptional pleasure in seeing the results of our own thoughts take concrete form as books, drawings, systems designs, and, yes, reengineered business processes. And what better starting point for this creative exercise than the "clean sheet of paper"?

The Misguided Lure of the "Clean Sheet"

Most people believe that artists produce masterpieces on clean canvases rather than use a paint-by-numbers approach. Seeing ourselves in the role of creators, or at least as competent artists, the clean-sheet approach has considerable appeal:

- ❏ Clean sheets offer an unrestricted opportunity for creativity: There appear to be few rules or limitations, no dumb questions, and no useless answers.
- ❏ Clean sheets allegedly promote new thoughts, as the bromide of the '70s contended: "Today is the first day of the rest of your life."
- ❏ With a clean sheet, there seems to be a complete lack of corporate baggage. We do not feel bound by past cultural paradigms. We can begin by discarding all of the outdated ideas of the past, along with unimaginative corporate mindsets and the parochial issues of the turf wars.
- ❏ Supposedly, clean sheets produce a vision of the future unimpeded by the way things happen now. After all, aren't current processes, procedures, and systems the problem?

We contend that *the lure of the clean sheet is indeed a false one.* We see it as an approach that can produce an exhilarating start on a clear day, followed by too many nights bumping into things in the dark. We will be more specific about this later in this chapter, but for the moment, it should be observed that Michaelangelo made preliminary sketches of his paintings and sculptures, and he made a lot of them before he was satisfied with his plan for the final masterpiece. And, for all we know, Mozart, genius that he was, may have quietly burned the contents of his wastebasket.

Methodology's Bad Rap

In contrast to the attractive, unfettered nature of a clean-sheet approach to BPR, most of us take a dim view of methodologies. We have used many of them for all kinds of work and we think we know them quite well. And this knowledge does not please us. Our perception of methodologies tends to be negative:

- ❑ First of all, we see unwanted restrictions inherent in a set of rules that dictate what we will do, how we will do it, and when we will do it.
- ❑ Next, we assume that methodologies are inflexible and have a very narrow focus: we tend to feel that they lead us to look for solutions or end results with blinders on. We assume that methodologies will always find what is obvious from the beginning. No chance of a breakthrough here! We may even think that the authors of a methodology begin by defining the desired result and then constructing a process to arrive at that end.
- ❑ Finally, and most importantly, methodologies are considered to be basically unimaginative. Since methodologies impose a step-wise process, there is no opportunity to really think, and isn't that the key to finding the breakthroughs?

Our philosophy holds that this is an incorrect and unfortunate view and unfairly disparages the value of the methodology as a good and appropriate tool. The negatives we see are probably the result of poor experiences, where we used flawed or inappropriate tools and got corresponding results. But, all is neither black nor white.

The clean-sheet approach is undeniably attractive, but its flaws are fatal. It appeals to our need to create, to innovate, to find the things that others have missed. It represents an absence of constraints, a divorce from the outmoded thoughts of the past. It does not look backward, only forward. *It is, however, an illusion.* It is far more difficult than it appears.

Ideas, even revolutionary ones, are not developed in a vacuum. Our thinking (or creativity, if you will) needs a frame of reference. We need to know what is being done, or has been done, in order to understand the way in which current practice fails.

In addition, we do need some kind of discipline so that we can order our thoughts and draw valid conclusions based on facts. If we sit in front of our clean sheet waiting for lightning to strike (the appearance of the breakthrough idea), we are more likely to experience the business analyst's equivalent of writer's block, not knowing when, where, or how to put pen to page.

Further, *the clean-sheet is more properly matched to a single visionary.* Reengineering, on the other hand, is a team activity. The reengineering process is difficult enough without having to evaluate and mediate the differences between multiple visionaries, each possibly pursuing very different, personal visions. Group dynamics being what it is, one "head visionary" will tend to emerge legislating oblivion for contrary visions. There is a real need to avoid this kind of tyranny and come to closure on specific issues, so that the group can move forward together. The clean sheet, by its very lack of discipline and process, does not satisfy these needs.

Unless deliberately structured to include specific checkpoints and feedback loops, *the clean-sheet approach is effectively uncontrolled.* It will lack ongoing validation of results, the opportunity for course corrections when needed. The sponsoring team must take the process on faith and wait for the final results.

At the same time, not all methodologies are good. The fault lies not so much in the idea of a methodology as in the way they are constructed and employed. In developing the Rapid Re methodology, we had in mind the classic definition of methodology: a systematic or clearly defined way of accomplishing an end (which can be applied to a science or an art). The "good" methodology is a road map that will help you get to where you want to go. It is not a description of what you will find when you get there. This distinction is crucial for any methodology, particularly in one designed for reengineering. Rapid Re does not have a preconception of what business process breakthroughs are but instead provides a process to help the analyst find the radical change that will make the competitive difference. As with any good road map, the methodology contains built-in protections against missing key road signs and blundering off in the darkness and confusion of a wrong turn. You always know where you started, where you want to go, and where you are at the present time.

A methodology such as Rapid Re provokes thought as opposed to constraining this essential process. In Rapid Re the reengineering team is prompted to understand, think about, and question such things as:

☐ Corporate and process strategies
☐ Customer expectations and perceptions

❑ Value-added aspects of core processes
❑ Potential for radical change
❑ Shortcomings of current processes and the potential for radical change
❑ Vision of what can be if customer expectations are met and shortcomings eliminated
❑ Opportunities for process combination and integration
❑ The contributing role of support processes
❑ Use (leveraging) of technology to enable radical change
❑ Organizational restructuring and process management
❑ Positioning and empowering the human resource
❑ SubVisions and implementation alternatives

Rapid Re does not provide *answers* for any of these topics but rather a means or manner of thinking about them: how to cast off unimportant limitations and how to evaluate opportunities, how to see and understand (vision) the nature and implications of change.

Any good methodology either produces an implementation plan or develops a set of considerations that will drive a subsequent plan. If you can't describe how to make the change (simple or radical), it will not happen. Certainly senior management will not bless (read "fund") the change.

In the end, it all comes down to producing a business case for any recommended change: what needs to happen, why it must happen, how it will occur, what it will take (time, resources, management, and cost) and the timing and quantification of tangible results. Only an appropriate methodology will develop this analysis in such a way (and in sufficient organized detail) as to convince the decision makers to proceed. The clean-sheet approach may intuitively feel good, but that will not be enough. The bright new thought may be right on the money, but it will usually require too great a leap in belief for the sponsoring team to literally "bet the company" and commit to its implementation without the structural support that a methodology invites.

Intuition vs. Method

Proponents of the clean-sheet or intuitive approach to reengineering believe that unrestricted use of imagination is the path to breakthroughs in business processes. We frequently liken this to the quest for the Holy Grail: an overpowering and compelling vision, but one that has not yet been realized. One knows what one wants, but how to get it remains a mystery.

As attractive as this unrestrained exercise in creative thinking may be, its limitations are severe: suitability only for small organizations and simple processes, nearly impossible to use as a team technique, difficult to reproduce as it lacks process and discipline, no checkpoint to ensure that original goals are being followed, insufficient detail for the required business case, and no basis for a credible transition and implementation plan. The lure of this intuitive process is unmistakable, but the reality is sobering.

The Rapid Re methodology, on the other hand, ensures you of a process that will guide you in selecting the best path from its road map, developing the necessary information to proceed, and providing ample opportunity to think rather than to accept the obvious.

How to Select a Methodology

What Exactly Is a Methodology?

Simply stated, a methodology is a systematic or clearly defined way of accomplishing an end. It is also a system of order in thought or action. When describing methodologies tailored just for BPR, we will be more specific. Our definition contains the further specifications that a successful methodology for BPR must:

❑ Begin with the development of a clear statement of corporate goals and strategies.

❑ Consider satisfying the customer as the driving force behind these strategies and goals.

❑ Address business processes, rather than functions, and align process and corporate goals.

❑ Identify value-added processes, along with those support processes that contribute to that value.

❑ Make appropriate use of proven and available management techniques and tools to ensure the quality of both information used and BPR "deliverables."

❑ Provide for the analysis of current operations and identification of processes that are not value-added.

❑ Provide for the development of "breakthrough" visions that represent radical, rather than incremental change; foster and provoke thought as the means of attaining and evaluating these visions.

❑ Consider solutions in which employee empowerment and technology are the basis for implementing the changes.

❑ Provide for the development of a complete business case to provide convincing information and arguments to the decision makers.

❑ Develop an actionable implementation plan to specify tasks, resources, and timing of events, following approval.

What Can You Expect From Using the "Right" Methodology for BPR?

At base, any good methodology should be a road map, that is, a
guide to finding the right path or road to our destination. This is opposed to some concepts of a methodology that are based on a description of what we will find when we get to our goal. In this last instance,
there is a predetermined result looking for the road that leads to it.

The methodology that suits our needs should guide us in developing complete and consistent answers, where the questions are pertinent
to the issue at hand. Information that is interesting in itself but not useful for reducing our issues to a solution merely wastes our efforts and
tends to confuse the analytic process that is at the heart of a good methodology.

Notice that we have twice used the word *guide*. This is deliberate.
The good methodology is just that—a guide—rather than a rigid set of
rules that must be followed exactly and in an inflexible order. This is
hardly analysis and certainly not *thinking*. If the methodology does not
permit let alone encourage thinking, then we shall only find the answers
that were predetermined by the author of the methodology.

When we consider appropriate methodologies for reengineering,
we will expect that they will feature both the empowerment of the human resource and the use of information technology as the prime enablers of radical change. At first it would seem that we have contradicted
ourselves here. Having previously said that a methodology should be a
guide for analytic thinking without a built-in bias toward an answer, we
now insist that our methodology use employee empowerment and information technology as accepted (actually, expected) features of the
reengineered process. This is not as inconsistent as it may seem for these
reasons:

❑ Reengineering begins from the premise that work has dramatically changed since the Industrial Revolution, when efficiencies and productivity were gained by breaking a job down into small individual tasks
that could be performed repetitively by low skilled labor.

❑ The pyramidal hierarchy of management needed to supervise and control workers who know nothing more than their own simple task is now itself hopelessly inefficient, having grown layer by layer as organizations expanded the size of the single-task labor force (the base of the pyramid). This type of management and supervisory organization expends most of its energies and time in elaborate controls and layer-to-layer communications, with unavoidable delays in decision making of all kinds. Given that work has already changed (with multiple tasks now contained within individual jobs), the old management structure is inappropriate. The exact opposite, *empowering* employees, will move decision making, communications, and control down to the level where the work is being done. This will make dramatic improvements in process time and efficiency.

❑ In any reengineered process, we are looking for radical change. Not only do we want to transform the way value-added processes work (tasks, responsibilities, sequences, etc.), but we need to make significant differences in the time it takes to respond to customers and market changes. Information technology (computing and communications) is the primary means of doing this.

What a BPR Methodology Will Not Do

No methodology of this kind should be a substitute for thinking. There are methodologies of the "shake the box, pour out the pieces, and they will assemble themselves into the answer" variety. That is definitely not what you want a reengineering methodology to do. It is critical that the methodology provide a vehicle for the analytic thought process rather than be a surrogate analyst.

Properly constructed, a BPR methodology is designed to guide the reengineering of business processes. Nothing else. It is not a means of resolving other important, but unrelated business issues, such as debt restructuring, new product development, business acquisitions, or global marketing strategies. BPR is concerned with the business process itself. When the process is "reengineered" correctly, optimal results should follow.

Methodology Selection Criteria

In addition to being a road map and a guide to business process reengineering, the most appropriate methodology should have other specific characteristics that are important to the BPR process and that will provide you with an effective and efficient tool. These criteria are used to evaluate methodologies that you will consider using. You should be looking for a methodology that:

❏ Is appropriate to the work at hand. In this we mean a true BPR methodology, not merely reworked industrial engineering or software engineering.

❏ Is flexible enough to address a range of applications, that is, not specific to just a service industry or a manufacturing/distribution company. It is also important that the methodology allows for skipping tasks that do not apply to your situation or those that represent work already completed. Flexibility is also required with regard to the order in which certain tasks are performed (within reason, of course) without compromising the final results.

❏ Is established in the market. Both vendor and methodology should have a positive reputation and track record. You want a methodology that has been used successfully by organizations like yours and in similar situations.

❏ Is learnable, in that it can be used by reengineering team members after a modest amount of training. This allows your organization to do the process reengineering without having to be totally dependent on outside "experts."

❏ Fixes roles and responsibilities of all those who will be involved in the BPR: reengineering team members and team leaders, sponsors, information systems management, stakeholders, suppliers and partners, and consultants.

❏ Identifies specific problems or opportunities by defining a business-oriented starting point of corporate goals and strategies, along with the extent to which current process goals and strategies are misaligned.

❏ Identifies key data for decision making, leading to the reengineered management structure and essential controls.

❏ Provides opportunity and guidance for analysis, prompting the reengineering team to question all aspects of business processes and their activities, both as they exist now, and later, once they have been reengineered.

❏ Provides a mechanism to identify and evaluate alternative visions of a reengineered process, with both a rating and ranking scheme.

❏ Determines valid performance measures to characterize current process characteristics, process goals derived from corporate goals, and the projected performance of the reengineered process.

❏ Produces actionable results by identifying action plans, responsibilities, resource requirements, priorities, dependencies, etc.

❏ Produces "affordable" results—those which satisfy the sponsoring team's original guidelines for acceptable reengineering costs, risks, and benefits realization time frames.

❏ Is complemented by support, in the form of training, third-party guidance and review, reengineering team membership, facilitation, and other type of consulting assistance.

❏ Has either a built-in tool set for reengineering team productivity or is adaptable to other commercially available tools (word processing, spreadsheets, databases, presentation graphics, data modeling, etc.)

We have discussed a selection process for a BPR methodology in the context of its purpose and use. We have emphasized the fact that radical change will place considerable stress on an organization. With this in mind and given that so many reengineering projects either fail outright or produce less-than-satisfying results, BPR cannot be classified as a low-risk undertaking. We believe that an appropriate methodology can provide the critical insurance against such mischances once the project has been started.

The Rapid Re Methodology

The big bang theorists contend that all matter that now exists was formed when the universe was formed, that none will be lost from here on out, and that no new matter will be created. If you subscribe to that theory, then whatever BPR actually is, it can't be anything new. In fact, on a less than cosmological level, many reengineering approaches are considered merely a repackaging of existing techniques under a name that suggests innovation but is really something of a deception.

The Rapid Re methodology *is* composed of a number of management techniques with which you are probably familiar. In fact, we are counting on just that familiarity to convince you that:

❏ Existing management techniques (process modeling, performance measurement, work flow analysis, to name a few) produce worthwhile results, although they are not ends in themselves as far as BPR is concerned.

❏ There is no need to invent any new techniques, as there are more than enough available for our purposes, and those that we have selected produce dependable results that have gained acceptance in both business and information systems.

❏ The Rapid Re methodology appropriately integrates and uses a number of these important techniques to develop and analyze the key information that allows us to identify opportunities for the radical change of value-added business processes. This integration has been done in a way that allows information to flow freely through the various stages of the methodology without restatement or any time-consuming translation.

❏ The resulting Methodology has a value that exceeds that of all of the "embedded" techniques.

Overview of Rapid Re

Rapid Re is a five stage, fifty-four-step methodology that enables organizations to achieve swift, substantive results by making radical changes in strategic value-added business processes. Included in the methodology is a set of integrated management techniques that are used to develop and analyze the information needed to identify opportunities and reengineer core business processes. The methodology has been designed to be used by reengineering teams in business organizations, without heavy dependence on outside experts. Each of the five stages addresses a logical part of the reengineering process and produces results that are used by subsequent stages. In brief, these stages are:

❏ *Stage 1—Preparation:* Appropriately begins with the development of an executive consensus on breakthrough business goals and objectives that represent the purpose for the existence of this reengineering project. Preparation also clearly establishes the essential linkage between breakthrough business goals and reengineered process performance, and defines project parameters regarding schedule, cost, risk, and organizational change. The Preparation Stage also assembles and trains the reengineering team and produces the initial change management plan.

❏ *Stage 2—Identification:* Develops a customer-oriented model of the business; identifies strategic value-added processes; and maps organizations, resources, and volumes to specific processes and priorities, and recommends specific processes as the highest impact reengineering targets.

❏ *Stage 3 — Vision:* Looks for the breakthrough opportunities in the processes; analyzes and structures them as "visions" of radical change.

❏ *Stage 4 — Solution:* Is actually divided into two nearly parallel substages: one to develop the technical design needed to implement the visions, and the other, the "social" design, which organizes and structures the human resources that will staff the reengineered process.

❏ *Stage 5 — Transformation:* Realizes the process visions (and subvisions for multiyear transitions), launching pilot and full production versions of the new processes.

We now look at how management techniques are used in these stages of the methodology. Before we begin, it is important to distinguish between several classifications of management techniques:

❏ Individual formal, procedural techniques are well-defined step sequences that produce a tangible result, such as process modeling, benchmarking, and work flow analysis.
❏ A combination of several procedural techniques under one descriptive title, such as information engineering, organizational restructuring, and project management.
❏ Nonprocedural techniques, such as motivation or facilitation.

Stage 1: Preparation

The purpose of this first stage is to mobilize, organize, and energize the people who will perform reengineering. This stage will produce a mandate for change; an organization structure and charter for the reengineering team; a game plan. In this stage, the management techniques identified in Figure 1-18 are used as follows:

❏ *Goal Seeking* is truly the foundation that establishes the corporate goals and objectives with which the various business processes must be aligned.
❏ *Facilitation,* which is used continuously during the lifetime of the reengineering project, is used here to assist management in making clear statements of corporate goals (particularly those related to customer satisfaction) and quantifiable objectives for such things as market share or profit margin.
❏ *Team Building* is directed toward organizing the members of the reengineering team into a working group and training them in

Figure 1-18. Stage 1: Preparation—management techniques.

Task	Management Technique
1.1 Recognize Need	
1.2 Develop Executive Consensus	• Facilitation • Goal Seeking
1.3 Train Team	• Team Building • Motivation
1.4 Plan Change	• Change Management • Project Management

the methodology. Included here also are the roles and responsibilities of all team members and others who are involved in the
overall project (sponsors, customers, partners, consultants, facilitators, etc.).

❑ *Motivation* is important in the development of interest and enthusiasm in the sponsors and reengineering team members to
encourage them to seek and understand the opportunity for
breakthrough changes.

❑ *Change Management* starts here with the development of the
change plan. In its original form, approximate time frames are
established for each activity of the project, and specific milestones, or review dates, are set for just the first stage. The
change plan will evolve in substance and detail as the project
progresses.

❑ *Self Assessment* analyzes the organization's strengths and weaknesses. Topics examined have included organization life cycle,
formal organizational structure, jobs/tasks and work, people,
and the organization's culture.

❑ *Environmental Assessment*, which is directed toward identifying
the external forces with which the business must contend. These
forces may offer either threats or opportunities to the business.
Such external forces include: economic, political, legal, social,

ethical, and technological forces at both the domestic and global levels.

❏ *Project Management* begins with this initial stage and continues throughout the project, requiring project leadership, planning, reporting, team member guidance, and issue resolution.

Stage 2: Identification

The identification stage develops an understanding of the business's customer-oriented process model. Identification produces definitions of customers, processes, and performance measures, and identifies value-adding processes. Typical work products of this stage include organization process maps, resource lists, volume and frequency data, and, most importantly, the designation of the processes to reengineer.

In this stage, several management techniques are used to gather data that will describe work as it is now being done. In many instances, subsequent stages will use the same techniques to support analysis of that data. The management techniques identified in Figure 1-19 are used as follows:

❏ *Customer Modeling* is perhaps the most crucial technique and is the first item of work for the team. The objective here is to gain a complete understanding of the customers, their relationship to the organization, and most important, their expectations. This is essential to identifying the value-added aspect of business processes, the extent to which they must change.

❏ *Performance Measurement* and *Cycle Time Analysis* are used in two ways: (1) to define the customer's performance expectations and (2) to quantify the measures of how work is now being performed (volumes, process times, etc.), identifying problems as they become apparent.

❏ *Process Modeling* produces graphic representations of individual processes and subprocesses showing the sequence of activities, identifying inputs and outputs and critical factors for success.

❏ *Supplier Integration and Partnership Programs* are used to extend the process model to include the relationship of suppliers and other business partners to the various processes.

❏ *Work Flow Analysis* complements process modeling, operating on the business model to identify critical activities necessary to make the process work and those which add value.

❏ *Organizational Mapping* takes the specific tasks and activities as-

Figure 1-19.   Stage 2: Identification—management techniques.

Task	Management Technique
2.1 Model Customers	• Customer Modeling
2.2 Define and Measure Performance	• Performance Measurement • Cycle Time Analysis
2.3 Define Entities	• Process Modeling
2.4 Model Processes	• Process Modeling
2.5 Identify Activities	• Process Modeling • Process Value Analysis
2.6 Extend Process Model	• Process Modeling • Supplier Integration & Partnership Programs
2.7 Map Organization	• Process Modeling • Workflow Analysis • Organizational Mapping
2.8 Map Resources	• Activity Based Cost Accounting
2.9 Prioritize Processes	• Process Value Analysis

sociated with processes and documents the actions taken and the responsibilities of various elements of the existing functional organization.

❑ *Activity-Based Cost Analysis* quantifies the labor costs associated with specific process tasks, based on current work volumes and staffing.

❑ *Process Value Analysis* is used to prioritize the processes based on the assumed potential of a process to meet the corporate goals and objectives. The analysis also considers the size of the improvement opportunity and the time, cost, and risk factors associated with radical change.

❏ *Change Management, Project Management,* and *Facilitation* are continuing techniques in this stage.

Stage 3: Vision

The purpose of this stage is to develop a process vision capable of achieving breakthrough performance for the processes selected to be reengineered. This stage identifies current process elements, problems, and issues; comparative measures of current process performance; improvement opportunities and objectives; definitions of what changes are required; and produces statements of the new process "vision." In this stage, the management techniques identified in Figure 1-20 are used as follows:

❏ *Work Flow Analysis* is used to further analyze the process in terms of the individuals performing discrete tasks and the technology (of any type) now being used. The process flow is now detail-mapped to identify inputs and outputs by activities and steps. For selected processes, the time dimension of the process will be investigated in detail.

❏ *Process Value Analysis* inspects the activities of each process to determine which have an impact on the value-added worth of the process itself. The impact can be positive or negative. Cycle time analysis is likewise employed in this evaluation of positive and negative impacts.

❏ *Benchmarking* is used to quantify existing performance factors, and where possible, compare them against competitors' practices. Benchmarking's most important role here, however, comes in producing new, fresh, creative ideas for optimizing a process.

❏ *Visioning* is the overall activity that describes the nature of a radically changed process composed of only those tasks and activities that actually add value. Visions can be described as the ideal process that would result if all performance measures were optimized. In the process of visioning, several alternate visions can be described and evaluated. The overall vision is for the complete change in the process. SubVisions are those transition

Figure 1-20. Stage 3: Vision—management techniques.

Task	Management Technique
3.1 Understand Process Structure	• Work Flow Analysis
3.2 Understand Process Flow	• Work Flow Analysis
3.3 Identify Value-Adding Activities	• Process Value Analysis • Cycle Time Analysis
3.4 Benchmark Performance	• Benchmarking
3.5 Determine Performance Drivers	• Work Flow Analysis
3.6 Estimate Opportunity	• Cycle Time Analysis
3.7 EnVision the Ideal (External)	• Visioning • Supplier Integration & Partnership Programs
3.8 EnVision the Ideal (Internal)	• Visioning
3.9 Integrate Visions	• Visioning
3.10 Define SubVisions	• Visioning

steps through which the total vision may be accomplished in stages over several years.

❑ *Change Management, Project Management,* and *Facilitation* are continuing techniques in this stage.

Stage 4A: Solution: Technical Design

The purpose of this stage is to specify the technical dimension of the new process. This specification will produce descriptions of technology, standards, procedures, systems and controls employed; designs for the interaction of social and technical elements; preliminary plans for development, procurement, facilities, tests, conversions, and deployment. In this stage, the management techniques identified in Figure 1-21 are used as follows:

☐ *Work Flow Analysis,* when used in this stage, analyzes the linkages among processes to identify opportunities for movement of steps, responsibilities, etc.

Figure 1-21. Stage 4A: Solution: Technical Design — management techniques.

Task		Management Technique
4A.1	Model Entity Relationships	• Information Engineering
4A.2	Re-examine Process Linkages	• Work Flow Analysis
4A.3	Instrument and Informate	• Information Engineering • Performance Measurement
4A.4	Consolidate Interfaces and Information	• Information Engineering
4A.5	Redefine Alternatives	• Information Engineering
4A.6	Relocate and Retime Controls	• Information Engineering
4A.7	Modularize	• Information Engineering
4A.8	Specify Deployment	• Information Engineering
4A.9	Apply Technology	• Information Engineering • Strategic Automation
4A.10	Plan Implementation	• Strategic Automation • Project Management

❑ *Information Engineering* is used in a variety of ways in this stage in defining the technical solution, particularly, where and how to apply technology as an enabler to implement the activities and steps of the revised (reengineered) process. These technologies range from management information through telecommunications, data capture, and expert systems. Information Engineering also is used to identify the elements of information in the system, the interrelationships of these information elements, and their relationships to the processes and activities which produce and consume them. These interrelationships suggest the necessary partitioning of the technical design into design units to support individual processes and activities. Information Engineering further specifies the interactions among these units so that system functions may be achieved.

❑ *Performance Measurement* helps identify appropriate places for process controls and performance data capture.

❑ *Strategic Automation* considers how the technical solution can be accomplished, addressing technology deployment and implementation options (use or adapt existing systems, replacements, outsourcing, etc.).

❑ *Change Management, Project Management,* and *Facilitation* are continuing techniques in this stage. Change management in particular will develop the implementation plan for the technical design solution.

Stage 4B: Solution: Social Design

The purpose of this stage is to specify the social dimensions of the new process. This stage produces descriptions of organization, staffing, jobs, career paths, and incentives employed; designs for the interaction of technical and social elements; and preliminary plans for recruitment, education, training, reorganization, and redeployment. In this stage, the management techniques identified in Figure 1-22 are used as follows:

❑ *Employee Empowerment* is used to define the responsibilities, particularly decision making, that can be redeployed to the level of the employee to move these actions close to the work being done.

Figure 1-22. Stage 4B: Solution: Social Design—management techniques.

	Task	Management Technique
4B.1	Empower Customer Contact Personnel	• Employee Empowerment • Skill Matrices
4B.2	Identify Job Characteristic Clusters	• Skill Matrices
4B.3	Define Jobs/Teams	• Team Building • Self Managed Work Teams
4B.4	Define Skills and Staffing Needs	• Skill Matrices
4B.5	Specify Management Structure	• Organizational Restructuring • Self Managed Work Teams
4B.6	Redraw Organizational Boundaries	• Organizational Restructuring • Organization Mapping
4B.7	Specify Job Changes	• Skill Matrices
4B.8	Design Career Paths	• Skill Matrices • Broadbanding
4B.9	Define Transitional Organization	• Organizational Restructuring
4B.10	Design Change Management Program	• Change Management
4B.11	Design Incentives	• Employee Rewards and Incentives
4B.12	Plan Implementation	• Project Management

❏ *Skills Matrices* are used to map required skills for each new position and define the job characteristic clusters that will give form to the process teams.

❏ *Team Building* now defines and structures the needed process teams, in terms of resources, responsibilities, staffing.

❏ *Self-Managed Work Teams* determine the way in which each process team will manage (plan, control, decide, etc.) the work produced by the team and the working of the team itself. This technique will also be used to explore the extent to which this approach is actually feasible.

❏ *Organizational Restructuring* and *Organizational Mapping* will now be used to "redraw" the organization that is appropriate to the management and operation of the new process.

❏ *Job Production* will be used to determine the skill needs and knowledge needs of each of the newly defined positions.

❏ *Broadbanding* can be used as a technique to design compensation systems based on similar payment for comparable work and responsibilities as opposed to hierarchical job titles.

❏ *Change Management, Project Management,* and *Facilitation* are continuing techniques in this stage. Change management in particular will develop the implementation plan for the social design solution and identify any barriers to change (along with possible "interventions" needed to remove such barriers).

❏ *Employee Rewards and Incentives* are used to break down some barriers to change and retain certain current operating expertise during the Transformation Stage.

Stage 5: Transformation

The purpose of this stage is to realize the process vision. This final stage produces pilot and full production versions of the reengineered process(es) and continual change mechanisms. In this stage, the management techniques identified in Figure 1-23 are used as follows:

❏ *Process Modeling* is used to complete the design of the business system. In doing so, it will model subprocesses and data, along with specific designs for applications, dialogs, and screens/reports, etc.

❏ *Information Engineering* will now implement the technical design from Stage 4A, by selecting technology platform(s), designing data structures and system structures, and defining prototypes

Figure 1-23.   Stage 5: Transformation—management techniques.

Task	Management Technique
5.1 Complete Business System Design	• Process Modeling
5.2 Perform Technical Design	• Information Engineering
5.3 Develop Test and Roll-Out Plans	
5.4 Evaluate Personnel	• Skill Matrices
5.5 Construct System	• Information Engineering
5.6 Train Staff	• Team Building • Just-In-Time Training
5.7 Pilot New Process	
5.8 Refine and Transition	
5.9 Continuous Improvement	• Continuous Improvement • Performance Measurement • Project Management

and roll-out plans. These designs can guide in-house system developers or be used as RFP (request for proposal) for outside assistance as appropriate.

❑ *Skills Matrices* in their final use, now address specific personnel and the strategies necessary to train or retrain them in order to place them in appropriate positions on the new teams. This can be viewed as a form of gap analysis.

❑ *Team Building* now comes full cycle and is used to organize and train the new process teams in their reengineered work assign-

Figure 1-24. Utilization of management techniques in Rapid Re.

Management Technique	1. Preparation	2. Identification	3. Vision	4A. Technical Design	4B. Social Design	5. Transformation
Project Management	X	X	X	X	X	X
Change Management	X	X	X	X	X	X
Facilitation	X	X	X	X	X	X
Goal Seeking	X					
Team Building	X				X	X
Motivation	X					
Customer Modeling		X				
Performance Measurement		X		X		X
Cycle Time Analysis		X	X			
Process Modeling		X				X
Process Value Analysis		X	X			
Supplier/Partner Programs		X				
Workflow Analysis		X	X	X		
Organizational Mapping		X				
Activity Cost Accounting		X	X			
Benchmarking			X			
Visioning			X			
Information Engineering				X		X
Strategic Automation				X		
Employee Empowerment					X	
Skill Matrices					X	X
Self-Managed Work Teams					X	
Organizational Restructuring					X	
Broadbanding					X	
Employee Rewards/Incentives					X	
Organization Mapping					X	
Technical (JIT) Training					X	

ments and functions as a team. Where appropriate, additional training will address specific technical aspects of the work, such as just-in-time concepts and operations.

❏ *Continuous Improvement* is now initiated as a program to identify and capitalize on opportunities for incremental improvement, following the implementation of the reengineered process(es).

❏ *Performance Measurement* assesses the actual quantifiable improvements that have been realized. This is done on an ongoing basis, since some key benefits will depend on the customer's reaction to the changes made.

❏ *Change Management, Project Management,* and *Facilitation* are continuing techniques in this stage. Change management is particularly important to charting the course through the transition of the old to the new and reengineered processes.

A summary of the management techniques used in the five stages of Rapid Re is charted in Figure 1-24.

Section II

Methodology

2

The Five Stages of Rapid Reengineering

We call our business process reengineering (BPR) methodology *rapid reengineering* or *Rapid Re* because it is designed to produce substantive results quickly, usually in six months to one year (See Figure 2-1.)

Gateway research has shown that senior managers of most companies have low tolerance for long projects, no matter how substantial the eventual benefits. Instead, they prefer quick wins, which may lay the foundation for future successes. At the same time, reengineering projects usually raise the level of stress in organizations, while everybody waits nervously to see how the project will affect them. Shorter projects shorten the period during which this stress must be endured. Rapid Re is grounded in these realities and so is designed to produce results rapidly. This is not to say that all of the improvement opportunities from a reengineering project can be attained within a year. Rather, Rapid Re is designed to realize those benefits that can be achieved in those time frames and then to set the stage for further improvement.

Rapid Re consists of five stages: Preparation, Identification, Vision, Solution, and Transformation. The stages are designed to be performed consecutively. The Solution stage is further divided into Technical Design and Social Design, the two of which are performed concurrently. The end of each stage represents a major milestone in the reengineering project. The stages are further divided into tasks—fifty-four tasks in all (see Figure 2-2).

Rapid Re can be customized to the needs of each reengineering project. Individual projects will skip, rearrange, or recombine tasks to meet individual needs or will give greater or lesser emphasis to some

(Text continues on page 50.)

Figure 2-1. Sample timeline.

Step	Month 1	Month 2	Month 3	Month 4	Month 5	Month 6	Month 7	Month 8	Month 9	Month 10	Month 11	Month 12

1. Preparation

2. Identification

3. Vision

4. Solution

5. Transformation

Near-term opportunities

Longer-term opportunities:
First SubVision

Figure 2-2. Stages and tasks.

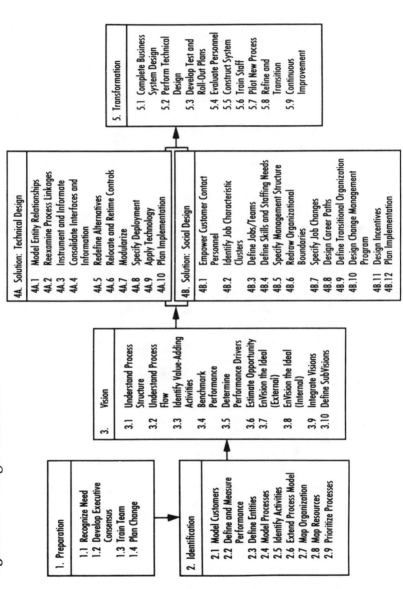

1. Preparation

1.1 Recognize Need
1.2 Develop Executive Consensus
1.3 Train Team
1.4 Plan Change

2. Identification

2.1 Model Customers
2.2 Define and Measure Performance
2.3 Define Entities
2.4 Model Processes
2.5 Identify Activities
2.6 Extend Process Model
2.7 Map Organization
2.8 Map Resources
2.9 Prioritize Processes

3. Vision

3.1 Understand Process Structure
3.2 Understand Process Flow
3.3 Identify Value-Adding Activities
3.4 Benchmark Performance
3.5 Determine Performance Drivers
3.6 Estimate Opportunity
3.7 EnVision the Ideal (External)
3.8 EnVision the Ideal (Internal)
3.9 Integrate Visions
3.10 Define SubVisions

4A. Solution: Technical Design

4A.1 Model Entity Relationships
4A.2 Reexamine Process Linkages
4A.3 Instrument and Informate
4A.4 Consolidate Interfaces and Information
4A.5 Redefine Alternatives
4A.6 Relocate and Retime Controls
4A.7 Modularize
4A.8 Specify Deployment
4A.9 Apply Technology
4A.10 Plan Implementation

4B. Solution: Social Design

4B.1 Empower Customer Contact Personnel
4B.2 Identify Job Characteristic Clusters
4B.3 Define Jobs/Teams
4B.4 Define Skills and Staffing Needs
4B.5 Specify Management Structure
4B.6 Redraw Organizational Boundaries
4B.7 Specify Job Changes
4B.8 Design Career Paths
4B.9 Define Transitional Organization
4B.10 Design Change Management Program
4B.11 Design Incentives
4B.12 Plan Implementation

5. Transformation

5.1 Complete Business System Design
5.2 Perform Technical Design
5.3 Develop Test and Roll-Out Plans
5.4 Evaluate Personnel
5.5 Construct System
5.6 Train Staff
5.7 Pilot New Process
5.8 Refine and Transition
5.9 Continuous Improvement

tasks. Furthermore, while the limitations of written language make it appear that each task within a stage is performed sequentially, the task ordering is only partial. Some tasks may be moved ahead of other tasks, some may be performed concurrently, some may be performed iteratively, and others not at all. Some tasks may even be moved between stages. For example, the full methodology assumes that Stages 1 and 2 (Preparation and Identification) have as their scope all of the key processes within a company. Stage 2 then ends with the prioritization of processes to reengineer. Then stages 3, 4, and 5 (Vision, Solution, and Transformation) are repeated for each process (or group of processes) selected for reengineering.

But sometimes (depending most often on who is the sponsor of the reengineering project) the scope of the project is not the entire company. It may be the processes of a business unit, a division, or even a functional department. Or, the specific process(es) to be reengineered may have been preselected. In these cases, the way in which the reengineering team is organized and the way in which it uses Rapid Re will both differ from what is described here.

Rapid Re does not assume any particular organization for the reengineering project team, although we give our recommendations in connection with Task 1.3. In particular, Rapid Re does not specify a specific outside consulting involvement. It is designed to be used by managers and professionals in most American companies without specialized consultants.

Companies have used Rapid Re themselves, with no outside help, after attending our American Management Association seminars. In other companies, the entire project team was trained by consultants who thereafter facilitated the work of the project team. In yet other companies, consultants are integral parts of the reengineering teams. Since Rapid Re is designed to be used in all of these settings, it must be accessible to the layperson.

For the same reason, Rapid Re was designed to require very few tools. Rapid Re can be performed with a pencil, paper, a flowcharting template, and a few simple paper forms. Although graphically enhanced for publication, the illustrations in this section were originally created with just such simple tools.

On a slightly more sophisticated level, spreadsheet programs can be used with Rapid Re for all the quantitative tasks, as well as for the presentation of qualitative data in tabular form. Project management programs can be used not only for planning and tracking the reengineering project, but also for simple process flow diagrams. Or, Rapid Re can be used with any or all of the categories of reengineering tools described in Chapter 9, which discusses where each tool can be used.

To illustrate the Rapid Re methodology, we use an extended example, The ABC Toy Company. This is not a single company but rather a composite of companies we have worked with as consultants. The example is somewhat simplified but retains enough characteristics of a real company that it illustrates all of the points we wish to make.

The ABC Toy Company is a manufacturer of blow-molded and injection-molded plastic figures of cartoon and comic book characters. It sells these figures through a direct sales force to national and regional toy and variety store chains. The business is highly seasonal. Every February there is a toy fair in New York City at which the toy manufacturers present their new lines to the buyers. Thereafter, customers place opening orders, to be delivered by Thanksgiving, for the Christmas selling season, which accounts for over one-third of annual sales. As store level or distribution center stocks fall, the buyers place reorders. All in all, ABC receives 80 percent of its orders in the last six months of the year. At present, ABC has $50 million in annual sales and 500 employees.

Until 1990, ABC had a 50 percent market share, with the balance going to its arch-competitor, XYZ Plastics. While ABC manufactures in the United States, XYZ sources its production in the Far East. As a result, XYZ's prices were somewhat lower than ABC's. But also as a result of the long lead times to place production orders and the long shipping times from the Far East, XYZ would often find itself with insufficient or "wrong" stock. That is, it was unable to fill customers' orders.

Since 1990, however, XYZ has improved its performance in filling customers' orders while keeping its prices below those of ABC. Consequently, ABC has lost market share, which is now 40 percent.

Using the ABC Toy Company as our subject, let us look at each of the five stages of Rapid Re starting with Stage 1: Preparation.

3

Stage 1: Preparation

The purpose of Stage 1 is to mobilize, organize, and energize the people who will perform reengineering. The Preparation stage produces a mandate for change; an organization, structure, and charter for the reengineering team; and a game plan.

The key questions answered by this stage include:

❑ What are senior executives' objectives and expectations? What is their level of commitment to this project?
❑ What should be the goals for this project? How aggressive can we make them without sacrificing realism?
❑ Who should be on the team? What mix of skills/capabilities should be represented on the team?
❑ What skills/capabilities are not represented by team members? How can they be developed or acquired?
❑ What reengineering skills will team members need to learn?
❑ What will we need to communicate to employees to earn their support and trust?

Stage 1, Preparation, consists of four tasks:

❑ Recognizing the need
❑ Developing executive consensus
❑ Training the reengineering team
❑ Planning the change

TASK 1.1—RECOGNIZE NEED

The need for reengineering is usually recognized as a result of a change: a market change, a technology change, or an environmental change. As a consequence of this change, a senior manager (the "sponsor") motivated by pain, fear, or ambition resolves to do something: reengineer. At this point the sponsor often recruits a facilitator.

Companies don't undertake reengineering because it is trendy or because it is elegant. They do so (often as a last resort) because they need to. This need is, in our experience, driven by one of three motives: pain, fear, or ambition. Companies feeling pain (e.g., low profits, shrinking market share) have to do something now. Companies feeling fear (e.g., aggressive competition, changing markets) have to do something soon. Companies feeling ambition (e.g., expand market share, enter new markets) have to do something now to realize their ambition soon. ABC Toy Company was feeling pain and fear: it had already lost ten points of market share and was concerned that it would lose more.

Business process reengineering (BPR) cannot be driven from the supply side, i.e., by internal or external consultants, industrial engineers, or systems personnel. The question of sponsorship of a reengineering project is key. Senior management must sponsor reengineering for several reasons. First, the impact of BPR is so broad that only senior management can sanction it. Second, reengineering usually involves a shift in culture, and it is uniquely senior management's role to set the culture. And third, reengineering requires leadership of the most visible sort.

The span of authority of the sponsor will constrain the scope of a reengineering project. That is, if the sponsor is the CEO or COO, the project may include any of the company's processes. If the sponsor is a business unit head, then the scope is generally confined to the processes within that business unit.

Sometimes, the sponsor may be the head of a functional department. In that case, the scope of the project will have to be the processes within that department, even if many of them cross departmental lines. A note of caution: Any mismatch between the scope of the reengineering project and the authority (whether direct or delegated) of the sponsor is likely to cause problems. Reengineering a functional department is particularly susceptible to such a mismatch. Reengineering the processes of a functional department presents special problems because the customers of the process are often people in other functional departments. It is often more difficult to get these internal customers to cooperate than it is to deal with external customers.

An executive generally must go through four stages—awareness, curiosity, interest, and belief—before he or she will commit to the sponsorship of a reengineering project, even when the need is perceived to exist. Most executives are already at the awareness or curiosity stages, at least. As of 1993, 80 percent of CEOs and COOs (but only 50 percent of human resources executives) that we surveyed were familiar with BPR. The numbers are certainly higher now, after front-page stories in the *Wall Street Journal*, a cover story in *Fortune*, and a best-selling book.

To move to the interest stage, an executive must have credible evidence that BPR has worked for others and recognition of a need that BPR might satisfy.

ABC Toy Company certainly recognized a need: to regain market share. And this was a need that reengineering might satisfy, because ABC management believed that improved performance was needed. It was confident that it had the right products for the right market. Improving performance is an issue at the operational level of the business. Choosing the right market to be in or the right products for a given market are issues at the strategic and tactical levels of the business. BPR is applicable to the operational level of a business, not the strategic or even the tactical. It can show a company how to do things right, but only in a limited way, what are the right things to do. It will not identify the markets a company should be in or the products it should develop. But it can give a company effective processes for making those decisions.

In order to move from interest in BPR to belief in it, an executive must be convinced that reengineering will help meet the company's perceived need. One way of accomplishing this is by demonstrating success within the company. Obviously, this is not possible for a first reengineering project. Another way is to show the executive a credible plan for carrying out the reengineering project, for it is not so much whether reengineering can work that they question, but whether "we" can make it work. A methodology really helps here, particularly one that is rich in checkpoints and milestone results.

> The ABC Toy Company was fortunate in that its CEO became the sponsor. She became convinced that only the rapid and radical redesign of strategic, value-added business processes could reverse the company's decline. And she recruited a reengineering consultant to facilitate the project.

Overall, slightly more than half of companies (54 percent) are using outside resources to assist their reengineering projects. Of those who aren't using outside resources, the most common reason (given by 70 percent of the executives we surveyed) was "We have the knowledge and expertise to handle the project in-house."

Interestingly, the larger the company, the more likely it is to use outside consultants (ranging from 43 percent for companies with sales below $100 million to 71 percent for companies over $1 billion). This is just the opposite of what one would expect; the larger companies should have more in-house knowledge and expertise. Perhaps this is a case of the larger companies knowing better what they don't know. Or, they may have more money to spend on, or more comfort in dealing with, consultants.

Our experience is that reengineering teams have a great deal of difficulty in starting BPR programs without experienced reengineering facilitation. In any case, we recommend that organizations use competent facilitators (whether internal or external) for at least the first two stages of reengineering.

TASK 1.2—DEVELOP EXECUTIVE CONSENSUS

Once the executive decides to sponsor a reengineering project, the next step is to build an executive consensus in its favor. This may be accomplished informally over a period of time through one-on-one or group meetings, casual conversations over meals, memoranda, sending people to reengineering seminars, talking to peers at other companies and to consultants, by reading, and through a hundred other activities. At minimum, the executives who must be brought into the consensus typically include the CEO, COO, CFO and senior human resources (HR) executives. The chief information officer is often also in the group. Also, the group has to include the potential process owners.

Most processes are cross-functional and interorganizational; because most companies are organized along product and/or functional lines, there are unlikely to be assigned "process owners" in an unreengineered company. But they are needed in the reengineered company, as we shall see in Task 4B.5. Therefore, the sponsor needs to think about who the likely candidates for process ownership are and bring them into the consensus as well. All of this sometimes takes several months. In other cases, if the sponsor is powerful and the management team close-knit, it can be completed in a week or two.

At this point, it is necessary to bring the key players together to define the reengineering project. This has been successfully accomplished in an executive workshop. This (usually) one-day working meeting includes the sponsors, the process owners, and the facilitator. Its purposes are to educate the management group in the methodology and terminology to be used; secure leadership and support for the project; define the issues to be addressed; identify other stakeholders; and set goals and priorities for the project. This working meeting also organizes the reengineering team and develops its mandate.

Figure 3-1 shows a typical executive workshop agenda. The discus-

Figure 3-1.   Typical agenda at executive workshop.

0800 – 0810	Introduction of attendees
0810 – 0825	Sponsor statement of problem
0825 – 0930	Introduction to business process reengineering
0930 – 1000	Restatement of problem in BPR terms
1000 – 1015	Break
1015 – 1100	Historical approaches to improvement
1100 – 1130	Critique of historical approaches
1130 – 1200	Define issues
1200 – 1300	Lunch
1300 – 1400	Discuss issues
1400 – 1430	Priorities and goals
1430 – 1500	Stakeholders
1500 – 1515	Break
1515 – 1530	Reengineering team characteristics
1530 – 1630	Agreement on reengineering team composition
1630 – 1700	Team mandate

sion of historical approaches to improvement is important to avoid confusing reengineering with previous company improvement initiatives such as automation, quality, and rightsizing. If the management team doesn't understand the differences and why the previous approaches are unlikely to produce the kinds of performance breakthrough needed now, then it is unlikely to support either the project itself or the kinds of changes the reengineering project is apt to bring about.

ABC Toy Company management identified four business goals, in priority sequence:

1. Regain a 50 percent market share in the next year.
2. Capture a 70 percent market share within three years.
3. Restore gross profit to the average that it had been during the "good" years 1985–1990.
4. Produce a return on investment (ROI) of 20 percent.

Notice that these goals have several characteristics that make them good goals for a reengineering project. First, they are specific and tangible: there will be no question of whether they are attained. Second, they are quantitative. Third, there are specific time frames for their attainment. And fourth, they will represent a *breakthrough* for ABC Toy Company. While any one, or even two, of these goals might be attainable by previous improvement means, it was clear to everyone that something radical—like reengineering—would be necessary to achieve them all concurrently.

On the other hand, the business goals are purely financial; they provide no clue to the organizational behaviors and changes that will be necessary to reach the goals. This is a disadvantage in a real reengineering project but an advantage in an example.

In a real reengineering project, management will almost always have some idea of the kinds of nonfinancial goals, or at least directions, necessary to attain the financial goals. These often include ideas about customer service, speed and accuracy of performance, quality, employee empowerment, greater availability of information, flattening of the organization, decentralization (or, alternatively, centralization), more extensive use of technology, and so forth. These nonfinancial goals, if not overspecified, can be helpful at the start because they are more suggestive and inspirational than sterile financial goals. In any case, the nonfinancial goals must be included in the Vision which is the product of Stage 3. But for our purposes, it is better for the ABC Toy Company to have only financial goals. Then we can see better how the nonfinancial goals enter the Vision.

In addition to the business goals, the management team also must develop a list of relevant issues concerning the conduct of the project, in order to give appropriate guidance to the reengineering team. These issues include the time, cost, risk, and social dimensions of change.

The first of these issues is time. Figure 2-1 shows the time line for a typical reengineering project, but different companies will have different needs and expectations for results. That time line usually starts from a distinct event that signals the start of something new as opposed to business as usual.

In our experience, companies to date have not undertaken major change programs on a continuous basis. Rather, it seems that their culture, organizational forms, and practices are frozen in place, like a crystal, with a high degree of resistance to change. Then, some shock occurs that unfreezes everything. This can be the replacement of a senior executive. It can be the emergence of a new competitive threat. It can be a hostile takeover attempt. It can be a financial surprise. Or, it can be any other event that convinces the sponsor that things have to change. The shock can be anything that creates sufficient pain, fear, or ambition to cross the threshold of resistance to change.

For the ABC Toy Company, it was the election of a new CEO. The former CEO was a second generation member of the family that controlled ABC. The shrinking market share of ABC convinced the board of directors that something different had to be done, and it recruited the new CEO.

The unfreezing represents, to mix metaphors, a window of opportunity for a company. For a relatively brief period of time, the situation is so fluid that significant change is possible. Thereafter, conditions will refreeze in a somewhat different form. The idea is to ensure that the new form represents a breakthrough in performance over the old one and not merely an incremental change. It has been truly said that "The window of opportunity opens slowly and closes rapidly."

The time available for the reengineering project may depend solely on the sponsor's patience. Or it may depend on other events. For example, a company may have to reengineer its customer service process in order to support a new product whose introduction date has already been set. Or a company may have to reengineer and improve performance in order to avoid being sold by its parent or to command a better price. Or it may need to reengineer to keep a commitment to investors, customers, employees, or other stakeholders.

Generally, the time frame for the project should be set between six and eighteen months. Less than six months is not enough time to do the redesign and transformation. If eighteen months have elapsed without significant results, the window of opportunity is likely to have closed.

For the ABC Toy Company, the timing needs and expectations were incorporated in the business goals: Recapture market share in one year and add an additional twenty share points in three years.

The second issue is cost. Our research shows that nearly two-thirds (65 percent) of companies do not budget for programs such as BPR. For those companies, this means that funding will have to be diverted from other areas, the company will have to accept lower profitability, it will have to borrow money, or, ideally, the reengineering project will have to be self-funding. Although the Rapid Re methodology is intended to make reengineering projects self-funding in about a year, this intention is not always realized in practice. Management must tell the reengineering team how much it is willing to spend on the reengineering project and at what rate. This may very well act as a constraint on the reengineering team's plans.

The ABC Toy Company executives decided that they were willing to make moderate investments in reengineering initially and then heavier investments as the reengineering results started to manifest themselves.

The third issue is risk. What happens if the reengineering project fails? Or if it is only partially successful? It would be reassuring to know that in the event of failure, things would revert to the *status quo ante*, but that isn't always possible. During the first four stages of reengineering, a company will have adequate opportunities to change direction or discontinue the project without major impact. But once the Transformation stage is under way, and particularly after the pilot implementation is complete, it may be more difficult to undo the work of the reengineering project.

Remember that reengineering is about *breakthroughs*, not about incremental change. And breakthroughs often require one to let loose of the tried and true. The reengineering team needs to understand management's appetite for risk.

ABC's management told the reengineering team that management was willing to undertake highly risky initiatives if the team could produce the results management wanted.

The fourth issue is the social dimension, and it is closely related to the risk issue. The social issue is, how much disruption are we willing to cause in people's lives? At least three different aspects of the social issue must be considered: employee redundancy, employee reskilling, and business partners.

One of the primary objectives and key benefits of BPR is the improvement of productivity. This usually means that a reengineered process requires fewer people to perform it than the process it replaces. What happens to the people made redundant? Will there be other jobs for them within the company? Will the excess people be severed, or will there be a natural attrition?

For the employees remaining in the reengineered process, their lives will change as well. In general, jobs in reengineered processes are broader, requiring more responsibility and greater skill. Stature and compensation within the reengineered organization comes less from whom you supervise than from what you do. There is more autonomy and less supervision. Promotions will flow from the acquisition of skills and not from performance. How will the employees react to all this? Are there labor agreements or regulations that constrain these kinds of changes? Is the current work force educable, or will we need to acquire some skills by hiring new people?

Business partners, such as vendors, suppliers, joint ventures, and customers may also be affected by reengineering. What kinds, and how much, of changes are permissible in these relationships? Clearly, a company has less control over its business partners than its own employees.

The reengineering team will need to understand the ground rules that management sets down for the social issues.

For the ABC Toy Company, which prided itself on having a "family relationship" with its employees, management directed the reengineering team to focus first on those changes that would be relatively easy on the employees. Management definitely preferred a warm bath to a cold shower.

ABC management was less concerned about changing relationships with vendors and customers. On the vendor side, ABC saw itself as one of many customers of each of its principal vendors and it felt that it had a broad range of choices in each vendor category. So ABC felt that it could find appropriate vendors that would accommodate whatever business process changes would be necessary to achieve its goals.

On the customer side, ABC management anticipated substantial change, because it was to be the improvement of ABC's performance on *activities valued by the customer* that would enable ABC to recapture and expand its market share.

Other companies may have entirely different situations than ABC's with respect to their customer and vendor relationships. The point is that management must explicitly recognize and delimit the scope and nature of the alterations that are acceptable to the relationships with business partners in order to give the reengineering team appropriate direction.

The agenda for the executive workshop may seem very ambitious for a one-day meeting, and it is. If there has been no prior consensus building and no activities to take the executives through at least the awareness, curiosity, and interest states with respect to reengineering, then it is unlikely that all of this work can be accomplished in one day or in one meeting. In that case, it is probably better to conduct several meetings over a period of time.

The last part of the executive workshop is concerned with assembling and chartering the reengineering team. In the Rapid Re methodology, we see the possibility of three different kinds of reengineering teams. The first is the team that executes stages 1 and 2, Preparation and Identification. Since we conceptualize these stages as part of a company-wide reengineering project and as providing a broad view of existing processes, the members of this reengineering team should be selected for the breadth of their understanding of the business. The second kind of reengineering team is the one that executes Stages 3 and 4, Vision and Solution. Since we conceptualize these stages as addressing only one or a small number of related processes at one time, the members of this reengineering team should be selected for the depth of their understanding of the specific processes to be reengineered and for their creativity. The third kind of reengineering team is the one that executes Stage 5, Transformation. The members of this reengineering team should be selected for their implementation skills. In practice, a company will seldom form entirely new teams at each point. Rather, the original team members usually provide the core of the later teams, thereby providing continuity.

Because the ABC Toy Company is fairly small and simple and because most processes crossed all of the departments, the same team was used for the first four stages.

Selection of the "right" people for the reengineering teams is one of the critical success factors in a reengineering project. But we have gotten ahead of ourselves! First, we must answer the question, why use teams?

Since most processes are cross-functional and interorganizational, a team is needed that represents all of the functional disciplines involved. The team members must not only provide information about their respective areas and how they are involved in the process, they must also *represent* their areas. This means that they must present the viewpoints, priorities, and interests of their constituencies. This requirement leads immediately to the two characteristics we seek in selecting team members: knowledge and stature. The team member must not only know about his or her own department, he or she must be perceived as someone who will represent that department's interests in a balanced and nonpartisan way.

BPR is not a program that a company can delegate safely to an outsider, such as a management consultant. It must be done by a company's own people. Only then is it likely to take root. Insiders have the detailed knowledge of what exists that outsiders lack. This is both a strength and a weakness, because it is harder for an insider to see that what exists is broken or illogical. More importantly, insiders have credibility. They are "us." They understand the culture of the organization, its values and beliefs. They can translate the imperatives of reengineering into a language that the company can understand.

On the other hand, outsiders—whether they be consultants, employees from a different division, or new hires—play an invaluable role in BPR projects. They bring a fresh perspective and the creative naïveté to ask, "Why do we do things this way around here?" Not having been part of the problem, they can more easily see the solution. They also lack a vested interest in the status quo. Consultants, whether internal or external, can also often bring specific methods, tools, and experience to the reengineering project. Sometimes, outsiders will have to be added to the reengineering teams to supply required skills, knowledge, or experience that is lacking among the insiders. In general, we have found a balanced mix of five or six insiders to one outsider is about right for a reengineering team. Depending on the specific project, there may be a need for full-time facilitation and/or support, usually provided by external or internal consultants.

As with many other corporate projects, BPR projects face the common dilemma that the people best suited to perform the work of the project are usually the ones who can least be spared from their normal duties. It helps to understand that there is no good solution to this problem and that any accommodation will be a compromise.

The members of the team must also be given enough time to do the work of the project. Some of the people in our reengineering seminars have told us that their reengineering team assignments were for as little as 10 percent of their time! That is barely enough to account for the loss of productivity from switching tasks. Full-time assignments for all team members are probably neither feasible nor desirable at most companies, since we want team members to stay involved in the processes they will be reengineering. But something on the order of half-time, on average over the life of the project, is necessary for meaningful contribution and progress. It appears to be better to obtain this half-time average through a mix of some full-time people and some less–than–half-time people, rather than having all team members work half-time, particularly during the Preparation and Identification stages. And in the early weeks of the project, it is better for all team members to be available close to full-time.

A very important requirement is for the reengineering team to have its own meeting room. The members will want to draw and hang many charts and documents to reference, and it is simply not effective for them to keep moving. A dedicated work space also enables the part-time team members to "drop by" whenever they can.

The ABC Toy Company's reengineering team is shown in Figure 3-2. It includes representatives of the three departments—operations, marketing, and finance and administration. It includes staff and managers at different levels (supervisor, manager, director). It includes people with different backgrounds and different personalities.

This makeup is fairly typical of a reengineering team for the first stages. It is rare that a team will include the executive level. And it is

Figure 3-2. ABC Toy Company reengineering team.

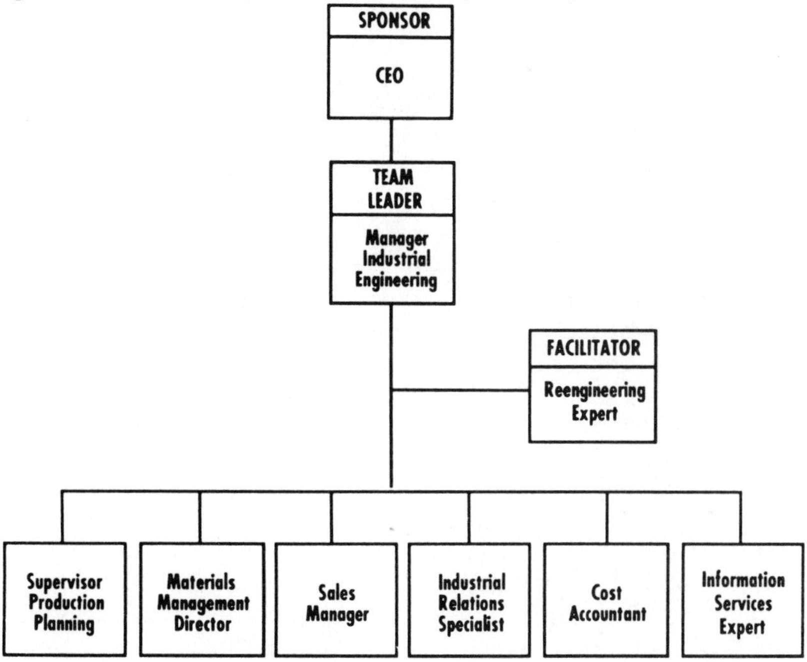

common to confine team membership to managers and professionals in the early stages, although inclusion of line workers in the Transformation stage is a good idea. Depending on the business and the company culture, there may be an opportunity to include line workers even here. Some companies even include customers, suppliers, and union representatives on their reengineering teams, although that is more likely in the later stages when the team is focusing on a single process.

ABC's CEO nominated the manager of industrial engineering as the team leader for several reasons. First, she thought that he had the broadest view of the organization because he had worked on improvements in all areas of the company. Second, she thought that by virtue of his training he would be more process oriented than other people, and he was accustomed to following a methodology. Finally, she believed that of all the jobs in the company, her own and the industrial engineer's were least likely to change. Therefore, he should not have a vested interest in the status quo.

The ABC executives recognized that reengineering was likely to change the way in which people work, the requirements of jobs, the way people are evaluated and motivated, etc. Therefore, they selected an industrial relations specialist for the project team.

They also recognized that information technology was likely to be an important part of the reengineered processes. For a long time, all of ABC's systems and procedures had been manual. Recently, several personal computers were installed in the order processing, inventory control, warehouse, and controller's areas. The first two had had independent consultants develop simple applications for them. The warehouse used a spreadsheet program, and the controller's area installed an integrated accounting package (billing, accounts receivable, accounts payable, and general ledger). Because ABC had no one who was knowledgeable about information technology, they retained one of the independent consultants with whom they had worked to participate on the reengineering team as an "information services expert."

Because this was the first project of its kind at ABC, as well as one of the most important programs it had ever undertaken, management wanted to ensure that the reengineering project went smoothly. It felt that the best way to ensure this was to hire a reengineering expert to act as a facilitator. Actually, it had already hired the management consultant to facilitate the executive workshop. It simply authorized him to continue with the reengineering team.

Once the reengineering team has been organized, it is ready to receive its charter—its mandate from the executive group. The last task of the executive group at this point is to give the reengineering team its mandate. That mandate can be issued in one of several ways depending on the company culture and timing issues. Several examples of how the mandate was issued in real projects follows.

In one company with which we worked, the reengineering team had actually been selected prior to the executive workshop, when the kind of project that was needed was originally conceptualized as a system replacement project. Management came to recognize that a more radical redesign of business processes was really needed, so they reconceptualized the project as BPR. When we facilitated the executive workshop, we were able to validate the composition of the project team, although we recommended that a human resources representative be added. In this case, the reengineering team was brought into the executive workshop at the end of the day and received its mandate directly from the two executives who were sponsoring the project: the CFO and the operations executive. The latter explained the business objectives. The former discussed management's expectations with regard to time, cost, risk, and social disruption, i.e., the project acceptance criteria. This worked very well.

In another project, senior managers decided to sponsor a reengineering project and educated themselves about reengineering by reading, attending one of our public seminars, and inviting us to make a half-day presentation. They then selected the reengineering team and told it why it had been selected. After we facilitated the executive workshop, we began the team training. It was not until we had trained the team on reengineering concepts, an overview of the methodology, and Stage 1: Preparation, that the team received its mandate. The CEO made an articulate and convincing business case that reengineering was needed, drawing on the key business indicators for the past ten years and current projections for the next two. He then presented the business goals and project acceptance criteria. The team felt that the business logic was so compelling that the CEO should give his presentation a second time, it should be videotaped, and the tape should be shown to all employees as the initial step in the communication plan.

Our point is that in this, as in all the tasks of Rapid Re, the specific approaches used and time allowed should fit the particular business circumstances and culture of the organization.

Task 1.3—Train Team

This task equips the reengineering team to undertake its mission. It includes defining management's expectations; building teamwork; learning the approach; selecting the manual and/or automated tools to be used in the project; adopting a common terminology; working through reengineering examples; and, finally, assuming responsibility for the project.

Figure 3-3 shows a typical agenda for a three-day training session for a reengineering project team, such as that of the ABC Toy Company. This is the minimum time required to equip the reengineering team with the knowledge they will require to proceed. The three days are allocated

Figure 3-3. Typical agenda for team training.

Day One - Morning	Day Two - Morning	Day Three - Morning
• Review of agenda	• The Vision Stage	• The Solution Stage: Technical Design
• Definition of processes	– Understanding process flow	
• Reengineering concepts and terminology	– Identifying value-adding activities	– Principles of system design and information flow
• How reengineering differs from previous improvement projects	– Determining performance drivers	– The role of information and technology in process flow
• Overview of methodology	– Estimating the opportunity	– Applying technology
• Examples	– Formulating a vision and defining subVisions	– Planning implementation
• Tools		• The Transformation Stage
• Project parameters		– Realizing the process vision
– Business goals and objectives		– Test and roll-out planning
– Why is reengineering necessary?		– Refinement and continuous improvement
– Acceptance criteria and time line		

Day One - Afternoon	Day Two - Afternoon	Day Three - Afternoon
• The Preparation Stage	• The Solution Stage: Social Design	• Begin project planning and change plan
– What has happened so far	– Principles of employee empowerment	– Anticipate resistance
– How the team training fits in	– Identifying skills, staffing needs, job changes, career paths, and incentives	– Establish communications
– What needs to be planned		– Develop project plan
• The Identification Stage	– Aspects of organizational structure	– Define specific roles and responsibilities
– Modeling customer needs	– Planning implementation	– Prepare schedule and scope
– Defining and measuring performance		
– Modeling processes		
– Prioritizing processes		

as follows: one-half day to organize the team, bring all team members to the same level of understanding of BPR concepts, and to communicate and discuss the mandate given the reengineering team by executive management; two days to learn this methodology; and one-half day to begin using the methodology.

This time budget is based on several assumptions: (1) that the trainer is the same management consultant who facilitated the executive workshop, (2) that the reengineering team members have some familiarity with BPR, for example, by having read a book such as this one, and (3) that the team members know each other. If any of these conditions are not present, more time must be allowed for the team training.

One advantage of this type of training is that all of the examples and applications of the methodology can be made specifically relevant to the needs of the project.

In order not to burden the reader at this point with the necessity of learning the automated tools that one can use with the Rapid Re methodology, the ABC project team has decided to conduct its reengineering project without using automated tools. Chapter 9 describes the available categories of reengineering tools, how to apply them with the Rapid Re methodology, and the issues surrounding their use. In practice, if a reengineering team decides to use automated tools, it may need to allocate significant amounts of time to learning them, if they are already in use in the company. If they are *not* already in use, the reengineering team will also have to spend time in researching, procuring, and installing the tools.

TASK 1.4—PLAN CHANGE

The last task of the reengineering team in the Preparation stage is to develop the overall plan for the remainder of the project. This plan should be fairly detailed for Stage 2, Identification. It will, of necessity, be more general for the remaining phases because the Identification stage will determine which processes and in what sequence to reengineer and because the composition of the reengineering team may change at the end of the Identification stage.

This task explicitly recognizes that there will be resistance to the changes that the reengineering project introduces and that the change must be managed if the project is to be successful. It initiates change management by identifying the stakeholders and their interests. It defines how communications will be managed to ensure that the stakeholders are kept informed in a constructive way. It identifies methods of assessing the extent of buy-in by various stakeholders and methods of intervening if buy-in is inadequate. This task also develops the project plan and schedule and defines project management methods, if these have not been specified already.

One of the major factors causing the current interest in BPR is the growing recognition by management that highly committed organizations outperform highly compliant ones and that technology has become and will continue to become cheaper and easier to use. These two factors—technology and people—are the keys to transforming business processes. Neither, alone, is the driver of BPR. Applying technology without social reengineering is merely automation. Applying social change without technical reengineering is merely a reorganization or a total quality management technique. Only the holistic approach, the joint design of the technical and social aspects of processes, is BPR, and it is BPR that is most likely to produce breakthroughs in performance.

Many reengineering projects make the mistake of "technocentricism." They say things like "We're reengineering; we've acquired image processing" or "We're reengineering; we're moving to client/server platforms." Certainly technology is a key *enabler* of BPR. But technology is not reengineering. Reengineering changes the business processes—the way the work is done. Applying technology to current processes has been rightly called "paving the cow path."

Perhaps one of the reasons that many practitioners fall into the error of technocentricism is that technology is, in a very real sense, easier than social change. After all, in many cases the choice between technical alternatives is fairly clear cut. And there is usually an objective way of determining whether the solution is working or not.

By contrast, the social side of processes is far more imprecise and problematic. It involves not only all the eccentricities of organizations but also the infinite variety of individual personalities. That is why we have found, in providing advisory services on the management issues that arise when technology is applied to business, that the human issues are inevitably more difficult than the technical ones. Far more BPR projects (or other improvement programs, for that matter) have failed because of inadequate attention to the social issues than because of technical issues.

BPR means change, and people don't like change. We will not change simply because there is a compelling business argument in its favor. We only change when we believe that it is in our best interest to change. One of the major tasks of the reengineering team is to design and execute a change management program that aligns the interest of the company with the interests of the stakeholders.

The most powerful tool that management (and its agent, the reengineering team) have in managing change is *communication*. The one thing that every company can be certain of is that once a reengineering project begins, everyone will know about it. Instantly. There is no such thing as "stealth reengineering." So the choice is not between communication and no communication. It is between unmanaged communication and managed communication. With unmanaged communication, the goals, procedures, and impact of the project will all be misunderstood. Rumors will abound. People's worst fears will run rampant. Productivity and morale will sink. And resistance, if not opposition, to change will harden. With managed communication, a company has at least a chance of circumventing these events.

A communication plan should be the first order of business for the reengineering team. And, as with any communication plan, it needs to begin by identifying the stakeholders. Whom will the reengineering project affect? How? What are their interests in the outcome? What questions are they likely to have? The underlying question for all employees is, "How will this affect my job, my compensation, and my career?"

Not all of the questions can be answered at this stage of the project, but the team must recognize that they will need to be answered eventually. Failure to provide answers leaves a vacuum in which people are invited to provide their own answers, which are likely to be erroneous. The communication plan must specify:

- ❑ *What* information people will need. This may vary by audience.
- ❑ *When* this information will be available.
- ❑ *How* to get this information to the people that need it.
- ❑ *Feedback mechanisms* that will let the project team know that the information has been received and understood and that will let the recipients submit questions, comments, and suggestions.

The feedback mechanism is very important for three reasons. First, it provides the reengineering team with a "sanity check" on what it is doing. Second, it provides an assessment mechanism. And third, it gives the recipients a sense of participation that a one-direction communication channel does not.

The initial communication by the reengineering team is critical, because it sets the tone and context for the entire project. The initial communication should be delivered as early in the project as possible and should contain the following eight elements:

1. Why the reengineering project is needed.
2. What the scope of the project is.

3. What results management expects. (Where the results include a
   change in competitive position, management may want to be cir-
   cumspect here.)
4. Who was selected to be on the reengineering team and why.
5. What will happen during the project and when.
6. What involvement people will have in the project.
7. What can be told now about how reengineering will affect all
   involved.
8. When the rest of the story can be told.

This communication is best delivered in two parts. Points 1 through 4
should be delivered by the reengineering project sponsor to underline
the importance of the message. Points 5 through 8 should be delivered
by the members of the reengineering team in order to give people a
sense of who they are and their commitment to the project.

Both the tone and the content of the communication are important.
The tone should be serious, reflecting the importance that the project
will have to many people's lives. It should be realistic, neither overly
optimistic nor overly pessimistic, but reflecting the probability of success. It should acknowledge ignorance and uncertainty where they exist
but state in a positive way how knowledge will be acquired and concepts
tested.

The tone of the initial communication should reflect the idea that
"we are all in this together." It should not imply blame for anyone (even
former employees) for the current situation, and it should not single out
any group for praise either. It should not have any of the characteristics
of a pep rally or a sales pitch. If the company's culture includes periodic
communication channels (e.g., meetings or newsletters), then it might
make sense to adopt their format. On the other hand, if reengineering
is likely to change the culture, for example to a more participative form,
then the format should so reflect. The idea is to give the employees a
preview of what the culture will be at the end of the reengineering.

The initial communication (and all subsequent change management
activities) should follow the precept: *Speak as if your audience is convinced,
act as if they are skeptical.* The content of the initial communication and
the subsequent work of the project should reflect another precept: *Say
what you are going to do, and do what you say.* This does not mean that the
reengineering team needs to be too detailed and specific. It does mean
providing as much of the big picture as possible and saying when the
pieces will come together. Where possible, the initial communication
should include statements of the commitments that management is pre-

pared to make at this point. But these should be firm commitments, not mere hopes.

One CEO announced a reengineering project by announcing, "When this is all over, half of us will have our jobs. But if we don't do it, none of us will." This declaration succinctly included the need for the project and the extent of management's commitment to the employees. Another CEO said, "We are going on a journey on which we will carry the wounded and shoot the stragglers."

At the ABC Toy Company, the factory was closed late one afternoon so that both first- and second-shift employees could attend and all employees were assembled in the auditorium of the local high school. The CEO made the opening remarks and introduced the project team. Then she turned the meeting over to the project team, who shared in presenting the project plan. Questions from the audience were solicited and answered by both the CEO and the project team members. Some of the answers were, "We don't know yet."

During the meeting, the CEO made the following specific commitments:

1. If the number of available jobs is reduced, all current employees will be fairly evaluated for the remaining jobs.
2. Appropriate training will be provided to enable current employees to fill new jobs. Current employees will be preferred to new hires.
3. All employees will be kept informed of the coming changes in jobs, organization structure, and staffing levels.
4. Employees losing their jobs will be given as much notice as possible. They will receive the company's normal termination benefits plus enhanced ones. They will also receive assistance from industrial relations in getting a new job. This will include assistance with resume preparation, research, interviewing skills, references, and a company-sponsored job fair for other local employers.

Another project with which we worked was for a global financial services company with 350 offices in the Americas, Europe, Africa, and Asia. The project involved the design, construction, and deployment of new systems that would affect every employee in every office. Because of the geographic spread of the company, the kind of town hall meeting conducted by the ABC Toy Company was clearly out of the question. So the initial communication consisted of an introductory announcement letter from the CEO to every office, followed by a flyer from the project team. The flyer was also retained as an ongoing communication vehicle. Each issue of the flyer invited comments, questions, and suggestions from the readers, and subsequent issues printed the questions with their answers. Additionally, management formed two advisory groups for the project, both with global representation. Both groups met with the project team at important milestones. The duties of the group members were to advise the project team, to act as spokespersons for their respective organizations, and, equally important, to provide a communication channel back to those organizations from the project team.

Clearly the ABC Toy Company and the global financial services company required different communication plans. But the purpose of those plans was the same: to gain and maintain the trust, cooperation, and participation of the stakeholders.

It should be apparent that, in order to communicate the information described, the project team will have to develop its project plan and its project management plan. These are often incorporated, along with background material and the initial change management plan, in a formal report and/or presentation to management. Figure 3-4 is a typical outline for such a document. Usually, this document is used to obtain management's concurrence in the project plan and precedes the initial communication activity.

As shown in Figure 3-4, two parts of the Change Management Plan remain to be discussed: assessment and intervention. The purpose of the assessment activity of change management is the determination of the extent of buy-in to the change; the purpose of the intervention activity is raising the level of buy-in.

An effective communication plan will create an environment that encourages people to buy in to the proposed change, but individual reactions will vary. Some, particularly those who foresee their condition as improved or unchanged, will support the proposed change with varying degrees of enthusiasm or acceptance. Others will react with boredom, disbelief, apathy, resignation, disappointment, anger, or hostility. To make matters worse, many of these reactions will be hidden. Some people are more expressive than others; they let you know what is on their minds. Others keep their own counsel. The danger is in thinking that someone who opposes the project is actually in favor. These passive-aggressive types may pay lip service to the goals and approaches of the reengineering project while they secretly behave in ways ranging from noncooperation to guerrilla warfare. Some may be so un-

Figure 3-4. Typical outline of change plan.

I. Purpose	III. Project Management
A. Background	A. Reporting relationships
B. Issues	B. Project reviews
C. Project goals	C. Progress reporting
D. Scope	
E. Team charter	

II. Project Plan	IV. Change Management Plan
A. Tasks	A. Stakeholders and their interests
B. Resources	B. Communication plan
C. Deliverables	C. Assessment plan
D. Responsibilities	D. Intervention plan
E. Schedule	

settled by the change that they become highly stressed. Stress is generally the result of ambiguity, which is why another purpose of the communication plan is to resolve ambiguity. This all leads to the need to actively assess how the stakeholders are reacting to the reengineering project. Once an accurate assessment has been made, an effective intervention can be planned.

At this stage of the project, neither assessment nor intervention can be planned in detail. Too little is known of what the change entails, whom it will affect and how, and their likely reaction. These issues will be revisited during Stage 4B, Social Design in Task 4B.10—Design Change Management Program, where change management is planned for the actual implementation of the reengineered process(es) during the transformation stage.

There are three reasons to begin planning assessment and intervention at this point in the Preparation stage. The first is to get the reengineering team to begin thinking about the related issues. The second is to identify and acquire the resources needed for assessment and intervention and to include their cost in the project budget. And the third is to begin the more limited assessment and intervention activities that may be needed during the first four stages of reengineering.

Examples of assessment tools that a reengineering team may wish to use are:

- ❏ Confidential employee surveys
- ❏ Focus groups
- ❏ Informal conversations
- ❏ Bulletin boards (physical or electronic)
- ❏ Attendance trends
- ❏ Monitoring of suggestions, comments, and questions
- ❏ Interviews

Examples of intervention tools include:

- ❏ Coaching
- ❏ Incentives
- ❏ Negotiation
- ❏ Discipline
- ❏ Individual or group counseling
- ❏ Training and education

At this point, the reengineering team is ready to move to Stage 2: Identification.

4

Stage 2: Identification

The purpose of this stage is to develop and understand a customer-oriented process model of the business. The identification stage produces definitions of customers, processes, performance, and success: identification of value-adding activities; a process map of organization, resources, volumes, and frequency; and the selection of the processes to reengineer. The key questions answered by this stage include:

- ❏ What are our major business processes?
- ❏ How do these processes interface with customer and supplier processes?
- ❏ What are our strategic, value-adding processes?
- ❏ Which processes should we reengineer within ninety days, within one year, subsequently?

The Identification stage, like the Preparation stage, is designed to be performed once per reengineering program. Thereafter, the reengineering team (or teams) can address individual processes or groups of related processes. In other words, the Identification and Preparation stages enable a company to decide which processes to reengineer in which sequence, and the Vision, Solution, and Transformation stages then are repeated once per each of those processes.

There may well be certain reengineering projects in which the current processes are well understood and the priorities for reengineering them are clear-cut. In those projects, it could be appropriate to move from Preparation directly to the Vision stage. In that case, however, the Vision stage would have to be expanded to cover some of the work that we have defined as part of the Identification stage.

Tasks 2.1 and 2.2 are devoted to understanding customers and their needs and wants, and how these translate into measures of process performance. Tasks 2.3, 2.4, 2.5, and 2.6 are devoted to identifying and understanding a company's processes. Tasks 2.7 and 2.8 are devoted to understanding how a company's organization relates to, and how a company's resources are utilized by, its processes. Finally, task 2.9 is devoted to determining the priorities to be attached to reengineering each process.

The state of the reengineering team's process understanding and the scope of its mandate will determine the extent to which the team needs to perform these tasks. In our experience, most companies, and particularly those companies just beginning reengineering programs, do not have a good understanding of their current processes.

Traditionally, companies are organized around functions and/or products. And most of the company's resources, procedures, systems, practices, and finances, etc. are structured organizationally. So it is often very difficult for the people in a company to identify and understand:

- ❏ What processes exist
- ❏ How they are related
- ❏ How processes correspond to functions and organizations
- ❏ What "process performance" means
- ❏ How each process contributes to, or detracts from, business goals
- ❏ Which people are involved in each process
- ❏ What resources are required in each process
- ❏ Where and when each process begins and ends
- ❏ Which processes are purely internal and which processes involve business partners such as customers and suppliers
- ❏ Which processes add value to a company's products or services, and which are support or administrative processes
- ❏ Which processes are important to a company's business strategy

Lacking this understanding, a reengineering team will find it difficult to identify a company's processes and to select the most important ones to reengineer.

There are a large number of ways that the work of a company can be structured into processes, because most processes consist of subprocesses. Some companies have identified as few as a half dozen major processes and other companies over a hundred. These differences are not necessarily a reflection of the relative complexity of the businesses but rather a function of the approach taken to identify the processes.

Some organizations have attempted to develop process classification schemes to help companies identify their processes (Figure 4-1). The schemes are exhaustive. They are likely to identify a large number of processes, since they do not attach relative importance to any of the processes. In our experience, most unitary companies can be described adequately by just five to twenty major processes. This same rule of thumb applies to divisions or subsidiaries of larger organizations. The question then becomes, what are the five to twenty processes? The methodology for the Identification stage is designed to answer that question.

Recap

This recap is for those readers referring to this chapter without having read Chapters 2 and 3.

The Preparation stage included recognition of the need to reengineer, usually as a result of a change, and usually motivated by pain, fear, or ambition. It also included the creation of an executive management consensus in favor of reengineering; the selection, chartering, and training of a reengineering team; and the early work of the reengineering team in producing a project plan and the beginnings of a Change Management Plan to address the anticipated social difficulties that reengineering inevitably creates.

> The ABC Toy Company felt that the best way to recapture and expand market share was to improve its customer service performance through reengineering. ABC management defined ambitious financial goals and chartered a reengineering project team with cross-functional membership, under the sponsorship of the CEO, and including an outside information technology consultant and a reengineering facilitator.

TASK 2.1—MODEL CUSTOMERS

This task identifies the external customers, defines their needs and wants, and identifies the various interactions between the organization and its customers.

It is entirely appropriate that business process reengineering (BPR) start with the customer, because all of the things that a company wants—profits, prestige, the psychic rewards of success—ultimately stem from the customer. These are the payoff from playing the game called business. On the other hand, the price of being a player in the

(Text continues on page 80.)

Figure 4-1. Process classification scheme: operating, management, and support processes.

1. Understand Markets and Customers

1.1 Determine customer needs and wants
- 1.1.1 Conduct qualitative assessments
  - 1.1.1.1 Conduct customer interviews
  - 1.1.1.2 Conduct focus groups
- 1.1.2 Conduct quantitative assessments
  - 1.1.2.1 Develop and implement surveys
- 1.1.3 Predict customer purchasing behavior

1.2 Measure customer satisfaction
- 1.2.1 Monitor satisfaction with products and services
- 1.2.2 Monitor satisfaction with complaint resolution
- 1.2.3 Monitor satisfaction with communication

1.3 Monitor changes in market or customer expectations
- 1.3.1 Determine weaknesses of product/service offerings
- 1.3.2 Identify new innovations that are meeting customers needs
- 1.3.3 Determine customer reactions to competitive offerings

2. Develop Vision and Strategy

2.1 Monitor the external environment
- 2.1.1 Analyze and understand competition
- 2.1.2 Identify economic trends
- 2.1.3 Identify political and regulatory issues
- 2.1.4 Assess new technology innovations
- 2.1.5 Understand demographics
- 2.1.6 Identify social and cultural changes
- 2.1.7 Understand ecological concerns

2.2 Define the business concept and organizational strategy
- 2.2.1 Select relevant markets
- 2.2.2 Develop long-term vision
- 2.2.3 Formulate business unit strategy
- 2.2.4 Develop overall mission statement

2.3 Design the organizational structure and relationships between organizational units

2.4 Develop and set organizational goals

3. Design Products and Services

3.1 Develop new product/service concept and plans
- 3.1.1 Translate customer wants and needs into product and/or service requirements
- 3.1.2 Plan and deploy quality targets
- 3.1.3 Plan and deploy cost targets
- 3.1.4 Develop product life cycle and development timing targets
- 3.1.5 Develop and integrate leading technology into product/service concept

3.2 Design, build, and evaluate prototype products or services
- 3.2.1 Develop product/service specifications
- 3.2.2 Conduct concurrent engineering
- 3.2.3 Implement value engineering
- 3.2.4 Document design specifications
- 3.2.5 Develop prototypes
- 3.2.6 Apply for patents

3.3 Refine existing products/services
- 3.3.1 Develop product/service enhancements
- 3.3.2 Eliminate quality/reliability problems
- 3.3.3 Eliminate outdated products/services

3.4 Test effectiveness of new or revised products or - services

3.5 Prepare for production
- 3.5.1 Develop and test prototype production process
- 3.5.2 Design and obtain necessary material and equipment
- 3.5.3 Install and verify process or methodology

3.6 Manage the product/service development process

4. Market and Sell

4.1 Market products or services to relevant customer segments
- 4.1.1 Develop pricing strategy
- 4.1.2 Develop advertising strategy
- 4.1.3 Develop product messages to communicate benefits
- 4.1.4 Estimate advertising resource and capital requirements
- 4.1.5 Identify specific target customers and their needs
- 4.1.6 Develop sales forecast
- 4.1.7 Sell products or services
- 4.1.8 Negotiate terms

4.2 Process customer orders
- 4.2.1 Accept orders from customers
- 4.2.2 Enter orders into production and delivery process

5. Produce and Deliver for Manufacturing Oriented Organization

5.1 Plan for and acquire necessary resources or inputs
- 5.1.1 Acquire capital goods
- 5.1.2 Hire employees
- 5.1.3 Obtain materials and supplies
- 5.1.4 Obtain appropriate technology

5.2 Convert resources or inputs into products
- 5.2.1 Develop and adjust production process (for existing process)
- 5.2.2 Schedule production
- 5.2.3 Move materials and resources
- 5.2.4 Make product
- 5.2.5 Package and store the product
- 5.2.6 Stage the product for delivery

5.3 Make delivery
- 5.3.1 Arrange product shipment
- 5.3.2 Deliver products to customers
- 5.3.3 Install (if specified)

5.4 Manage produce and deliver process
- 5.4.1 Document and monitor order status
- 5.4.2 Manage inventories
- 5.4.3 Assure quality
- 5.4.4 Schedule and perform maintenance
- 5.4.5 Monitor environmental constraints

6. Produce and Deliver for Service Oriented Organization

6.1 Plan for and acquire necessary resources
- 6.1.1 Hire employees
- 6.1.2 Obtain materials and supplies
- 6.1.3 Obtain appropriate technology
- 6.1.4 Acquire capital goods

6.2 Develop human resources skills
- 6.2.1 Define skill requirements
- 6.2.2 Identify and implement training
- 6.2.3 Monitor and manage skill development

6.3 Deliver service to the customer
- 6.3.1 Confirm specific service requirements for individual customer
- 6.3.2 Identify and schedule resources to meet service requirements
- 6.3.3 Provide the service to specific customers

6.4 Ensure quality of service

7. Invoice and Service Customers

7.1 Bill the customer
- 7.1.1 Develop, deliver, and maintain customer billing
- 7.1.2 Invoice the customer
- 7.1.3 Respond to billing inquiries

7.2 Provide after-sales service
- 7.2.1 Provide post sales service
- 7.2.2 Handle warranties and claims

7.3 Respond to customer inquiries
- 7.3.1 Respond to information requests
- 7.3.2 Manage customer complaints

8. Develop and Manage Human Resources

8.1 Create human resource strategy
8.2 Ensure employee involvement
8.3 Train and educate employees
8.4 Recognize and reward employee performance
8.5 Ensure employee well-being and morale
8.6 Manage relocation of personnel
  • 8.6.1 Manage movement of international personnel
  • 8.6.2 Manage movement of domestic personnel

9. Manage Information

9.1 Manage information systems
9.2 Evaluate and audit information quality

10. Manage Financial and Physical Resources

10.1 Manage financial resources
  • 10.1.1 Develop budgets
  • 10.1.2 Manage resource allocations
  • 10.1.3 Design capital structure
  • 10.1.4 Manage cash flow
10.2 Process finance & accounting transactions
  • 10.2.1 Process accounts payable
  • 10.2.2 Process payroll
  • 10.2.3 Process accounts receivable, credit, and collections
  • 10.2.4 Close the books
10.3 Report information
  • 10.3.1 Provide external financial information
  • 10.3.2 Provide internal financial information
10.4 Conduct internal audits
10.5 Manage the tax function
  • 10.5.1 Ensure tax compliance
  • 10.5.2 Plan tax strategy
  • 10.5.3 Employ effective technology
  • 10.5.4 Manage tax controversies
  • 10.5.5 Communicate tax issues to management
  • 10.5.6 Manage tax records
10.6 Manage physical resources
  • 10.6.1 Manage facilities
  • 10.6.2 Plan fixed asset additions
  • 10.6.3 Manage risk

11. Execute Environmental Management Program

11.1 Formulate environmental management strategy
11.2 Ensure compliance with regulations
11.3 Train and educate employees
11.4 Implement pollution prevention program
11.5 Manage remediation efforts
11.6 Implement emergency response program
11.7 Manage government, agency and public relations
11.8 Manage acquisition/divestiture environmental issues
11.9 Develop and manage environmental information system
11.10 Monitor environmental management program

12. Manage External Relationships

12.1 Communicate with shareholders
12.2 Manage government relationships
12.3 Build lender relationships
12.4 Develop public relations program
12.5 Interface with board of directors
12.6 Develop community relations
12.7 Manage legal and ethical issues

13. Manage Improvement and Change

13.1 Measure and monitor overall organization performance
13.2 Conduct quality assessment
13.3 Benchmark performance
13.4 Make process improvements
13.5 Manage change
13.6 Implement TQM

Version 7: American Productivity & Quality Center/International Benchmarking Clearinghouse.

game is to meet the needs of the customer fairly completely and fairly consistently. Today's competitive environment provides few niches in which a company can survive if it doesn't adequately serve its customers.

Some companies have described their reengineering programs as a matter of survival; others have described their programs more positively. But virtually all agree that whatever the announced objectives of the reengineering project, any process changes that don't enable the company to better meet the customers' needs and wants are unlikely to achieve any of the other objectives. The reason is simple. Although the primary focus of a reengineering project may be, say, cost reduction, customer satisfaction is a moving target. While your company is busy reducing costs, chances are the competition is improving customer service.

Customer service and customer satisfaction are the subjects of an extensive body of literature in their own right, which we will not attempt to reproduce here, since modeling the customer is only one of the fifty-four tasks in the Rapid Re methodology. Suffice it to say that reengineering must begin by understanding the customer: who he or she is, what he or she wants and needs, and what is important to him or her. This understanding is summarized in a customer model.

Sometimes, the necessary understanding of the customer already exists within the company, usually as a result of ongoing activities or special studies undertaken by marketing or sales. In that case, the reengineering team can obtain the necessary information internally, perhaps through a team member from marketing or sales. But they had better validate that understanding with the customers themselves. In other cases, the reengineering team will determine that there is inadequate understanding of the customer. Then it must obtain that understanding. Some techniques that reengineering teams have used to understand the customer are customer interviews, customer surveys, or by inviting key customers to actually participate in the reengineering project.

In compiling the list of customer needs and wants, the reengineering team must be careful to distinguish between what a customer says and what the customer means. This is the first issue. When a customer says that they want low price, for example, what they really mean is that they want low price at some threshold value of quality and performance. The literature and/or marketing professionals should be consulted in dealing with such issues.

A second issue is knowing who the customer is. Retailers and personal service companies, for example, deal directly with the ultimate users of their products and services. Many manufacturers, however, deal with resellers who are not the ultimate users. The reengineering team must understand and model this distinction.

The ABC Toy Company reengineering project team began this task by interviewing the vice president of marketing, several of the best salespeople (the manager of sales was a member of the reengineering team), and the customer service representatives. Then it conducted a brainstorming session with the salespeople at their regular monthly sales meeting. Finally, it visited about ten key customers and invited several to participate in a Customer Advisory Council, which was used throughout the project to validate process visions and implementation ideas.

The reengineering team recognized that the company's direct customers were the national and regional toy and variety store chains. Their needs were those related to selling a sizable volume of ABC's toys at a good margin (50 percent was the industry expectation) and with little hassle. This translated into a need for merchandise that was defect-free, attractively packaged, and available on the shelves when the customers came looking for it. This meant that opening orders had to be filled in time for the selling season (Thanksgiving to Christmas) and that reorders had to be filled within ten days. The direct customers also needed good consumer demand for ABC's products. One requirement for this demand to exist is that the products be advertised, customarily through cooperative advertising controlled by the retailer and partially paid for by the manufacturer through co-op advertising allowances.

The other requirement for the demand to exist is that ABC's products meet the needs and wants of the ultimate consumer. ABC's market research had previously identified two types of end user. The obvious one was the child who played with ABC's cartoon and comic book character toys. There were many such consumers, but their purchases were usually small—the one or two characters they favored. The less obvious end user was the collector, who might be any age. There are fewer collectors than children, but they make larger purchases—often all the characters in the line.

The collectors have a different set of wants and needs from the children. All that the children want is a good likeness of their favorite characters constructed so that it won't break easily. The collectors, however, want a broad variety of characters, with one year's edition clearly distinguishable from the next. They want fine detail. And they want a durable product, not so much one that would withstand rough handling (as in the case of the child) but rather one whose color and shape would not change over time.

ABC's market research had also shown that over 80 percent of the toys used by children were actually purchased by an adult, usually a parent. Although the child picked out or asked for the toy, the adult bought it. So adult consumers were actually a fourth type of customer. Their wants and needs were for the toys to have a reasonably low cost (perceived value), that they be available in convenient locations (wide distribution), and that they be safe.

Finally, the reengineering team identified all of the interactions between the company and its various customers and summarized the results of this task in a customer model (see Figure 4-2).

TASK 2.2—DEFINE AND MEASURE PERFORMANCE

This task defines customer-oriented measures of performance and determines current performance levels—both averages and variances. It

Figure 4-2.   ABC Toy Company customer model.

Customer	Adult Consumer	Child Consumer	Collector
• Attractive packaging	• Reasonably low cost	• Popular characters	• Variety
• Few defects	• Available in convenient	• Good likeness	• Perceptible differences year-to-year
• Opening orders accurately and completely	locations	• Rugged	but not within year
filled in time for selling season	• Safety		• Fine detail
• 50% profit margin			• Durable
• Reorders filled within ten days			
• Cooperative advertising allowances			

also examines existing standards of performance and identifies performance problems.

Only when the customers' needs and wants are understood can a company begin to define what "performance" means and how to measure it. Traditionally, many companies have developed performance measures that are oriented toward internal needs, such as product cost. Furthermore, for measurements to be useful management tools, they must be related to a reference point. When a measure has been in use for some time, the reference point may be a baseline (e.g., how we did last year) or a standard (e.g., the historical average, or how we think we should do). Increasingly, the standard is a benchmark (e.g., how some other company or another unit of our company is doing). When a new measure is introduced, it is often difficult to obtain a reference point at first.

The ABC Toy Company reengineering team identified four performance measures that it felt best measured the company's performance in those areas most important to the customers.

1. *The time from receipt of an order to its shipment.* There were two standards here, one for opening orders and one for reorders. On opening orders, the standard was six weeks, and ABC was meeting this standard 92 percent of the time. The problem was that orders received toward the end of the selling season were often late. On reorders, the standard was two weeks, and ABC was meeting this standard 85 percent of the time. The problem was that when a product or stockkeeping unit (SKU) was out of stock, it could take up to thirty days before it was replenished by a manufacturing production run.
2. *The percentage of orders shipped as ordered, i.e., accurately and completely.* The standard here was 100 percent for both opening orders and reorders. For opening orders, actual performance was 95 percent, since most orders were filled directly from the production schedule, which was created from a blend of actual orders and sales projections. On reorders, however, performance was only 80 percent. Substitutions and back orders were common.
3. *The rate of merchandise defects.* The standard was 1 per 10,000. On initial production runs, the standard was exceeded. Actual defects were 1 per 20,000. However, on reruns of production, to fill some late opening orders and

most reorders, actual defects were 1 per 2,000. Quality control was much better on the long, start-of-season production runs.
4. *The time needed to post claims and allowances to the customer's account.* Here the standard was by the next statement cycle, and the standard was being met in excess of 99
   percent of the time, except for items in dispute.

At the completion of this analysis, the ABC reengineering
team knew that, from the customer's perspective, something
would have to be done to the processes involved in filling reorders.

TASK 2.3—DEFINE ENTITIES

This task identifies the entities, or "things" with which the organization
deals. An entity is an abstraction that is realized in one or more specific
instances. For example, the entity "employee" may have the instances
"Tom," "Dick," and "Harriet." In addition, entities have attributes that
describe them, e.g., Social Security number, birth date, address. Other
entity attributes relate to the state that the entity is in, e.g., employed or
retired. Some entities, like customers and employees, are relatively permanent—they continue to exist and we continue to be interested in them
for a relatively long time. Other entities, such as orders or checks, are
transactions—they exist and we are interested in them for a relatively
brief time.

This task also defines the states that each entity can be in, and correlates state changes with interactions, that is, it identifies which interaction causes each state change. If you find this abstraction strange, you
are not alone. Most people to whom we teach the methodology have a
similar reaction. Yet this abstraction is an important part of the Rapid Re
methodology.

The purpose of this task is threefold. The first purpose is to force
the reengineering team to look at the work of the business in a new way,
in terms of processes instead of functions. Much of the BPR literature
calls for the reengineering team to "break frame," or do "breakthrough
thinking" or to "shift paradigms," but it doesn't tell the reader *how* to
do these things. Actually, one can't shift paradigms; one can only experience a paradigm shift. And the purpose of the abstraction is to encourage such a shift by presenting the familiar in an unfamiliar way,
much as your neighborhood looks if you've ever seen it from a balloon
or small plane.

The second purpose of this task is to provide an assured method of identifying a company's processes. Processes emerge from the analysis of state change sequences; that is, a process is a series of activities that convert business inputs into business outputs by changing the state of one or more entities of interest.

The third purpose of this task is to begin to identify the information needed in the reengineered processes and how to organize that information. Since entities are the "things" of interest, they are the obvious candidates for information records. That is, we will need a set of information (its attributes) of each instance of each entity, e.g., each employee, each machine, each order. And among the attributes must be those that describe its state (active or retired, idle or loaded, received or shipped).

Information, as will be seen in Chapter 6, is one of the key enablers of business transformation. It can enable new products, new services, and new processes. So the reengineering team must begin to understand information at an early stage of the project.

At the ABC Toy Company, the reengineering team struggled with the definition of the entity called "product." Products were what the company sold, so they had to be important. Members of the reengineering team agreed that the two entities they spoke most about in their daily work were customers and products. What they discuss about products was how to design, make, and sell them.

The initial list of product states that the reengineering team came up with was as follows:

1. Product idea
2. Licensed character
3. Design model
4. Production model
5. Mold
6. In production
7. In stock
8. Out of stock
9. Picked
10. Packed
11. Shipped

The initial list of interactions that the reengineering team thought caused these state changes was as follows:

1. Market research report or suggestion
2. License agreement with copyright holder
3. Product design
4. Product design test and approval
5. Mold design
6. Production order release
7. Quality inspection and warehouse receipt
8. Sales order picking
9. Sales order picking
10. Packing of picked sales order
11. Shipping of packed sales order

The appearance of "sales order picking" as the interaction causing two different state changes—from "in stock" to "out of stock," and from "in stock" to "picked"—bothered the reengineering team. So they started to examine what these states really meant. "Out of stock" was unambiguous: It meant that the number of pieces of the product in inventory was zero. But what did "in stock" mean? As it was commonly used at ABC, "in stock" meant that there was sufficient inventory to fill the sales orders on hand. And what did "picked" mean? At any given time, some of the sales orders were picked while others were not.

These considerations led the reengineering team to conclude that its original concept of the product entity had to be replaced by three other entities: product, SKU, and sales order.

The product entity could have the states:

1. Product idea
2. Licensed character
3. Design model
4. Production model
5. Mold

with the same state-change/interaction relationships as before.

The SKU entity could take on many different states, represented by the number of pieces of the product on hand, on back order from customers, on production order from manufacturing, and allocated to orders in-house but not yet picked. The interactions that affected these state attributes or variables were sales order (and back order) booking, changing and picking, and production order placement and receipt.

Figure 4-3 shows the states and interactions for the sales order entity, as well as three of the others that the reengineering team defined.

TASK 2.4—MODEL PROCESSES

This task defines each process and identifies its state change sequence. It defines the process objectives and critical success factors. It identifies the process inputs and outputs, as well as any additional stimuli that cause a state change.

Figure 4-3. ABC Toy Company entities and states.

Entity Name	Customer	Order	Molding Machine	Claim Transaction
Type:	Permanent	Transaction	Permanent	Transaction

States and Interactions:	• Balance
	  - invoice
	  - payment
	  - adjustment
		• Booked
		  - order
		  - change
		
		• In Process
		  - release
		
		• Picked
		  - pick
		
		• Packed
		  - pack
		
		• Part Shipped
		  - shipment
		
		• Full Shipped
		  -shipment
		
		• Received
		  - receipt
		
		•Billed
		  - invoice
		
		•Completed
			• Installed
			  -installation
			
			•Scheduled
			  - production
			    schedule
			
			• Loaded
			  - job order
			
			• Empty
			  - job
			    completion
				• Submitted
				  -claim
				
				• Rejected
				  - rejection
				
				• Accepted
				  -acceptance
				
				• Adjusted
				  -adjustment
				
				• Paid
				  -adjustment

At the ABC Toy Company, the reengineering team defined ten processes, which it called:

1. Develop Product
2. Manufacture
3. Fulfill Orders
4. Service Customer Request
5. Maintain Customer Account
6. Develop Human Resources
7. Compensate
8. Fund
9. Comply
10. Acquire Customer Orders

The Develop Product process, for example, took the product entity through the state change sequence: product idea ➡ licensed character ➡ design model ➡ production model ➡ mold. Similarly, the Fulfill Orders process took the order entity through the state change sequence: booked ➡ in process ➡ picked ➡ packed ➡ part shipped ➡ full shipped ➡ received ➡ billed ➡ completed.

This is not the only set of processes that the team could have defined, nor are their names the only ones that could have been assigned, but they will do. Also, this set of processes did not exhaust all of the things that the ABC Toy Company did. For example, activities such as the design and construction of a factory or warehouse, the purchase of machinery, or the remaindering of surplus stock were not included in any of the processes. Rather, the team selected these ten processes because they felt these were the *major* processes, the ones performed on a daily basis, and the ones that would have the greatest impact on the ultimate success or failure of the company.

The language that a reengineering team chooses to describe the concepts with which it is dealing is very important, for it can either constrain or enable innovative thinking about the business. Entities, being things, should be described by noun or noun phrases, e.g., "customers," "sales order." Processes, being action, should be described by verbs or verb phrases, e.g., "manufacture" or "fulfill orders." It is best to use strong verbs, in the active voice and the imperative mood, because these most accurately portray the dynamic nature of processes. The object of the verb is usually an entity. Sometimes, the object is implied, as in "manufacture" (product) and "compensate" (employee). Sometimes the object of the verb is generalized, as in "develop human resources," where "human resources" is meant to encompass both the entities "employee" and "applicant."

The reason for using these linguistic devices is that they help the reengineering team to keep the abstract concepts straight. Also, they avoid confusion between the process perspective and the traditional functional/organizational perspective. For example, if a process is called Order Fulfillment or Order Processing, it is easy to confuse it with a function or organization of the same name. Not so if we call the process Fulfill Orders or Process Orders.

From this point on, our ABC Toy Company example will use the Fulfill Orders process. We have chosen to use this process in preference to one of the others because it should be more understandable to most readers (including people in service businesses), and because it was the top priority process for ABC, as they will have discovered in Task 2.9.

Once the state change sequence that comprises a process is identified, the next step is to think about the factors that cause the state change. In some cases, these are internal to the process itself. For example, in Fulfill Orders, the transition from picked to packed is caused by the activity of packing, which is clearly part of Fulfill Orders. In other cases, the factors are external to the process, in which case we call them *stimuli*. One type of stimulus is a transactional type entity, which we then call an *input* to the process. For example, the receipt and logging of a new sales order is the stimulus that initiates the Fulfill Orders process and places that order in the state "booked." The order is also the input to the process. An entity that is created by a process is an *output* of the process. Often, an entity is an output from one process and an input to the same or another process. For example, a pick list is output when the order moves from the "booked" to the "released" state. The pick list, annotated to indicate what has been picked, is then an input to the "picked" state.

In addition to identifying the state change sequence, inputs, outputs, and stimuli, the reengineering team must decide on the process objectives and the critical success factors for the process. Sometimes these are obvious. But other times they require deep and original thought, since the process perspective is so new.

Figure 4-4 shows the Fulfill Orders process model for the ABC Toy Company.

TASK 2.5—IDENTIFY ACTIVITIES

This task identifies the major activities needed to effect each state change. It also determines the extent to which each activity adds value,

Figure 4-4. Fulfill orders: process model.

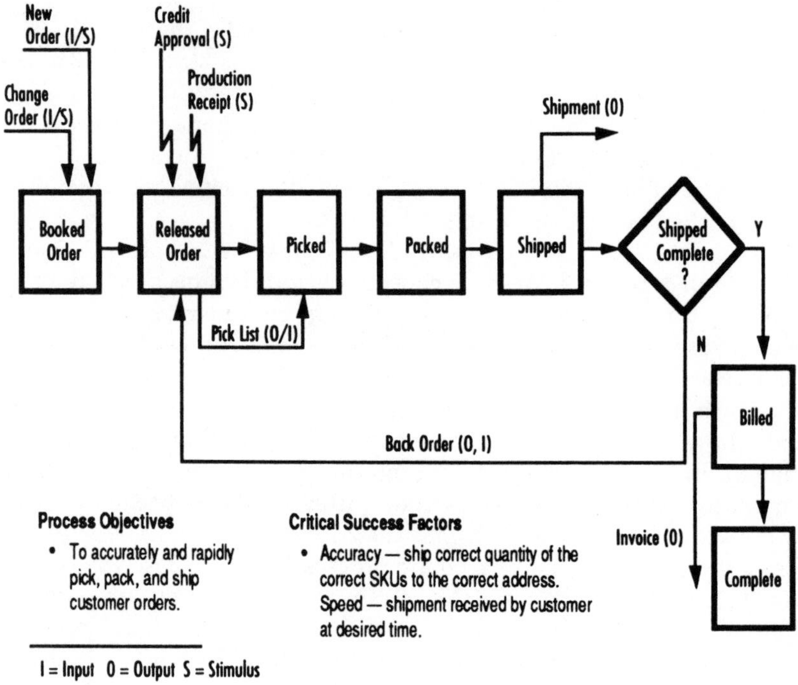

that is, the extent to which the activity contributes to meeting a customer want or need. *Value-adding activities* usually have three characteristics: they accomplish something the customer cares about, they physically change an entity, and it is important that they be done right the first time.

Figure 4-5 shows the list of activities for the Fulfill Orders process at the ABC Toy Company. Notice that only eight of the twenty-three activities are value-added. Fully two-thirds of the activities are internal administration or support!

TASK 2.6—EXTENDED PROCESS MODEL

By this point in the Rapid Re methodology, the process states have served their purpose. We have identified state variables as attributes of

Figure 4-5. Fulfill orders: major activities.

State Change	Activities	Value Added	State Change	Activities	Value Added
Booked	Identify customer – Add if new Identify salesperson – Find commission rate Assign order number If change order, make changes	+	Released to Picked	Pick SKUs Mark as picked Update inventory Prepare back order	+
Booked to Released	Check customer credit If necessary, demand prepayment or COD Check inventory – Allocate if necessary Create pick list Assign ship date Schedule warehouse	 + +	Picked to Packed Packed to Shipped	Check order Prepare shipping documents Pack order Determine shipping method Determine freight charge Consolidate shipments Ship	 + +
			Shipped to Billed	Prepare invoice Mail	+ +

+ = value added

the associated entities. And we have used the state change sequence to identify the processes. Therefore we will now shift focus from the process states to the state transitions and the activities performed in moving from state to state.

In the case of the Fulfill Orders process model, the reengineering team at ABC replaced the boxes marked Booked Order, Released Order, Picked, Packed, Shipped, and Billed with a series of boxes marked Book Order, Release Order, Pick, Pack, Ship, and Bill. The activities in Figure 4-5 formerly listed for the state change Booked are now associated with Book Order. Those associated with the state change Booked to Released are now associated with Release Order, and so on.

Some of the greatest opportunities to improve both customer service and process efficiency come from integrating a company's processes more closely with those of its customers. Well-known examples of this include Procter & Gamble's integration of its outbound logistics with Wal-Mart's in-store inventory and Baxter Health Care's integration of its order processing with the supplies management processes of its hospital customers.

In order to uncover these opportunities, it is necessary to extend the boundaries of the process model to include its interfaces with customers' processes. For example, Fulfill Orders interfaces with the customers' purchasing at one end and with their accounts payable at the other end. This task also identifies internal and external suppliers and their interactions with the processes.

> In ABC's Fulfill Orders process, the accounts receivable and inventory control organizations are internal suppliers to the process. They provide, respectively, customer account balances and notification that back-ordered products have now been produced.
>
> Also in the Fulfill Orders process, the credit reporting agency Dun & Bradstreet and a variety of common carriers are external suppliers to the process. Dun & Bradstreet provides credit information, and the carriers provide carriage of the shipment and associated paperwork.

At this point, the process model begins to reveal that certain individuals and groups within the organization are both suppliers and customers. The process takes the form:

EXTERNAL SUPPLIER ➻ INTERNAL CUSTOMER/SUPPLIER ➻ INTERNAL CUSTOMER/SUPPLIER ➻ INTERNAL CUSTOMER/SUPPLIER ➻ EXTERNAL CUSTOMER

This very important and powerful insight will serve as a key enabler of BPR. It means that all of the tools, techniques, and perspectives that we bring to improve service to external customers can also be used to improve service to internal customers. In other words, by treating each participant in the process as the customer of the participants who supply him, the optimization of work flow and efficiency become synonymous with optimization of customer service. This is entirely consistent with the well-known observation that the best customer service is provided by those organizations in which the customer contact personnel are themselves well served.

Just as effective management of a process from the customer perspective requires measurement of (external) performance, so too does it require measurement of internal performance. The task therefore identifies additional measures of performance oriented toward the internal customers, and incorporates these into the process model as well.

Figure 4-6 shows the extended process model for Fulfill Orders.

TASK 2.7—MAP ORGANIZATION

This task defines the organization(s) involved in each major activity and the type of involvement (e.g. "responsible for," "provides input to," "receives notification from," etc.). It therefore defines the process/organization boundaries.

Figure 4-7 is an organization chart for the ABC Toy Company. It is somewhat oversimplified in that it omits many functions that can be found in other (usually larger) companies. These include advertising, corporate planning, corporate secretary, information services, internal audit, legal, licensing, print shop, public affairs, quality, safety, security, and stockholder relations.

There are many ways to represent the process/organization information. We prefer to use a matrix, although other methods might be preferable if the matrix is very large and very sparse. Figure 4-8 shows the organization versus activity matrix for Fulfill Orders.

TASK 2.8—MAP RESOURCES

This task estimates the head count and expense dollars in each major activity of each process. It also estimates transaction volumes and frequencies. This information is used to compute estimated annual costs per activity and process and unit costs per transaction. A very important word in the preceding description is "estimate." Great precision is not needed at this time. The primary purpose of this task is to obtain a "first cut" of the utilization of resources by each process in order to understand the relative resource intensity of each process. This understanding will be used in Task 2.9 to help determine the priorities for reengineering various processes.

A second purpose of this task is to obtain a baseline for process resource utilization. This may be compared with similar estimates for

(Text continues on page 96.)

Figure 4-6. Fulfill orders: extended process model.

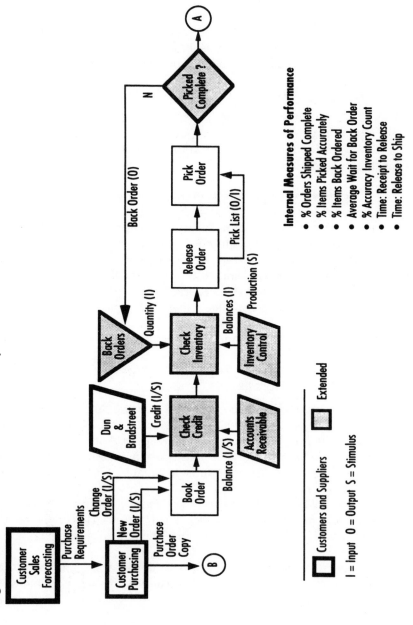

Internal Measures of Performance

- % Orders Shipped Complete
- % Items Picked Accurately
- % Items Back Ordered
- Average Wait for Back Order
- % Accuracy Inventory Count
- Time: Receipt to Release
- Time: Release to Ship

Customers and Suppliers

Extended

I = Input   O = Output   S = Stimulus

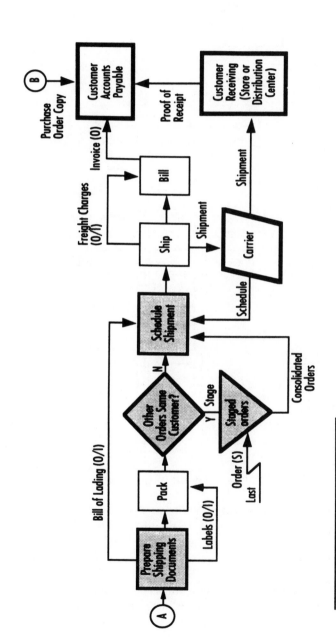

Purchase Order Copy

Customer Accounts Payable

Customer Receiving (Store or Distribution Center)

Proof of Receipt

Invoice (O)

Freight Charges (O/I)

Bill

Ship

Shipment

Carrier

Shipment

Schedule

Schedule Shipment

Consolidated Orders

Bill of Lading (O/I)

Other Orders Same Customer?

N

Y Stage

Staged orders

Order (S)

Lost

Pack

Labels (O/I)

Prepare Shipping Documents

A

B

☐ = Customers and Suppliers   ▨ = Extended

I = Input   O = Output   S = Stimulus

Figure 4-7. ABC Toy Company organization chart.

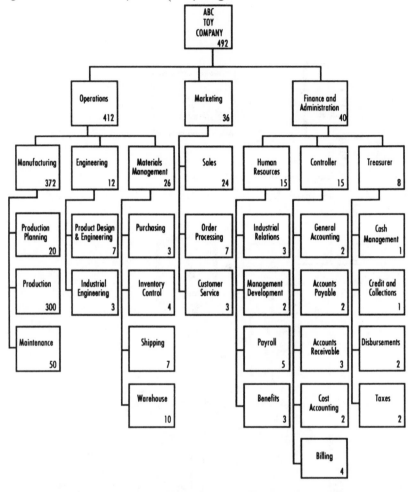

the reengineered process to obtain a measure of the improvement that reengineering will produce.

The methodology of this task is very similar to that of activity-based costing. If a company has recently performed an activity-based costing analysis, then it is likely already to have much of the information that this task requires. For companies that have not performed activity-based costing, the results of this task are likely to be eye-opening. Most companies have never analyzed what specific business processes are costing them. And many have never determined the unit costs of performing various activities.

Figure 4-8. ABC Toy Company organization map.

	Organizations	1. Identify Customers	2. Identify Salespersons	3. Assign Order Number	4. Make Changes, if nec.	5. Check Credit	6. Make Demands, if nec.	7. Check Inventory	8. Create Pick List	9. Assign Ship Date	10. Schedule Warehouse	11. Pick	12. Mark as Picked	13. Update Inventory	14. Check Order	15. Check Order	16. Prepare Shipping Docs	17. Pack Order	18. Determine Ship Method	19. Determine Freight	20. Consolidate Shipments	21. Ship	22. Prepare Invoice	23. Mail
Marketing	Sales	I	I				N																	
Marketing	Order Processing	R	R	R	R				R	N			N		R		R			N				
Marketing	Customer Service																							
Materials	Inventory Control				N			R						R	N									N
Materials	Shipping																R	R	R	R	R	R		
Materials	Warehouse								N	R	R	R	R	I										
Mfg	Production Planning													N	N									
Finance & Admin	Accts. Receivable	I			I																			
Finance & Admin	Credit & Collections				R	R																		
Finance & Admin	Billing								I					N						N			R	R

KEY
R = Responsible R =
I = Provides Input I =
N = Is Notified N =

Figure 4-9 shows the table that the reengineering team prepared for the Fulfill Orders process. FTE means full-time equivalent personnel. Frequencies of performance for each activity were determined by interviewing the personnel involved in the process. This method was also used to obtain the FTE counts: Each person was asked to estimate how much of his or her time was spent on each activity and process in which he or she was involved. To determine the annual labor costs, the team multiplied the FTE numbers by the average fully loaded payroll cost, by job grade, which it obtained from payroll section. In order to obtain the annual purchases' dollar amounts, the team looked at the previous year's 1099 reports for each major vendor, and, together with the purchasing supervisor, allocated those amounts to the processes and activities.

Most of the volume numbers came from the order log. The total number of orders per year was obtained by subtracting the first order number in January from the last order number in December. The average number of orders per day was then the total number divided by the number of working days in the year. The

Figure 4-9. Fulfill orders: resource map.

Activity	Frequency	Volume		FTE	Annual	Annual	Annual	Unit
		Avg	Peak	Count	Labor $	Purchase $	Total $	Cost
1. Identify Customer	Daily	80	200	0.4	23,200		23,200	1.16
2. Identify Salespersons	Daily	80	200	0.4	23,200		23,200	1.16
3. Assign Order Number	Daily	80	200	0.1	5,800	10,000	15,800	0.79
4. Make Changes, if nec.	As needed	5	50	0.1	5,800		5,800	4.64
5. Check Credit	M,W,F	80	200	0.5	39,000	15,000	54,000	2.70
6. Make Demands, if nec.	M,W,F	5	20	0.1	7,800		7,800	6.24
7. Check Inventory	Daily	400	2,000	1.2	80,400		80,400	0.80
8. Create Pick List	Daily	80	200	1.0	58,000	2,000	60,000	3.00
9. Assign Ship Date	Daily	80	200	0.2	10,400		10,400	0.52
10. Schedule Warehouse	Daily	80	200	0.8	41,600		41,600	2.08
11. Pick	Daily	400	2000	5.0	260,000		260,000	2.60
12. Mark as Picked	Daily	80	200	1.0	52,000		52,000	2.60
13. Update Inventory	M	2,300	4,000	0.4	26,800	2,000	28,800	1.04
14. Prepare Back Order	Daily	25	50	0.3	17,400	1,000	18,400	2.94
15. Check Order	Daily	80	200	1.0	48,000		48,000	2.40
16. Prepare Shipping Docs	Daily	80	200	2.0	116,000	10,000	126,000	6.30
17. Pack Order	Daily	80	200	2.0	96,000	250,000	344,000	17.20
18. Determine Ship Method	Daily	20	100	0.5	24,000		24,000	4.80
19. Determine Freight	Daily	80	200	0.5	24,000		24,000	1.20
20. Consolidate Shipments	As needed	5	10		nil	nil	nil	nil
21. Ship	Daily	80	200	2.0	96,000	1,000,000	1,096,000	54.80
22. Prepare Invoice	Daily	80	200	2.0	94,000	4,000	98,000	4.90
23. Mail	Daily	80	200	1.0	47,000	6,000	53,000	2.65
							2,500,000	

KEY
nil = negligible
blank = none

maximum number of orders per day was obtained by scanning the order log for September, which was the highest revenue month.

To find the number of line items per order, the reengineering team took two samples of orders, one in September and one randomly distributed throughout the year. The first sample consisted almost entirely of opening orders, and they averaged ten items per order. The second sample consisted of both opening orders and reorders, and they averaged five items per order. Similar methods of sampling, interviewing, and estimating were used to obtain the other volume statistics.

TASK 2.9—PRIORITIZE PROCESSES

This task weights each process by its impact on the business goals and priorities set in Task 1.2, Develop Executive Consensus, and by the resources consumed. It considers these, as well as the time, cost, difficulty, and risk of reengineering in a multidimensional approach to setting priorities for reengineering the processes. Once the priorities are set, the task also schedules Stages 3, 4, and 5 for each selected process.

As described in the introduction to this Identification stage, sometimes a reengineering team will know what processes the company has and which are most in need of reengineering. In those cases, much of the work of the Identification stage can be deferred safely to later stages. Other teams will start out pretty much in the dark as to what their processes are and which are most important to the business changes they seek. In that case, they will probably want to do a fairly full Identification stage to ensure that they miss nothing important. Still other teams will find themselves in intermediate positions, with a partial understanding of the processes and a limited scope. In that case, they will want to do most of the Identification stage, but only for those processes within their project scope.

This task is designed to enable the reengineering team to develop recommended priorities for reengineering, obtain executive concurrence, and move ahead. Development of priorities for reengineering is a complex task, requiring multifactor analysis and trade-off analysis. Ultimately, it requires sound business judgment. There is no algorithm guaranteed to produce the "right" answer, nor is one company's right answer the right answer for another company. The three major components of the analysis are:

1. *Impact:* the current and potential contribution of each process towards the company's business goals
2. *Size:* the resources consumed or utilized by each process
3. *Scope:* the time, cost, risk, and social change implicit in reengineering each process.

In order to assess the impact of reengineering a process, the reengineering team will have to identify the business opportunities that they foresee coming from the redesign of each process. Some of these opportunities will be obvious, when the current process clearly is deficient or no longer adaptive. Other opportunities will require greater thought. But it is essential that the team identify the specific ways in which reengineering can be expected to improve things. Management will not be satisfied with vague generalizations or promises of benefits to come. Further, the team must *quantify* the expected benefits, with the understanding that these are preliminary estimates.

Quantification of benefits is one of the requirements most resisted by reengineering teams, because their members are accustomed to only making quantitative estimates after much greater analysis than the Identification stage permits. When we encounter such resistance, we begin by asking them, "Is it safe to say that the benefit from such-and-such opportunity is somewhere between one cent and one hundred million dollars?" Once they acquiesce, it is simply a question of negotiating the end points of the interval with which they feel comfortable.

Figure 4-10 shows the chart prepared by the ABC Toy Company reengineering team to summarize the major improvement opportunities that they believed were available through reengineering. As is often the case, several of the anticipated benefits would come from reengineering more than one process. The team also decided to make single-point estimates of the benefits, rather than use a range.

Figure 4-11 shows the chart prepared by the ABC Toy Company reengineering team to prioritize the processes. It chose to use a 10-point scale to express the relative contribution of each process to management's business goals for the reengineering project. The only resources that it felt were important were people and money. Other teams might consider other resources such as machinery or space. For time, risk, and social change factors, the team selected a simple triage scheme (short-medium-long, low-medium-high, easy-medium-hard, respectively). For the cost factor, the team adopted the scheme (found in most restaurant guides) of using the symbols $, $$, $$$, and $$$$ to indicate increasing levels of expense.

Many managers and professionals share the misconception that greater precision and accuracy than that illustrated here is needed to make important decisions such as which processes to reengineer in which order. In our experience, this kind of rating system is perfectly adequate. Furthermore, there need not be unanimity in all of the ratings. Team members will often disagree whether a particular score

Figure 4-10. ABC Toy Company summary.

Opportunities	Major Processes	DP	MP	FO	SC	MA	HR	CE	FB	CR	AO	1	2	3	4	Estimated Benefits
		Processes Impacted										Related to Goals				
Improve timeliness of shipments	FO		X	X							X	X	X			2.5 MM (5% of sales)
Improve accuracy of shipments	FO		X	X							X	X	X			5 MM (10% of sales)
Improve customer satisfaction	FO		X	X	X	X						X	X	X	X	4 MM (8% of sales)
Provide "one-stop shopping"	FO			X	X							X	X	X		1 MM (2% of sales)
Reduce defects	MP	X	X										X	X		5% of sales
Reduce product cost	MP	X	X											X	X	5% of COG
Improve product quality (detail)	MP	X	X										X	X		30% of sales
Reduce write-offs	AO			X							X			X	X	0.5 MM
Reduce selling costs	AO										X			X		10% of selling costs
Increase productivity	AO										X		X	X		Included in previous
Increase sales calls per customer	AO										X	X	X			10% of sales

Processes Key

DP - Develop Product
MP - Manufacture
FO - Fulfill Orders
SC - Service Customer Rqst.
MA - Maint. Cust. Acct.
HR - Develop Hum. Res.
CE - Compensate
FB - Fund
CR - Comply
AO - Acquire Cust. Ord.

Goals Key

1 - Regain market share
2 - Capture 70% share
3 - Maintain gross profit
4 - ROI 20%

Figure 4-11. ABC Toy Company process priorities.

Process	GOALS				RESOURCES				FACTORS				Priority
	Regain Market Share	Capture 70% Share	Maintain Gross Profit	ROI 20%	FTE	$	Time		Cost	Risk	Social		
Develop Product	0	8	5	5	15	2,500,000	Med.		$$	High	Easy		3
Manufacture	0	9	7	7	375	29,300,000	Long		$$$$	Med.	Hard		2
Fulfill Orders	8	9	9	9	22.5	2,500,000	Med.		$$	Med.	Med.		1a
Service Customer Request	6	8	5	5	9	700,000	Short		$	Low	Easy		1b
Maintain Customer Account	3	3	3	3	8.5	1,000,000	Short		$	Low	Easy		
Develop Human Resources	4	6	4	4	6.5	765,000	Long		$	Med.	Hard		
Compensate	3	5	3	3	11.5	1,350,000	Med.		$	High	Hard		
Fund	3	3	3	3	9	1,060,000	Med.		$	Med.	Easy		
Comply	1	1	1	1	7	825,000	Med.		$	Med.	Med.		
Acquire Customer Orders	7	7	8	8	36	5,000,000	Med.		$$$	High	Med.		1c

KEY

0 = No Impact
10 = Maximum Impact

should be a 7 or an 8, or a medium or a low. Most of the time it won't matter. When it does matter, the team may choose to do additional analysis. But remember that one of the greatest risks for a reengineering (or any other) project is "paralysis by analysis." It is usually better to make a reasoned business decision and move on.

Another common error is to attempt to reduce a complex, multifactor analysis to a single numeric function. Usually, teams try to do this by assigning numeric scores to each factor for each process, then assigning weights to each factor, and finally summing up the weighted factor scores to obtain a total score for each process. This is pseudo-scientific nonsense! What is the relative weight of meeting a strategic business goal as compared with doing it quickly? Or of reengineering an expensive process as opposed to one in which the change will be easy? What is needed is explicit consideration of these factors and the tradeoffs among them. The truth about "quick," "good," and "cheap" is that you can only have two of them.

> The ABC Toy Company reengineering team rated the processes Fulfill Orders, Manufacture, and Acquire Customer Orders as the ones with the greatest impact on the stated business goals. Other processes had considerably less impact. These three were also the largest processes in terms of people and cost. While management had expressed a willingness to accept greater risk, the Fulfill Orders and Manufacture processes represented only medium risk. The Acquire Customer Orders process represented high risk because it was almost entirely visible to the customers and would have an immediate impact on them.
>
> The team decided that the Manufacture process was not a good candidate for early reengineering. It would take a long time, be expensive, and be a difficult change. The Acquire Customer Orders process was both riskier and more expensive than the Fulfill Orders process, so the latter became the team's choice for first priority, even though it represented medium difficulty of change, and management had expressed a preference for easy change.
>
> Second priority was assigned to Service Customer Request, which was seen as a "quick win" with a fairly high impact on the business goals. The third priority went to Acquire Customer Orders, since the team felt that reengineering the first two processes would have demonstrated success and given management the confidence to up the ante. For similar reasons, the team nominated the Manufacture process for fourth priority. The Develop Product process filled out the top five.

In order to validate its ratings of the time factor, the reengineering team prepared preliminary plans and schedules for the remaining reengineering stages for each of the five processes.

At this point, the reengineering team presented the results of the Identification stage to its project sponsor, the CEO, and to her direct reports, the vice presidents of operations, marketing, and finance and administration. (These four made up ABC Toy Company's management committee.) The management committee approved and accepted all of the reengineering team's recommendations and asked the team to begin immediately on reengineering the Fulfill Orders process.

5

Stage 3: Vision

The purpose of this stage is to develop a process vision capable of achieving breakthrough performance. The Vision stage identifies current process elements such as organization, systems, information flow, and current process problems and issues. The Vision stage also produces comparative measures of current process performance, improvement opportunities and objectives, a definition of what changes are required, and a statement of the new process "vision."

The key questions answered by this stage include:

- ❏ What are the primary subprocesses, activities, and steps that constitute our selected process(es)? In what order are they performed?
- ❏ How do resources, information, and work flow through each selected process?
- ❏ Why do we do things the way we do now? What assumptions are we making about our current work flow, policies, and procedures?
- ❏ Are there ways to achieve our business goals and address customer needs that seem impossible today, but if could be done, would fundamentally change our business?
- ❏ Consider the boundaries between our processes and our business partners, i.e., customers, suppliers, strategic allies. How might we redefine these boundaries to improve overall performance?
- ❏ What are the key strengths and weaknesses of each selected process?
- ❏ How do other companies handle the processes and associated complexities?
- ❏ What measures should we use when benchmarking our performance against best-in-class companies?

❑ What is causing the gap between our performance and that of best-practice companies?

❑ What can we learn from these companies?

❑ How can the results of visioning and benchmarking be used to redesign our processes?

❑ What are the specific improvement goals for our new processes?

❑ What is our vision and strategy for change? How can we communicate our vision to all employees?

The Vision stage, and the stages that follow it, are designed to be performed once for each business process (or closely related set of processes) that is to be reengineered. This is different from the Preparation and Identification stages, which are designed to be performed once per reengineering program. At the conclusion of the Identification stage, the original reengineering team may split itself into a number of subteams, each charged with reengineering one process. New people may also be added to be subteams at this point.

The "vision" that is the goal and product of the Vision stage is more than an idea and less than a design. It is an articulation of the purpose of reengineering the process. A well-defined vision should have the following characteristics:

❑ It should be comprehensible by a management audience that understands the business.

❑ It should describe the primary features that distinguish the reengineered process from the current process.

❑ The description should include both the social aspect (e.g., organization, staffing, jobs) and the technical aspects (e.g., technology, systems, procedures) of the process.

❑ It should state—at least qualitatively, and preferably quantitatively—how the performance of the reengineered process will be improved.

❑ It should be motivational and inspiration. The stakeholders should feel that the vision is a goal worth aspiring to.

❑ It should be apparent that the vision represents a break with the thinking and assumptions that led to the current process.

Some writers on reengineering begin their description of the process of reengineering with the development of a process vision. And there are cases where companies initiated reengineering projects when a reengineering "champion" sold their vision of a new process. But most companies follow the developments outlined in this methodology: first recognizing the need for radical and discontinuous change in the way they do business; then identifying the processes that constitute that way; and only then developing a clear understanding of where they need to go.

The vision stage consists of ten tasks:

3.1 —Understand Process Structure
3.2 —Understand Process Flow
3.3 —Identify Value-adding Activities
3.4 —Benchmark Performance
3.5 —Determine Performance Drivers
3.6 —Estimate Opportunity
3.7 —EnVision the Ideal (External)
3.8 —EnVision the Ideal (Internal)
3.9 —Integrate Visions
3.10—Define subVisions

Tasks 3.1 and 3.2 are devoted to understanding the structure and flow of the current procedure. Please note that we have used the word "understand" rather than "analyze." Here (as well as elsewhere) we choose our words very carefully, because the way we speak about something often bounds the way we can think about it. By using "understand" rather than "analyze," we mean to develop enough information about the current process to determine what it is for, how to define "good" performance, and what is wrong with the current process. We don't want to "analyze" the current process, because we intend to replace it with the reengineered process.

Task 3.3 identifies the value-adding activities within the process so that these can be enhanced, while nonvalue-adding activities are minimized. Tasks 3.4 and 3.5 are devoted to benchmarking the performance of the current process and to determining the factors responsible for that performance. Task 3.6 estimates the size and nature of the opportunity to improve performance by reengineering the process, and Tasks 3.7, 3.8, and 3.9 develop the vision of the process necessary to achieve that opportunity. Finally, Task 3.10 develops "subVisions" for the process, that is, self-consistent depictions of intermediate process implementations.

Recap

This recap is for the use of those readers referring to this chapter without having read Section Two, Chapters 2 through 4.

After recognizing the need for reengineering and mounting a team to do it (Preparation), the first order of business is to identify the current processes that a company employs and the ways in which the processes utilize resources and interact with the organization. Next, the reengineering team needs to determine how the processes affect the business goals and the time, cost, and risk involved in changing the processes. This analysis leads to the decisions on which processes to reengineer in what order (Identification).

To determine how a process affects a company's business goals, it is usually necessary to understand the needs and wants of the company's customers, since it is in satisfying these needs and wants better, faster, or less expensively that a company's business goals are best advanced. Our ongoing example, the ABC Toy Company, determined that the Fulfill Orders process had the greatest impact on its business objective of expanding market share.

TASK 3.1—UNDERSTAND PROCESS STRUCTURE

This task expands our understanding of the static aspects of the process modeled in Tasks 2.4 through 2.6 by identifying all activities and steps in the process; identifying all involved organizations and primary job functions; preparing a matrix of activities/steps versus organization/jobs; and by identifying systems and technology used and applicable policies. Some reengineering teams—those that start with an understanding of their company's processes and a mandate to focus on a single process— may start their work at this point.

Process structure is defined in terms of activities, steps, inputs, outputs, and stimuli. We need to define *activities* as the major subdivisions of a process. Each activity represents a unit of mental and/or physical work and produces a result (its output). Each activity uses the physical and/or informational output of other activities (its inputs). If an input is from outside the process and it also initiates an activity, we call that input a *stimulus*. *Stimuli* are special kinds of inputs that trigger an activity.

Steps are further subdivisions of activities. One of the questions that first-time reengineering teams invariably ask is "How detailed should our study of the current process be?" The objective of Tasks 3.1 and 3.2 is to develop sufficient understanding of the way current processes work to ensure that their reengineered replacements truly represent major improvement. The level of detail needed to achieve this understanding will vary but will always be less than that required to fix the current process. That is why we use the term "understand" rather than "analyze" in the title of these tasks.

In general, the level of detail should be sufficient to answer the following questions:

- ❑ What organizations and jobs are involved in the process? What pieces of work are done by each job?
- ❑ What policies apply to the performance of the process? In which piece of work does each policy apply?
- ❑ What technology is used in the process? In which piece of the work is the technology used?

The ABC Toy Company's Fulfill Orders process wound its way through all three of the company's departments. It began in the order processing section of the marketing department, where three jobs, order editor, order clerk, and back-order clerk, worked on the process. It was then worked on by the credit manager in the credit and collections group under the treasurer in the finance and administration department. Next, it was worked on by the inventory supervisor in the inventory control group of the materials management section in the operations department. After returning to the order processing section for the creation of paperwork, the process then wound its way through the warehouse and shipping groups of materials management. The physical order was handled by the warehouse worker and dockhand, and the accompanying paperwork was worked on by a warehouse clerk, a shipping clerk, and a traffic manager. Finally, the process returned to the billing group under the controller in the finance and administration department, where it was worked on by a billing clerk. All told, eleven different jobs in six different departments were involved in the process.

The technology used in the Fulfill Orders process ranged in vintage from the 1870s (prenumbered ledgers, self-advancing numbering stamp, telephone, and typewriter) to the 1980s (personal computer applications).

The policies that governed the Fulfill Orders process were:

- ❑ Each ship-to location of each customer shall have a unique customer number.
- ❑ Salespersons shall be paid commissions in accordance with a defined schedule.
- ❑ Each order shall be credit checked. Credit actions shall be determined by a defined credit policy.

❑ Scheduling of inventory replenishment production order shall be governed by the production plan.

❑ Beginning-of-season opening orders shall be shipped within six weeks of receipt. Reorders shall be shipped within two weeks.

All in all, the ABC Toy Company reengineering team identified twenty-three activities and eighty-three steps in the Fulfill Orders process. The information developed during this task could be represented in many ways. We have found a matrix format to be useful. Figure 5-1 shows part of the Fulfill Orders process.

Task 3.2—Understand Process Flow

This task expands our understanding of the dynamic aspects of the modeled process by identifying primary decision points and subprocesses, identifying flow variations, preparing a matrix of inputs/outputs and stimuli against activities/steps, and establishing timing.

In this task we explicitly recognize that the process is not performed the same way every time. Rather, variants typically are put into practice under differing circumstances. We call a series of activities/steps performed together conditionally a *subprocess*.

In the Fulfill Orders process, there are four potential subprocesses:

1. A new customer subprocess, which is performed when an order is received from a new customer
2. A change order subprocess, which is performed when the order received is not new but rather modifies a previously received order
3. A credit risk subprocess, which is performed when the customer's credit is insufficient to ship the order as requested
4. A consolidate orders subprocess, which is performed when more than one order to the same customer ship-to address is in hand

Also in this task the inputs and outputs of the process are explicitly listed.

A second major purpose of Understand Process Flow is to make a list of the process inputs and outputs. Although we all have a good intuitive notion of inputs and outputs, a little exposition might be appropriate here. The entities, or "things," with which processes deal are of two types. The first type is physical and relatively permanent in nature. It includes entities such as customers, employees, machines, and prod-

Figure 5-1. Fulfill orders: process structure.

Activities/Steps	O.1 Order Editor	O.2 Order Clerk	O.3 Backorder Clerk	C.1 Credit Manager	I.1 Inventory Supervisor	W.1 Warehouse Clerk	W.2 Warehouseperson	S.1 Shipping Clerk	S.2 Traffic Manager	S.3 Dockhand	B.1 Billing Clerk	Systems & Technology	Policy
5. Credit Check													
5.1 Get D&B new customer				X								Phone	
5.2 Check account balance				X								Aged Trial Balance	
5.3 Determine credit action				X									Credit Policy
6. Make Demands, if necessary													
6.1 Contact customer				X								Phone	
6.2 Negotiate payment				X								"	
6.3 Hold order				X									
6.4 Mark order COD				X									
6.5 Split order				X									
7. Check Inventory													
7.1 Determine availability					X							PC dBase Application	
7.2 Allocate					X							"	
7.3 Update availability					X							"	
7.4 Reorder					X							Production Order	Production Plan
8. Create Pick List													
8.1 List in warehouse sequence	X											PC Paradox Application	
8.2 Palletize	X											"	
9. Assign Ship Date													

Job Functions

ucts. The second type is transactional and informational in nature. It includes entities such as orders, invoices, and paychecks. While these entities also have physical reality, as deposits of ink on paper or electromagnetic impulses, it is primarily the information they carry that is important to us.

If we are interested in the physical (permanent) entities, then we require information about them. The set of information about a permanent entity could be considered an entity itself, e.g., customer record or property record. Collections of information about entities are called *files*. Files corresponding to permanent entities are often used to store information that is repeatedly referenced.

The portions of processes performed in an office environment normally deal with transactional entities and the information about physical entities, while the physical entities themselves are dealt with in those portions of processes that are performed in plants, mills, laboratories, mines, smelters, etc. Often, a physical entity and a related informational entity will traverse the process together, e.g., a bank deposit and deposit slip, the goods to be shipped and a bill of lading.

In common parlance, we often fail to distinguish between the physical entity and the information about the entity, e.g., the customer and the customer record. It is usually clear from the context to which of them we are referring.

Inputs and outputs can be physical or informational, and the same entity can be both an input and an output. When a process takes an input, modifies the input item, and then outputs the modified item, we call that process output an *updated output*. When an activity produces a new output, we say that the entity is *created*. When an activity uses an input without updating it, we say that input is *read*.

The ABC Toy Company reengineering team identified fifteen information inputs/outputs in the Fulfill Orders process:

1. Order
2. Customer File
3. Order Log
4. Credit Report
5. Accounts Receivable File
6. Inventory File
7. Reorder
8. Pick List
9. Warehouse Model
10. Back Order

11. Bill of Lading
12. Shipping Labels
13. Invoice
14. Credit Approval
15. Production Receipt

Note that none of the inputs or outputs are physical in nature. This model of the Fulfill Orders process has made the handling of the physical goods implicit in the process of handling information about the physical goods. For example, the actual dispatching of warehouse personnel to pick cartons of product, load them on a pallet, and move the pallet to the shipping area is represented by the creation and updating of a pick list and the updating of the inventory file. The actual act of affixing labels to the cartons, loading them onto a truck, and dispatching the truck to the customer is represented by the creation of the shipping labels and the bill of lading.

In other words, the Fulfill Orders process model is a model of the information flow of the process. Although the activities and steps (e.g., pick and pack) describe actions taken on the physical entities, the physical entities themselves are not described among the inputs and outputs. The reason for this is that the ABC Toy Company reengineering team did not believe that, *in its particular case,* the physical aspects of the process warranted change. It felt that the materials handling technology being used was adequate and appropriate.

Other companies (or even other teams) could very well come to different conclusions. In that case, the process model *should* include physical inputs and outputs. The flow of a process, the major decision points, and the sequential or parallel execution of activities are best represented in a flow diagram, such as Figure 5-2, which represents the Fulfill Order Process.

The relationship between activities/steps and inputs/outputs is best represented by a matrix. Figure 5-3 shows part of the matrix for Fulfill Orders. When all of the inputs and outputs are informational, the relationships "create," "read," "update," and "delete," or "destroy" are often used to express the actions on the information. These are called CRUD matrices.

The third major purpose of Understand Process Flow is to establish the timing of the process. All processes do *not* need to be timed, and the degree of accuracy and level of effort required will both vary even for

Figure 5-2. Fulfill orders: process flow.

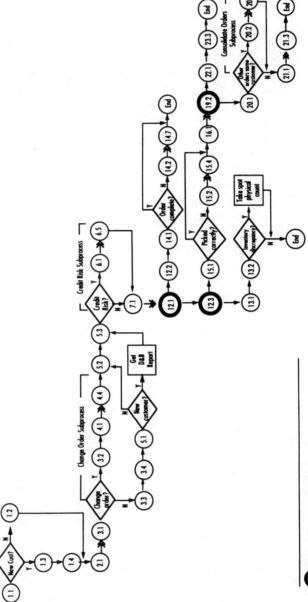

⬤ Activities that enable parallel activity chains

→ Some detail not shown

Figure 5-3.   Fulfill orders: process flow.

Activities/Steps	Inputs/Outputs	Order	Customer File	Order Log	Credit Report	Credit Approval	Production Receipt	Timing			
								In Queue	In Process	Actual Process	Out Queue
1. Identify Customer	S							1 hr.			
1.1 Look-up customers	I	I									
1.2 Retrieve customer number	I								5 min.	5 min.	
1.3 Assign new number	I										
1.4 Develop customer info.	I	C							2 days	20 min.	
2. Identify Salespersons											
2.1 See if salesperson assigned	I								2 min.	2 min.	
2.2 Record salesperson	U										
2.3 Determine commission rate	U								1 hr.	2 min.	
3. Assign Order Number											
3.1 See if order change	I								5 min.	5 min.	
3.2 Find original order number				I							30 min.
3.3 Assign next order number	SU			I				30 min.	1 min.	1 min.	
3.4 Log order				U					5 min.	5 min.	
4. Make Changes, if necessary											
4.1 See if order released				I					2 hrs.	4 min.	
4.2 Put shipping hold	U										
4.3 Revise order	U								15 min.	15 min.	
4.4 Revise commission	U										

KEY
S = Stimulus
I = Input
C = Created Output
U = Updated Output

those processes that *do* need timing. Whether or not a reengineering team chooses to time a process depends upon the way they define the performance of the process during the Identification stage.

If the external customer-oriented measures of performance defined in Task 2.2 (Define and Measure Performance) or the internal customer-oriented measures of performance defined in Task 2.6 (Extended Process Model) include the time dimension, then the reengineering team will usually want to time the process.

Timing a process means assigning times to each activity, or, if more accuracy is required, to each step of the process. When the steps within an activity are performed by different individuals, it is usually necessary to determine timing at the step level. The time required to complete a unit of work in an activity or step may be decomposed into the following components:

❑ *Transit time.* This is the amount of time needed for the inputs to the activity or step to reach it.
❑ *In-queue time.* This is the interval of time from when the inputs are received until they are acted upon.
❑ *In-process time.* This is the interval of time from when work begins on the inputs until work is completed on the outputs.
❑ *Actual process time.* This is the actual amount of time that work is done to convert the inputs to outputs. By definition, the *actual process time* must be less than or equal to the *in-process time.*
❑ *Out-queue time.* This is the interval of time from when the outputs are completed until they begin to transit to the next activity or step.

Teams should define the "unit of work" in the way that provides the most flexibility. If a process currently works on transactions in batches, the team will have greater flexibility in designing the new process if they think of the timing for each transaction in the batch. On the other hand, if the new process design is unlikely to unbundle the batch, it may be better to think of the timing of the whole batch. In manufacturing, for example, individual products are usually produced in batches or lots. Yet some companies have set as a design goal the ability to efficiently manufacture in lot sizes of one. Each team must choose the unit of work definition that best suits its situation.

The same holds true in the way different teams will *measure* time. For some, an average will suffice. For others, they may need to know the range of times, i.e., minimums and maximums. Yet others may want timing statistics such as mean, median, mode, and variance.

The *elapsed time* of an activity or step is the sum of the transit, in-queue, in-process, and out-queue times. It is often instructive to look at two ratios: that of the in-process time to elapsed time, and that of actual process time to in-process time. Frequently, these ratios are only a few percent. When the first ratio (in-process/elapsed) is low, this strongly suggests that a good way to improve the speed of the process would be to reduce the transit, in-queue, and out-queue times. When the second ratio (actual process/in-process) is low, it suggests that one should try to increase the portion of the time that the activity or step is actually working. In many processes, improvement in these ratios provides far higher improvements in elapsed time than does improvement in the speed with which the actual work is done.

Timing information can also be combined with volume and frequency information (compiled during Task 2.8: Map Resources) to calculate the *utilization* of process resources such as people and machines. Utilization represents the percentage of its capacity that a resource is used. The formula for calculating utilization is:

$$\text{Utilization} = \frac{(\text{actual process time per unit of work}) \times (\text{units of work per unit time})}{(\text{units of resource}) \times (\text{available time per unit time})}$$

Obviously, if utilization can be improved, the process may require fewer units of the resource.

At ABC Toy Company, the reengineering team had identified two external customer-oriented measures of performance that were time-related: time from receipt of order to shipment, and time to post claims and allowances. This led them to conclude that they needed to time the Fulfill Orders process and the Maintain Customer Account process. Figure 5-3 also shows the timing for a portion of the Fulfill Orders process. The reengineering team decided that average times would suffice.

In the portion of the Fulfill Orders process shown in Figure 5-3, new orders flow through activities 1, 2, and 3. The in-process time for an order in these three activities is 2 days, 1 hour, and 18 minutes, while the total elapsed time is 2 days, 3 hours, and 18 minutes. So the ratio of in-process to elapsed time is 89.6 percent. This ratio shows that transit and queuing have little impact on this portion of the process.

The ratios of actual process to in-process times tell a different story, however. For most of the steps, the ratio is 100 percent. But for Step 1.4 (Develop Customer Information), it is only 2.1 percent. And for Step 2.3 (Determine Commission Rate) it is only 3.3 percent. The problem in both cases is that the Order Editor has to telephone someone else (the customer, salesman, or sales manager) to obtain the needed information, and they are frequently unavailable. So this analysis showed that better means of obtaining the information could improve the speed of the process.

From Task 2.7 (Map Organization), the team had found that eight Order Editors, on average, were involved in performing the Fulfill Orders process. From Task 2.8 (Map Resources) the team found that an average of 80 orders per day were processed, and of these, five were change orders. From Figure 5-3, the Order

Editors were spending 34 minutes per order on steps 1.1 through 3.2 (Steps 3.3 and 3.4 were performed by Order Clerks), and 19 minutes per change order on Steps 4.1 through 4.4. Since these are the *only* activities performed by Order Editors, their utilization was calculated as:

$$\frac{34 \text{ minutes} \times 80 \text{ orders/day} + 19 \text{ minutes} \times 5 \text{ orders/day}}{8 \text{ Order Editors} \times 7 \text{ hours/day} \times 60 \text{ minutes/hour}}$$

or 83.8 percent. This told the team that the Order Editors were utilized fairly heavily. If productivity was to be improved, the team would have to find more efficient ways of performing the work of Fulfill Orders.

TASK 3.3—IDENTIFY VALUE-ADDING ACTIVITIES

This task assesses the impact of each activity of the process on the external performance measures for the process to identify activities that add value, those that do not, and those that are purely for internal control. If the reengineering team has performed the tasks of the Identification stage, it will have already understood the needs and wants of the process customers and defined external measures of process performance. If not, the reengineering team must perform the equivalent tasks at this point.

Because the Identification stage dealt with all of a company's major processes, it was necessary then to understand all of the customer's needs and wants. Now in the Vision stage we deal only with one or a few processes, so the team may need only to understand the customer's needs and wants addressed by the selected process. But since these relationships can be subtle and complex, it is better to start with as full an understanding of wants and needs as possible.

For the ABC Toy Company, the direct customers wanted attractive packaging, few product defects, a 50 percent profit margin, cooperative advertising allowances, opening orders accurately and completely filled in time for the selling season, and reorders filled within ten days. Of these, only the last two are addressed by the Fulfill Orders process.

The team identified two measures of the process performance in meeting the customer's wants: cycle time, defined as the time from receipt of an order until shipment, and accuracy, defined as the percentage of orders shipped exactly as ordered.

In this task, the reengineering team identifies the activities and steps that add (or subtract) value in the process. Once these are known and understood, they will point the way for reengineering the process following the general principles: Enhance the value-adding activities, and seek to eliminate the nonvalue-adding activities. Indeed, the ratio of value-adding to total steps gives a good measure of the opportunity for reengineering: the lower the ratio, the greater the opportunity for improvement. Ratios in the range of 10 to 30 percent are common. (For the Fulfill Orders process, it is twenty-three out of eighty-three steps, or 28 percent.)

The easiest way to identify the value-adding steps is to consider the impact of the step on each of the performance measures for the process. Will the performance of the step have a positive impact on the performance measure? If so, the step will meet the definition of value-added: It does something the customer wants. The step might also have negative impact, or no impact at all, on the performance measure.

Nonvalue-adding steps may be categorized further as "control" and "other." The "other" category includes housekeeping, administration, communication, and coordination activities. Both control and other steps are candidates for elimination or for integration into value-adding steps. Decisions on other steps can usually be made within the context of the process itself, whereas decisions on control steps may require a broader context: The reasons that the control is there may not be apparent from inside the process. Indeed, from the perspective of the process, many controls actually impede performance. Figure 5-4 illustrates this task for the Fulfill Orders process.

The purpose of this task is to help the reengineering team ask the key questions "Why do we do things the way we do?" and "Is this really necessary?" and "What are we doing that actually degrades process performance?" Sometimes, as in Step 15.2 of Figure 5-4, a step will have a positive impact on one performance measure and a negative impact on another performance measure. Repicking an order that has been picked incorrectly will improve accuracy but lengthen cycle time. Here the trade-off between shipping an incorrect order sooner and a correct order a little later is obvious, but this isn't always the case.

TASK 3.4—BENCHMARK PERFORMANCE

This task compares both the performance of the organization's processes and the way those processes are conducted with those of relevant peer organizations to obtain ideas for improvement. The peer organizations may be within the same corporate family, they may be comparable com-

Figure 5-4. Fulfill orders: activities value.

Activities/Steps	Performance Measures		Activity Type		
	Cycle Time	Accuracy	Value-Adding	Control	Other
14. Prepare Back Order					
14.1 Determine if complete		+	X		
14.2 Determine if customer accepts backorders		+	X		
14.3 Estimate availability					X
14.4 Contact customer, if necessary		+	X		
14.5 Write back order				X	
14.6 Suspend back order				X	
14.7 Adjust inventory				X	
15. Check Order					
15.1 Check against pick list		+	X	X	
15.2 Re-pick, if necessary	–	+			X
15.3 Adjust pick list, if necessary				X	
15.4 Forward correction, if necessary					X
16. Prepare Shipping Documents					
16.1 Compute cube and weight					X
16.2 Prepare bill of lading					X
16.3 Prepare labels					X
17. Pack Order					
17.1 Repack cartons, if necessary	–				X

KEY

+ = Positive impact

– = Negative impact

X = Type of activity

panies, industry leaders, or best-in-class performers. The task consists of identifying relevant peers, determining their process performance and the primary differences in their processes that account for the performance differences, and assessing the applicability of those process differences to our processes. The purpose of this task is to ask the important questions: Why do we do our process the way we do, whereas they do their process differently? Can we learn something from them?

Benchmarking has become a subject with its own literature. It became popular in the mid to late eighties as a part of the quality movement and is a required activity for any company aspiring to the Malcolm Baldrige National Quality Award. We take no position on whether the kind of benchmarking described in the literature is worth doing. Certainly some major corporations, preeminently Xerox Corporation, have made it a way of life.

What is clear to us, however, is that "classical" benchmarking is neither feasible nor necessary for business process reengineering (BPR). Classical benchmarking is not feasible because it takes too long and requires too many resources for a reengineering project. We allow only a month to six weeks for the entire Vision stage, and a benchmarking project can take that long to train the team members and select the companies to benchmark. Nor is classical benchmarking necessary for reengineering, in our view, for we are using it only to help us to ask, "Why do we do things the way we do?" and to get ideas on better ways to do things.

For those readers not familiar with benchmarking, the following outline should suffice:

1. Select an area of your business to benchmark. When reengineering, the "area" should be a process.
2. Decide the most important measures of the performance of the process.
3. Measure your own company's performance of the process.
4. Find other companies that are performing the process better than your company, as determined by the selected measures.
5. Understand how the process works at the better performing companies.
6. Decide whether the process features that make the other company's process better will work in your company.
7. Implement what you have learned.

In classical benchmarking, enormous amounts of time can be spent in researching other companies; in selecting and measuring performance variables; in normalizing results to ensure apples-to-apples comparisons; and in negotiating, arranging, and conducting reciprocal site visits with multiple companies. This amount of time and effort is simply not available in most BPR projects. Instead, we suggest a more rapid and modest approach to benchmarking—one that readily sacrifices rigor and precision for speed and coverage.

Our benchmarking approach relies primarily on secondary and tertiary information sources and infrequently on primary sources. Even then, the method of acquiring information is more likely to be by telephone than by an on-site visit. We begin with a simple observation: People who have accomplished something significant, such as a novel or breakthrough approach to a business problem, generally like other people to know about it. One has only to attend an industry or professional conference or to read professional journals and the trade press to confirm the truth of that observation. So the first source of benchmarking information is the business literature. When you have winnowed some likely leads, you can telephone the authors. They are usually delighted to be called; I know that we are. A second good source of information is your major customers and suppliers. Often they are also the customers and suppliers of other companies, sometimes of your competitors. Sometimes they themselves have a process similar to the one you are attempting to reengineer. It is important to stress in this connection that benchmarking is *not* industrial espionage. You should never ask others for information that you are unwilling to supply about your own company. A third good source of information is your employees and applicants. Sometimes they have direct experience with the companies you are trying to benchmark. Sometimes they network with people who have such experience. A fourth good source of information is vendors. If a vendor has provided products and/or services to others with good results, it is likely to approach your company as well. So listen to the vendors and ask for references. There are also organizations that facilitate the exchange of information. The U.S. Department of Defense is one; the International Benchmarking Clearinghouse is another.

The purpose of all this benchmarking activity is twofold: first, to provide additional insights into the idiosyncrasies of your own practices, and second, to get ideas on how to do them better. To accomplish this purpose it is not necessary to have precise numerical measures of relative performance. It is sufficient to know the relative performance in a general way. If company X appears to have 15 percent better performance than our process, it doesn't matter if it is really 10 percent or 20 percent. First of all, we must allow for the overly generous estimate. Second, we must allow for the possibility that we and company X measure performance differently. Finally, we are seeking breakthroughs in performance, and 10 to 20 percent doesn't count as a breakthrough. So we would probably conclude that company X doesn't perform the process much better than we do. But if the margin were 50 percent, we would definitely want to take a closer look.

Also, it is not necessary to have a detailed understanding of the other company's process in order to accomplish our purpose. Rather, it is necessary only to understand the main features and tactics taken in the process that distinguish it from ours. Much more important is the issue of whether the differences are applicable to our own process, that is, whether the other company's approach is relevant to our own situation. There are no easy guidelines here. Confining your search to companies in your own industry is more likely to ensure the relevance of what you find but less likely to discover the ideas that will prove to be a breakthrough for your industry. In one famous example of benchmarking outside your own industry, when Xerox wanted to benchmark its order process, it went to L.L. Bean.

The ABC Toy Company reengineering team selected six companies to benchmark. The first, naturally enough, was their arch competitor, XYZ Plastics. The other five were selected because they appeared to provide superior order fulfillment. Two of the companies were in the toy business, and three were not. Figure 5-5 shows the table that the ABC reengineering team prepared to summarize the results of its benchmarking exercise.

The first conclusion that the team drew from this information was that there was an opportunity to widen ABC's advantage over XYZ in order fulfillment performance. And XYZ was unlikely to be able to close the gap as long as they continued to manufacture overseas and outsource warehousing. The second conclusion was that the factors that enabled the other two toy companies to perform so well were simply not present at ABC. And the third conclusion was that some specific technology—handheld terminals and electronic data interchange (EDI)—and business arrangements (store level reorders) appeared to contribute to exceptional performance.

TASK 3.5—DETERMINE PERFORMANCE DRIVERS

This task defines the factors that determine the performance of the process by identifying:

❑ Sources of problems and errors
❑ Enablers and inhibitors of process performance

Figure 5-5. Fulfill orders: benchmark.

Company	% Orders Shipped Complete	% Items Picked Accurately	% Items Back Ordered	Avg. Wait for Back Order (days)	% Accuracy Inventory Count (Annual Physical)	Average Days Receipt to Release	Average Days Release to Ship	Notes on Differences
ABC Toy Company	95*	97	1.5	22	75	15	15	All mfg. in Asia.
	80	99	23	15	—	5	5	Uses public warehouse.
XYZ Plastics	90	98	8	40	—	5	15	
	75	98	30	30	—	5	10	
Acme Model Aircraft	99	99.5	1	10	98.5	1	2	Relatively low seasonality.
	99	99.5	1	10				Predictable demand.
Top Notch Toys	99.7	99.9	nil	n.a.	95	1	10	Assembler of pre-cut
	99.2							parts. Made to order.
Ultimate Electronics	98	99.9	4	7	99.5	2	1	Over 100K SKUs†. Handheld terminals in warehouse.
Zenith Pharmaceuticals	99.9	99.9	0.5	3	97	0.5	0.5	Same day shipping. EDI from hospitals, distributors.
Growth Cosmetics	99.7	99.7	1.3	2	98	1	5	Automatic store reorders. Weekly scheduled shipments.

* Note: Upper figure pertains to new orders   † = Stock Keeping Units
Lower figure pertains to reorders
SKU = Stock Keeping Units

KEY

nil = negligible
— = not available
n.a. = not applicable

❏ Dysfunctions and incongruities
❏ Activity or job fragmentation
❏ Information gaps or delays

Actually, the performance drivers are not defined as a result of an additional analytic effort. Rather, they emerge naturally from all of the work done before in reviewing and benchmarking the process. They come from a fresh (or a refreshed) set of eyes and brains looking at the process and concluding, "That just doesn't make sense. It would be better if. . . ."

When one looks at a business process and tries to understand why it is the way it is, one is conducting industrial archeology. For the business processes in most organizations were *not* engineered in the first place. Rather, they are historical accidents, accumulations of custom and practice with an overlay of systems and procedures. That is the reason that processes are often so very different in very similar businesses. The current processes embed a host of assumptions that are often no longer valid and that sometimes were invalid when they were made. Assumptions about the cost and capabilities of technology, about the limitations and motivations of human beings, about the most effective way of organizing and managing people and work. Sometimes the processes enshrine the political status in the organization at some prior time. Sometimes they continue doing work, the need for which has long since vanished.

This Determine Performance Drivers task, then, identifies the factors, characteristics, and elements of the process responsible for its performance deficiencies and assesses their impact.

At the ABC Toy Company, the reengineering team identified a number of problems with the Fulfill Orders process.

1. All orders were credit checked. Since the credit manager was semiretired and worked only three days per week, there was often a large queue of orders awaiting his attention. The average delay on opening orders was eight days, and on reorders it was three days.
2. Forty percent of all the orders were received with incomplete information. This required the order editor to contact the salesperson and/or customer and introduced additional delays and errors.
3. There were numerous errors in transcribing information from order to pick list to back order resulting in orders be-

ing shipped incorrectly, in accounting adjustments, and in inefficient use of warehouse personnel and space.

4. Orders were released to the warehouse on a first in, first out basis, regardless of the customer's requested ship date. This necessitated significant expediting activity to meet the customers' requests. In spite of this, 15 percent of opening orders and 30 percent of reorders were not meeting the customers' ship date. Extra work and rearrangement of goods in the warehouse were required for expedited orders.

5. There were significant discrepancies between the actual physical inventory counts and the book inventory. Sometimes this resulted in unnecessary back orders or production orders. Sometimes order processing personnel had to go into the warehouse to count the actual inventory on a spot basis. There was much reworking of records and documents.

6. Sales forecasts for reorders were inaccurate. This resulted in 23 percent of the items being back-ordered and substantial inventory write-downs when the remaining inventory was disposed of at the end of the season.

7. Eight percent of the orders were consolidated with a subsequent order from the same customer. Studies showed that this resulted in an average 11 percent reduction in freight costs on these orders. But the practice also caused an additional ten-day delay, on average, and significant work in moving goods and reworking documents.

While the team found other problems as well, these are a representative sample.

TASK 3.6—ESTIMATE OPPORTUNITY

This task uses all of the information developed so far in Stage 3: Vision to assess the opportunity for process improvement (or to expand on the initial assessment made in Task 2.9). It estimates the degree of change needed and the difficulty of the change, the costs and benefits of the change, the level of support for the change, and the risks of making the change. It also defines the near-term opportunities for improvement, which can be pursued immediately.

Figure 5-6 shows part of the document the ABC reengineering team created as a result of this task. Two of the opportunities were near term. The first, shown in the figure, was to establish

Figure 5-6. Fulfill orders: opportunities.

Opportunity	Change	Difficulty	Benefits	Costs	Support	Risks
Improve reorder sales forecast	Track store level reorders	Moderate	Better service. Lower write-off.	Store level order capture. Forecast model.	Operations: High Marketing: Low Customers: ?	Change may not work and failure would be visible to
Exception credit checking	Accept all orders up to established credit limit	Low	Reduce delays	Establish, maintain limits.	Operations: High Marketing: High Finance: Low	Sudden change in credit-worthiness
Eliminate transcription errors	Capture order electronically and update on-line	Moderate	Accuracy. Less labor.	On-line system	Moderate	Low
Optimize warehouse flow	Release orders "just in time"	High	Reduced cycle time. Better Service. More	On-line system. Sophisticated warehouse model.	High	Advanced technology for ABC

credit limits and initiate exception credit checking. The second was to discontinue consolidation of orders. But the ABC team was unsure whether the additional freight costs ($8,800 per annum) would be offset by the reduced complexity.

Notice that both the benefits and the costs of each opportunity in the example are expressed qualitatively and not quantitatively. Sometimes, enough information will be available to make a quantitative estimate. But even then, the estimate will usually be a range rather than a single point estimate.

The lack of quantitative data really presents no difficulties at this stage because the only purpose of this assessment is to decide, on a preliminary basis, which opportunities for improvement to incorporate into the process vision. In the next stage, Solution, specific design decisions will be made on how to accomplish the process vision. At that point, more reliable estimates of cost and benefit can be made. All the project team will be asking for in this stage is for the sponsor to accept the vision and authorize the team to proceed with the next stage.

TASK 3.7—ENVISION THE IDEAL (EXTERNAL)

This task describes how the process would operate with all of the external performance measures (defined in Task 2.2 or Task 3.3) optimized. In particular, it describes the behavior of those activities that interface with customers and suppliers.

TASK 3.8—ENVISION THE IDEAL (INTERNAL)

This task describes how the process would operate with all of the internal performance measures (defined in Task 2.6 or Task 3.4) optimized. It thus repeats Task 3.7, treating internal participants as customers and suppliers. This task also describes how key job functions would be performed to achieve ideal performance.

TASK 3.9—INTEGRATE VISIONS

It is possible that the internal and external ideals conflict. This task identifies any such conflicts and trades off among the alternative capabilities to produce the most effective integrated vision. Tasks 3.7, 3.8, and 3.9 are usually performed concurrently, or at least iteratively. Regardless, the final integrated vision should be internally consistent and compelling.

The ABC Toy Company described its vision for the Fulfill Orders process in terms of the major components or subprocesses as follows:

Order Receipt

Initial opening orders will be taken by salespersons from chain buyers and submitted by mail or FAX. That is the current practice. However, reorders will be submitted directly by stores via FAX, EDI, or telephone. The customers may still have the orders drop shipped to the stores or to the chain's distribution center.

Order Entry

Orders will be captured electronically by an on-line data processing system. Master customer, item, and salesperson files are used to supply default information. All data are validated on-line. Credit checking is automatic and produces an exception report. The perpetual inventory balance is checked, and inventory is allocated to orders and back orders, and production orders are issued; customer notifications are produced automatically. All order entry functions are performed by a single customer service representative job.

Change Order

The original order will be displayed on-line for modification. All other capabilities of order entry are also available.

Credit Risk

The majority of orders will be approved automatically because they are under the credit limit. An expert system will suggest credit limits and credit actions. Eventually, the expert system will set credit limits and decide on all but a few credit actions.

Order Release

Pending orders for the same customer, including back orders, will be consolidated automatically. The customer's requested ship date, inventory availability, warehouse capacity, and staff availability will all be combined to produce a warehouse schedule that optimizes flow. Picking instructions will be sent on request to handheld terminals in the warehouse.

Picking and Packing

The warehouse worker will follow the instructions on the handheld terminal, confirming each pick action by scanning a bar code on the carton. After assembling the order in the shipping area, the warehouse worker uses the handheld terminal to transmit picking data to the computer, which produces labels and a bill of lading at the loading dock.

Shipping

An expert system determines the best method of shipping. The carrier is notified via EDI. The carrier's pickup time is factored into the warehouse schedule so that shipments arrive at the loading dock in proper sequence for loading and just in time for pickup.

Billing

Invoices are produced automatically. Some of the features of this vision—such as the handheld terminals, the use of EDI, and the store-level reorders—can be traced directly to the information obtained by benchmarking. Other features are a direct response to the opportunities seen for improvement. And some of the features are just blue-sky thinking.

The vision is heavily weighted toward the technical aspects of the process—technology, procedures, and systems. The only social feature is the new customer service representative job. Nevertheless, the vision is not driven by technology, it is enabled by it. That is to say, the reengineering team did not search for useful technical innovations and seek to use them in the process. Rather, it sought solutions to identified problems and found them through its awareness of available technology. This distinction is subtle but important.

TASK 3.10—DEFINE SUBVISIONS

This task examines the time frame for realization of the process vision and the possibility of defining successive subVisions between the cur-

Figure 5-7. Fulfill orders: subVisions.

SubVision	Cycle Time Impact	Accuracy Impact	Time Frame
Order processing system with order change capability. Perpetual inventory: allocations, backorders, reorders, customer notification. Credit limits used to produce exception report. Suggested order consolidation report. Shipping documents on request. Manual freight calculation, warehouse scheduling and routing. Automatic billing. Customer service representative.	-20%	+50%	1 year
Store-level reorders. EDI. Warehouse flow optimization. Expert routing system. Automatic freight calculations. Shipping documents on request. Automatic order consolidation.	-20%	+35%	2 years
Expert credit system. Hand held terminals in warehouse. Shipping documents automatically produced at loading dock. EDI link to carriers.	-10%	+15%	3 years
Total	-50%	+100%	3 years

rent process and the fully integrated vision. If defined, each subVision is associated with performance goals.

At ABC Toy Company, the team recognized that attainment of its full vision would require several years, so it examined alternatives that would provide some of the features and benefits earlier. Eventually it came up with the three-phase (or three sub-Vision) solution shown in Figure 5-7.

Decisions on which features to incorporate into each subVision were based on considerations of logical precedence, time, risk, cost, and benefits. Most of these factors were already assessed in Task 3.6. Estimates of the impacts on process performance were judgmental but heavily influenced by what the team learned from benchmarking.

At this point, the reengineering team completed Stage 3 by presenting its vision to the management committee, which authorized it to proceed with the design of a new process to fulfill the vision.

6

Stage 4A: Solution: Technical Design

The purpose of this stage is to produce a process design capable of achieving the process vision. This stage answers the question "How?" Developing the solution has two components, Technical Design and Social Design. Business process reengineering (BPR) is enabled by three factors or forces: technology, information, and human potential. BPR seeks to leverage these three forces into breakthroughs in process performance.

We often neglect to mention information as one of the enablers, subsuming it under the discussion about technology, because it is information technology that is most commonly used in BPR. But information is an enabler in its own right, and sometimes a nontechnical (e.g., manual) solution that provides better information is all that is needed. For example, if a worker repeatedly performs a task with no feedback on the quality of his or her work, the worker's performance is likely to be vastly improved when that feedback is provided.

Shoshanah Zuboff, in her book *In the Age of the Smart Machine* (New York: Basic Books, 1988), notes that information technology provides two distinct capabilities for improving the performance of work. The first, and more familiar, capability is automation: actually replacing manual tasks with machine tasks. Examples include calculation, printing, scanning, and control of machinery. The second capability is information. In order to automate, a computer must develop an electronic record of the process it is automating. Zuboff uses the example of the automation of a pulp mill. The computer maintained detailed data on the values of hundreds of physical variables in the process never before recorded. This information enabled the operators to optimize the process in ways that were impossible before. Zuboff uses the word *informate* to describe this potential application of technology. We call such applications of technology and information to improve a process Technical Design.

The third enabler of BPR is human potential. Although most business processes ultimately rely on human beings to carry them out, it has long been recognized that few processes fully utilize the potential of those human beings. Indeed, since the dawn of the Industrial Revolution, the organizing principle of work has been *specialization*. Specialization means that a worker is given responsibility for only one or, at most, a few closely related tasks. By specializing, the worker is expected to perform the task more efficiently than would a worker who was less specialized. Also, because the work is decomposed into a series of simple tasks, it becomes much easier to apply technology to such tasks (i.e., automate them) than it would be to automate more complex tasks.

Indeed, the principle of specialization worked wondrously well. Productivity exploded, invention abounded, and the world became enormously richer (and more populated). By the end of the nineteenth century, the principle of specialization was being applied to mental work as well as physical work by such industrial engineers as Frank Gilbreth and Frederick W. Taylor. Even professional and managerial work became specialized. And the business organization reflected this specialization by collecting specialists with similar skills into *functional organizations.*

There are only two problems with specialization. The first is that, because each person is responsible for only a piece of the work, no one is responsible for the work as a whole or for its products. This means that a large infrastructure had to be created to organize, direct, and control the work. Several different categories of workers emerged: those who do the work, those who manage those who do the work, those who seek to improve the way the work is done, those who support those who manage, etc. Since each of these workers is also doing work, the bureaucracy proliferated.

The second problem with specialization is that it fails to exploit human potential. We are not screw turners, auto mechanics, computer operators, managers, or accountants. We are human beings with a vast range of interests and capabilities. And the less of our abilities the job utilizes, the less of our potential it exploits. In the extreme, where workers are responsible for limited operations whose contribution to the overall result is unclear, alienation and diminished productivity result. Despite these drawbacks, the specialized, bureaucratic organization delivered higher productivity than earlier organizational models, and it flourished.

In recent years, however, this organizational model has come increasingly into question, mainly because it is essentially a *command and control* type of organization. That is, while work is done at the lowest levels of the organization, decisions are made at the highest levels. The workers are analogous to muscles; senior management is analogous to the brain. And middle management is analogous to the nervous system, since its primary function is to relay information upward and instructions downward.

The command and control organization is good at enforcing a high level of *conformance* but not very good at enforcing a high level of *commitment* among its members. That is why the archetypical command and control organization—the military—must resort to devices like intensive drilling and must promote values like "duty, honor, country." In actuality, even the military does not provide as rigid a command and control environment as it might appear. Military strategy is implemented at the corps level and above, and lower-level units generally have a good deal of tactical freedom. The last major conflict in which the generals tried to control actions at the lowest level—World War I—saw long periods of stalemate and needless waste of life.

The greatest weakness of the command and control organization is that it is inflexible and slow moving. The workers at the interface between the external environment and the organization have no power to respond to the changes they encounter. They must relay information, slowly and imperfectly, to the senior management, where decisions are made as to how to respond. Then these decisions must be translated into policies, procedures, and systems and relayed, again slowly and imperfectly: back to the workers who use them. Workers in this kind of organization tend to be risk averse. J. Laurence Peter observed that people in a bureaucracy are judged by their conformance to the rules, not by their performance in carrying out the mission of the bureaucracy. He tells a story about a bookstore clerk who was willing to cash a personal check (because Peter had ID and the rules said it was all right to do so) but not to cash a traveler's check (because the rules didn't mention them) even though the traveler's check was guaranteed and the personal check wasn't.

The command and control model is being seen as a less and less effective organization today because we live in an era of accelerating change. There is simply no time for the bureaucracy to respond. And the grand strategies and plans are overtaken by events more rapidly than anyone could have foreseen. Geopolitical, social, economic, cultural, and technological trends change with such rapidity and magnitude that some people see the environment as chaotic. In this type of environment, the only rational response is to develop organizational forms that are better able to react and deal with largely unpredictable events. These adaptive organizations are usually characterized by relatively short lines of communication between front line workers and senior management and by a great deal of responsibility and authority being pushed down into the ranks. This is the type of organizational design that usually emerges from BPR.

The technical and social designs for a business process must be congruent. That is, they must be mutually supportive of the process goals. Richard Walton, in his book *Up and Running* (Boston: Harvard Business School Press, 1989), describes several cases in which technically sound systems failed because they were incongruous with the organization in which they were implemented. It has often been observed that "Good people can make a bad system work; bad people can't make a good system work." Actually, this is not a comment on "bad" people, but rather on people whose skills, knowledge, orientation, authority, and responsibility were mismatched with the needs of the system.

Walton made another very important observation: Technology itself is neutral with respect to the role assigned human beings. Technology can be used to control people (e.g., monitor their behavior and performance) or to empower them (e.g., "informate" their work).

This discussion is all leading to the recognition that there are two sides to a design solution for a business process: the technical and the social. The technical design seeks to leverage technology and information in order to improve process performance. The social design seeks to leverage human potential to the same end. Since the technical and social designs must be congruent for maximum performance, the technical and social designs should be developed concurrently. This chapter covers technical design. Chapter 7 covers social design.

Recap

This recap is for those readers referring to this chapter without having read Section Two, Chapters 2 through 5.

Before beginning the design of a reengineered process, a reengineering team should have developed a Vision of the new process. The vision articulates the purpose of reengineering the process. It should be comprehensible to a management audience and clearly linked to the organization's business goals. It should include both technical and social aspects of the way the work will be done. It should state the performance goals for the new process and demonstrate that these represent a breakthrough. Finally, it should inspire the sponsors and other stakeholders to aspire to its realization.

The ABC Toy Company developed a vision for its Fulfill Orders process that it thought would help it meet its business goal of expanding market share. The vision was heavily weighted toward the use of information technology. It included an on-line order-processing system; expert systems for credit management, route selection, and warehouse scheduling; handheld terminals in the warehouse; and the introduction of electronic data interchange (EDI) with its customers. On the social side, the vision postulated a new customer service representative position that would assume responsibility for all order processing activities.

The reengineering team estimated that it would take three years to achieve this vision and that it would result in a 50 percent reduction in cycle time and a 100 percent improvement in accuracy. The team also described three subVisions that represented partial realizations of the vision after one, two, and three years, respectively.

Technical Design Stage Purpose and Tasks

The purpose of Technical Design is to specify the technical dimension of the new process. The Technical Design stage produces descriptions of the technology, standards, procedures, systems, and controls employed by the reengineered process. It (together with Stage 4B, Social Design) produces designs for the interaction of social and technical elements. Finally, it produces preliminary plans for systems and procedures development; procurement of hardware, software, and services; facilities enhancement; test, conversion, and deployment.

The key questions answered by this stage include:

❑ What technical resources and technologies will we need in the reengineered process?
❑ How can these resources and technologies best be acquired?
❑ What information will the reengineered process use?
❑ How will the technical and social elements interact? (e.g., the human interface of the system)

The Technical Design Stage consists of ten tasks:

4A.1 —Model Entity Relationships
4A.2 —Reexamine Process Linkages
4A.3 —Instrument and Informate
4A.4 —Consolidate Interfaces and Information
4A.5 —Redefine Alternatives
4A.6 —Relocate and Retime Controls
4A.7 —Modularize
4A.8 —Specify Deployment
4A.9 —Apply Technology
4A.10—Plan Implementation

Task 4A.1 develops an initial information model of the process. Tasks 4A.2 through 4A.6 represent templates or rules of thumb that can be applied to a process to identify better ways of performing it. These tasks are best performed concurrently and/or iteratively. Task 4A.7 defines the component parts of the reengineered process that can be moved independently in space, time, or organizational location. Then Task 4A.8 specifies the deployment. Task 4A.9 determines the applications of technology in the process. And finally, Task 4A.10 plans implementation of the technical elements of the reengineered process. Actually, Task 4A.10 is also part of the same task in Social Design 4B.12, which plans implementation of the social elements.

TASK 4A.1—MODEL ENTITY RELATIONSHIPS

This task identifies the relationships among entities. It also defines the direction and cardinality of the relationships, i.e., whether the relationship is one-to-one, one-to-many, or many-to-many, and which entity "owns" which other entity. Since entities are the "things" with which a process is concerned, the technical elements of the process includes information (i.e., collections of data) about the entities. This task is a first step in modeling the data.

In the ABC Toy Company's Fulfill Orders process, there were six entities: Customer, Order, Line Item, Product, Back Order, and Invoice. Each entity consists of one or more instances. For example, the entity Customer consists of the instances Toys R Us, Wal-Mart, etc. The entity Product consists of the instances Baby-Toots, Cobra Commander, etc. Each entity is represented by a set of attributes. Each instance of the entity is associated with a set of values for the attributes. For example, the entity Order would include the attributes "order number," "date of receipt," "shipping date," and "ship-to location." One instance of the Order entity might have the corresponding values: 12345; 08/15/93; 10/01/93; 123 West State Street, Topeka, KS.

Some of the attributes of the entity might describe its state. For example, an Order could be booked, released, or picked. Entities may have relationships. For example, the entity Customer has the relationship "places" with the entity Order. Every relationship implies a reverse relationship. For example, an order is "placed by" a customer. That is, relationships are directional and usually asymmetric. A relationship may be one-to-one, one-to-many, or many-to-many. For example, one customer may have many orders, but each order has only one customer. Also, relationships may be optional: At any given time, a customer need not have an order.

The entities and their relationships are the first level of an information model of the process. Subsequent levels, developed in Stage 5, specify the attributes and the logical implementation of the information model. For the purpose of this stage, however, we need only know the entities and recognize that the technical design will include a data store (file or table) of information about the entity. Figure 6-1 shows the entity relationship model for the Fulfill Orders process.

Figure 6-1.   Fulfill orders: entity/relationship model.

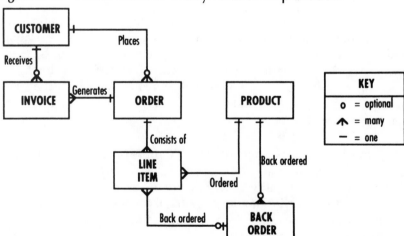

TASK 4A.2—REEXAMINE PROCESS LINKAGES

This task considers whether movement of steps among activities, activities among processes, or reassigned responsibility for steps would improve performance. It also identifies instances where better coordination among activities would improve performance.

The ideas behind this template or rule of thumb are very similar to those of Michael Porter in his books *Competitive Strategy* (New York: Free Press, 1984) and *Competitive Advantage* (New York: Free Press, 1985). Porter conceptualizes each company as a Value Chain consisting of direct activities such as inbound logistics, operations, outbound logistics, and sales and service. The value chain also contains indirect activities such as finance and administration, information services, and technology development that support the direct activities. Porter defines the value-added of a company as the difference between the value of the goods and services it produces and the value of the goods and services it consumes. (Porter's definition is equivalent to ours—something the customer is willing to pay for—because if the company didn't add value, no one would buy its products.) Porter gives numerous examples where the value added can be increased by integration or better coordination among activities. For example, better coordination between manufacturing and purchasing can lead to higher quality and higher yields in the goods produced.

Porter also noted that the suppliers and customers of a company also have their own value chains. And he saw additional opportunities to add value by integration or better coordination among activities *in different value chains*. For example, extending the manufacturing case just described, if the customer's demand for the goods were linked more closely with the manufacturer's manufacturing, and the manufacturer's purchasing were linked more closely with the supplier's production and outbound logistics, additional value could be created for all three companies. While Porter spoke of "activities" rather than "processes," his notions and ours are very similar. Sometimes, there is an opportunity for a business to transfer responsibility for work to its customers. Salad bars, automatic teller machines, and self-service gas stations are all examples of this responsibility transfer.

Sometimes, there is a better opportunity for a business to transfer responsibilities from its customers to itself. The retail business of Citibank basically worked by collecting deposits from its customers and then lending the money to other customers at a higher interest rate. When interest rates on deposits fell into the two to three percent range, deposits fell as well, as customers found other, more lucrative ways to invest their money. Citibank responded by establishing new retail investment services that help their customers invest in alternatives like mutual funds. If Citibank couldn't earn on the interest rate spread, they could at least earn fees. In essence, Citibank rethought the boundaries between its customers' processes and its own.

Sometimes, there is an opportunity for a business to transfer responsibility for work to its suppliers. Just-in-time inventory control is one example of this. So is Wal-Mart's agreement with Procter & Gamble for the latter to manage the former's inventory of Pampers.

Some suppliers specialize in providing services that wholly or partially replace activities formerly performed by their customers. We call these suppliers *outsource vendors,* and the act of using them *outsourcing.* Today, outsource vendors provide services such as catering, maintenance and repair, data processing, mail room operation, and operation of communications networks. The key question that a company must answer in outsourcing is where greater value can be added—by the outsource vendor or by themselves. Sometimes the answer is surprising. Although most banks consider data processing one of the activities that adds significant value because it is central to so many of the banks' major processes, Continental Bank chose to outsource its data processing. The *Harvard Business Review,* in reporting on this case, titled the article "Outsourcing the Crown Jewels."

These are examples of the movement of steps and coordination of activities among the processes of different organizations. There are many more opportunities to move steps and coordinate activities among the processes of the same organization. For example, *concurrent engineering* represents the coordination or integration of marketing, product development, product and process engineering, and manufacturing processes.

Sometimes an organization can reduce or eliminate a support process by incorporating it into a core, value-added process. Agway is an agricultural cooperative that had four lines of business: feed and grain, insurance, petroleum products distribution, and retailing. Their information services organization was viewed as a support activity and cost center. As such, it had difficulty competing for resources within the corporation. Information services management restructured the organization by spinning off the application development groups to the business lines they supported. Then they converted the remaining computer and network operations organization into a profit center selling services to external customers, thereby becoming a fifth line of business.

Sometimes an organization can resequence activities to eliminate the need for separate subprocesses. At the restaurants in Disney World, customers had to stand in one line to order food, in another line to pick up the food, and in a third line to pay for it. Disney established kiosks throughout the park where customers could order their food in advance, go to the restaurant, pick up their food, and pay for it. In a similar vein, Disney began prescooping ice cream for ice cream cones. These innovations both reduced the number of subprocesses and simplified the interface with the customer.

At the ABC Toy Company, the reengineering team recognized two opportunities in the Fulfill Orders process. First, better coordination would permit optimization of the warehouse work flow. For example, if order consolidation and customer requested ship dates could be better coordinated with the manufacturing production schedule, then both manufacturing and warehousing would benefit. Second, consolidation and automation of order editing, order processing, inventory control, and billing activities would improve accuracy and timeliness and provide better customer service.

The reengineering team also recognized two cross-process linkage opportunities. First, there was a Service Customer Request process that handled all customer calls. Most of these calls were routed to the order editors or to the accounts receivable personnel. The team decided that the Service Customer Request process could be eliminated. If the customer call was related to accounting issues, it would be handled by the Maintain Customer Account process. All other calls would be handled by Fulfill Orders. This would improve the speed and accuracy of the response and reduce effort. Second, the activities for soliciting, writing, and submitting store-level reorders would be transferred from the Acquire Customer Orders process to the Fulfill Orders process, permitting faster order fulfillment. At the same time, Fulfill Orders would pass information to the Manufacture process, which would permit more accurate sales forecasts and better production planning.

Task 4A.3—Instrument and Informate

This task identifies the information needed to measure and manage the performance of the process, defines places where the information can be stored (usually, files associated with the entities), and adds steps to the process, as needed, to capture, assemble, and disseminate the needed information. *Instrument* and *informate* are both transitive verbs.

By instrument we mean putting in place the instruments necessary to measure the performance variables by which we will manage the process. By informate we mean making the performance information available in a useful way. The instruments must provide a *complete* and *consistent* set of information.

The information must be provided in an understandable and useful way. Automobile manufacturers have largely discontinued the use of digital displays in automobiles because they provide unneeded accuracy and distracting detail. People who receive 300-page reports on a frequent basis are unlikely to use them; instead, contemporary process designs are more likely to include flash reports or displays, user-defined queries and reports, and exception reports and trend analysis.

In reengineering a process, the team should question everything, but especially the information flow. Often there are records kept or reports prepared and distributed that are totally unnecessary. A consultant, studying the processes of a small manufacturer, discovered that the warehouse manager was preparing a report each Monday morning of the previous week's consumption of wooden pallets and sending it to the CEO. The CEO was totally unaware of the report since, without his knowledge, his secretary (sure that he wasn't interested) was filing the reports. The warehouse manager didn't know why he was preparing the report; it had been among the duties explained to him by his predecessor. Everyone was puzzled until the CEO remembered that ten years earlier at a cocktail party, he had met a man who made pallets. The man said that he could offer the CEO a good price on pallets, how many did his company use? The CEO responded that he didn't know but would find out. That Monday, the CEO called the warehouse manager to prepare a report of the previous week's pallet consumption. And no one ever told him to stop!

Figure 6-2 shows some of the decisions that the ABC Toy Company made about instrumenting and informating its Fulfill Orders process.

TASK 4A.4—CONSOLIDATE INTERFACES AND INFORMATION

This task defines the process changes needed to reduce or simplify interfaces, both internal and external. It identifies and eliminates duplicate information flows, and with them, the reconciliation activities needed to figure out which of the duplicates to believe.

Most organizations have not previously had a process perspective. As a result, their attempts at proceduralizing, systematizing, and auto-

Figure 6-2. Fulfill orders: instrumentation.

Performance Information	Store	Processing
Number, percent, quantity, and dollar amount of items back ordered. Also as ratio to items ordered.	Order File	Automatic capture. Periodic reports. Exception reports when threshold exceeded.
Distribution of order cycle times, in days. Also for segments of the cycle.	Order File	Same as above.
Warehouse throughput and productivity.	Order File and Payroll	Periodic reports, current plus trend.
Accuracy of credit decisions. Credit problems for automated and manually approved orders.	Order File and Accounts Receivable	Same as above.

mating the work have usually produced a patchwork of incompatible partial solutions. It is not at all uncommon to see a business process supported by a combination of unrelated manual and computer systems. The ABC Toy Company's Fulfill Orders process is a good example: Although most steps were manual, the process also used three different and unrelated personal computer applications.

This fragmentation of the process information and work flow has several negative consequences:

❑ It creates additional work to translate information from the form required by one step into the form required by another. We often see people keying data into a computer program that they are reading from a report or document produced by another computer program.

❑ Errors and delays are introduced by the necessity for transcription.

❑ Since each of the systems typically has its own unique human interface, the people performing the process tend to become specialists or experts at the tools that they happen to use. Since these tools are often inaccessible or incomprehensible to the people who don't use them, the fragmentation is increased.

❑ Because each piece of the process is worked on by different people using different tools, the rate at which they can complete a piece of work differs. This introduces queues of work at each step. The result of fragmented processes is that the work spends more time waiting to be looked at and less and less time actually being performed. This leads to work processes requiring an order of magnitude more time than if the work were to be performed by one person. Most of the elapsed time is spent waiting in queues (in-baskets) or moving between queues, or waiting to be moved (out-baskets).

❑ The "location" of a specific transaction is difficult to determine. Often, all we know is that the transaction is "in process" until it emerges at the other end. Sometimes this necessitates adding another level of complexity to the process in order to locate and expedite selected transactions.

❑ The information used by different people and/or at different steps is inconsistent. Sometimes this is a result of transcription errors, sometimes of system incompatibilities, and sometimes of timing differences. Whatever the cause, it can result in erroneous processing. Again, additional complexity may be required in order to control this cause of errors.

❑ Sometimes, in order to overcome the process deficiencies, the solution is to develop a "traveler," a file of information that accompanies the transaction and accrues the additional information added at each step in the process. Sometimes, the people in the process resort to creating their own "unofficial" files of information because they don't trust the official files or because the official files lack some important piece of information they need. Both of these solutions add work, additional opportunities for error, and a risk that the process will run out of control.

A provocative example can be found in a brief story that might bear the title "Physician, heal thyself." There was an internationally known management consulting firm that used an automated system for capturing all time and expenses by client assignment. The only trouble was, the automated system didn't validate that the time and expenses were assigned to the right assignment, and it didn't produce any reports until a month later. Since the consultants were interested in billing their clients promptly, they had to use a manual system that recorded time and expenses from the same input documents used in the automated system. Since the head consultants knew who was working on the assignment and the computer didn't, the manual system was much more accurate. Not only did they have to do the record keeping and billing manually, they also had to waste time a month later making adjustments to the automated records so that they would agree with the manual records, in order that the automated management reports would be accurate.

Because of the inherent fallibility of manual systems, it was common to introduce redundancy into manual processes in order to maintain control. Double entry bookkeeping, which was invented in the Middle Ages, is a good example. Many of these same control devices were carried over into automated systems. At first, when automated systems were fairly unreliable, these controls made good sense. Today, however, there is less need for them.

The very design of a system can reduce or eliminate the need for some controls. For example, when computer systems were batch oriented and operated on sequential files, one sequential file was written by one program to be read by the next. And we often produced control totals of the records on each file and compared them to ensure that no records were lost or misprocessed. With direct access files, however, each program operates on the same records, so that there may be no need for the control totals or comparisons.

Similarly, with batch systems we often created control totals of transactions and shipped them off to the computer. When the computer report came back, we compared our control total for the batch with that calculated by the computer, in order to ensure that the computer processed all of the transactions. With on-line systems, however, we can *see* whether the computer is processing each transaction.

Each time that we introduce redundancy, we not only create the additional work to do the same thing twice, we create the additional work to make sure that the two are still the same. These kinds of controls are needed far less often today, yet they keep appearing in our business processes.

Information technology provides other opportunities to reduce process fragmentation by consolidating interfaces and information. Desktop computer graphic user interfaces (GUIs, pronounced "gooeys") like Microsoft Windows, IBM OS/2 Presentation Manager, or Unix X-Windows provide standard and intuitive "look and feel" for a wide variety of application programs. This makes the tools used in one step of a process easier and more understandable for people who don't normally perform that step—reducing the need for specialty system operators.

Similarly, the use of common information stores accessed by different people, often in different locations, ensures that they are working from and on the same information. Database management systems for data and text, imaging systems for graphics and pictures, voice storage systems for audio, and multimedia systems for all types of information can be used for common stores. Telecommunications, both wired and wireless, can deliver that information wherever it is needed. When these types of process improvements are made at the interface with the customer, they can provide significant advantages.

Loew's Corporation, which operates a chain of movie theaters, began wondering why customers should be able to buy advance tickets to sporting events and the stage, but not to the movies. It developed a system that allowed customers to order their tickets by telephone, using a credit card to pay for them, and pick up the tickets at the box office. For $1.00 more, the customer could have a reserved seat. This proved very popular, for Loew's had simplified the customer interface and added value by eliminating the need for the customer to stand in line for the ticket or, even worse, being turned away because a showing was oversold.

As a consequence of automating the ticket purchase, Loew's discovered that it had informated the process. Before, it had no way of knowing the demand for a particular show. It only knew how many tickets were sold. It had no way of knowing how many people were turned away or turned off by the long lines. So its decisions on which screen or screens to show each film were only partially informed. The new system allowed it to measure demand much more accurately so that it could make better decisions on screen allocation. At the same time, it had access to information on which films customers attended. So it could, if it chose, use this information to market new films to likely customers.

At the ABC Toy Company, the use of centralized customer, inventory, and order files by the order processing system dramatically simplified the interfaces and information of the Fulfill Orders process (see Figure 6-3).

TASK 4A.5—REDEFINE ALTERNATIVES

This task evaluates the continued need for special cases (if any) in the process. If needed, it considers segregating the special cases in separate processes. In other words, this task seeks to replace a single complex process with one or more simpler processes.

Sometimes this task determines that a single process should be split into two, by segmenting the process inputs and creating parallel flows. Federal Express used to have a single process. Simplified, it worked like this: Every evening trucks picked up packages and delivered them to an

Figure 6-3. Fulfill orders: interfaces.

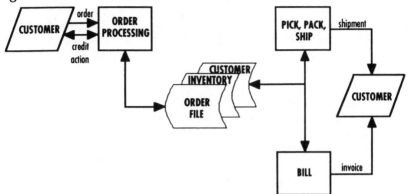

airplane, which flew them to the operations center in Memphis. There they were sorted and put back on airplanes which flew them to their destination city. Then trucks picked them up and delivered them to the specified address, generally by 10 A.M. the next day. This process worked very well for Federal Express and its customers, but the company recognized an opportunity for improvement. The trucks were idle from the time they dropped off the last package in the morning until they picked up the first package in the evening. Similarly for the airplanes. And the operations center was idle from the time the last plane left until the first plane arrived. Federal Express recognized that it could provide nonpriority service, for delivery in the afternoon or on the morning of the second day, at a lower cost by utilizing the unused capacity. When it instituted the additional services at reduced cost it stimulated additional demand and additional profits.

Sometimes this task determines that two separate processes should be joined into one. A postal distribution center had separate processes for handling packages and letters. The packages were handled by automated equipment that scanned the destination zip code (with workers correcting any misreads) and routed the packages over a series of conveyer belts that ultimately deposited each package in a large canvas shipping basket containing other packages for the same zip code. Letters were also handled by automated equipment that scanned the destination zip code (with workers correcting any misreads) and sorted the letters by zip code. Batches of about one hundred letters with the same zip code were then banded and deposited in a bin. Postal workers took the banded letters and walked to an area occupied by many canvas shipping baskets, each prominently marked with a destination zip code. The workers then threw the banded letters toward the appropriate basket. Most of the time, they were accurate. Sometimes, they were not. A consultant visiting the distribution center realized that the banded letters with a single zip code were actually a package! He recommended that the letter process feed directly into the package process and this was done, both improving accuracy and eliminating unnecessary labor.

At the ABC Toy Company, the Fulfill Orders reengineering team realized that the use of credit limits and an expert system could triage all orders. The majority of orders would be below the credit limit, so they could be approved automatically. The largest portion of the orders above the credit limit could be assigned credit actions automatically that the customer service representative could handle. Those very few remaining orders, the difficult credit decisions, could easily be handled by the treasurer, so that the need for the credit manager was eliminated.

Also, since the order processing system would automatically recognize a change order and present the original order for modification at the front end of the process, there was no longer a need for a separate change order subprocess.

TASK 4A.6—RELOCATE AND RETIME CONTROLS

This task seeks to reduce the number of nonvalue-added activities in the process by simplifying the control structure of the process. It accomplishes this by integrating controls into value-adding activities, by replacing error detection with error avoidance, and by moving error detection closer to the point of occurrence of the error. This task also reviews the logical relationships among activities in order to find opportunities to perform in parallel activities currently performed serially. Obviously this would increase the speed of the process.

When we use manual systems, we have largely serial processes, because all of the information necessary to process a transaction must move through the process with the transaction. Different people can't work on the transaction at the same time because the "file" can be in only one place at one time. Organizations using such systems often have large, centralized filing departments that store and retrieve the files as needed. You can imagine the problems that arise when a transaction arrives that requires a file that was checked out to process an earlier transaction that is not yet completed!

Sometimes this task determines that activities formerly performed serially should be performed in parallel. IBM Credit Corporation was losing business because it took too long to process a lease application through the activities of configuration, credit checking, pricing, and document preparation. It automated and informated the process with a central database that permitted it to perform several of the activities concurrently.

Clearly it is better to avoid errors than to correct them. Many of the templates discussed in the preceding tasks are designed to avoid errors by reducing or eliminating the need for transcription, by providing the same information in the same way at each point of the process, by simplifying the interfaces, etc. But when errors can't be avoided (and they are, after all, inevitable) they should at least be detected as close to the point of error as possible. The reason is obvious: The further from the point of occurrence an error is detected, the more difficult it is to correct. That is because all of the intervening work may have been corrupted by the error. Several studies have shown that in computer systems development, an error in specification of the requirements will cost about two hundred times as much to correct after the system is implemented as it would cost to correct at the requirements stage.

Ideally, an error should be caught and corrected as soon as it is made. Early data processing systems used "check digits" on identifiers like customer and product numbers to provide partial protection against transcription errors. Today, on-line systems can provide immediate validation of entered transactions. If the person entering the transaction is also the person initiating it, the transaction can be immediately corrected. Even if the transaction is being entered by someone else, it can be rejected or suspended so that no damage is done.

When errors are not corrected close to the point of occurrence, tremendous process difficulties may result. We worked with a railroad that had about 600 people in its revenue accounting department. This department bills shippers for each shipment and also accounts for the division of revenues with other railroads, since about half of all shipments are carried by more than one railroad. We found that about one-third of those 600 people were dedicated to correcting the errors made by the other two-thirds. It wasn't enough to correct the errors introduced by the 400 people, for they were a small fraction of the problem. The errors began much earlier in the process, when a salesperson negotiated a contract with a shipper. The contract might specify operating conditions that the operations department couldn't meet or didn't know about. Then, too, the contract had to be reviewed and approved by the legal department, which could add weeks of delay. After that, the accounting department had to calculate the contract rates. Meanwhile, the shipper began shipping, expecting to be served and billed in accord with the contract. Since operations didn't know about the contract, it didn't provide the contracted service. Since accounting didn't know about the contract, it used the wrong rates in calculating the freight bill. Naturally, when the customer received the bill it rejected it as erroneous. The same thing happened when the participating railroad got its allocation of the revenue. Hence the 200 people correcting errors.

To remedy this situation we had to reengineer the entire process—from marketing and sales through operations to legal to operations to accounting. Only then were we able to eliminate most of the errors and most of the work done by those 200 people. Interestingly, this also eliminated a lot of work for the shippers and participating railroads, namely all those people checking and returning our bills.

TASK 4A.7—MODULARIZE

The purpose of this task is to define parts of the reengineered process that can be deployed independently. This partition of the process, if one exists, enables the process to be distributed in space (e.g., by decentralizing it) and/or in time (e.g., by substituting process parts in moving from one subVision to another).

The formal analysis of this task consists of determining the dependencies among the activities of the revised process and of determining interactions between activities and entities. This analysis allows the clustering of activities by related changes and by time/space adjacency, so that modules can be defined for movement and for implementation.

At the ABC Toy Company, by the time the reengineering team had completed Task 4A.6 for the Fulfill Orders process, it had reduced the original twenty-three activities to seven: Electronic Data Interchange (EDI) Order Receipt, Order Entry, Check Credit, Schedule Warehouse, Pick and Pack, Ship, and Bill. EDI Order Receipt was clearly a separate module, since the rest of the process didn't depend upon it. Until it was implemented, orders could continue to arrive as they had always had, by FAX or mail.

Order Entry was also a module, but one that could be implemented in two versions—with and without automatic consolidation of orders. Similarly, the Check Credit module could be implemented with or without the expert credit system. Schedule Warehouse could be implemented with or without automatic scheduling and Pick and Pack with or without handheld terminals.

The Ship module had two submodules: automatic routing and freight calculation and carrier EDI. The Bill module had no submodules.

Each of the modules and submodules were specified by considering activities and steps and ways of performing them that go together. It simply doesn't make sense to partition the process any further. Schematically, the technical design of Fulfill Orders looks like Figure 6-4.

TASK 4A.8—SPECIFY DEPLOYMENT

This task uses the modules defined in the previous task to evaluate structural alternatives (e.g., centralized versus decentralized) and implementation alternatives (e.g., first subVision versus second subVision). Analysis of these alternatives then leads to the selected deployment of each module in space, time, and organization. Note that this task is conducted concurrently with Task 4B.6—Redraw Organizational Boundaries.

Figure 6-5 shows the list of modules for the Fulfill Orders process and the organizational and implementation alternatives that the reengineering team thought feasible. Clearly, all of the basic modules—Order Entry, Check Credit, Schedule Warehouse, Pick and Pack, Ship, and Bill—must be present in the first subVision. Of the nonbasic modules, the Check Credit expert system, the Pick and Pack handheld terminals, and the Ship carrier EDI could be implemented with any subVision. But automatic consolidation of orders had to be implemented no later than the second subVision, and automatic warehouse scheduling and automatic route selection and freight calculation could be implemented no earlier than the second subVision because the latter depended upon the former.

Based on these considerations, the reengineering team decided to implement EDI Order Receipt, Automatic Order Consolidation, Automatic Warehouse Scheduling, and Automatic Route selection and freight calculation with the second subVision. This left the expert credit system, handheld terminals, and carrier EDI for implementation with the third subVision. The team thus reaffirmed the scope of the subVisions originally defined in Task 3.10.

Which organizations should be responsible for which modules was clear in most cases: marketing should be responsible for order receipt and entry, operations for all of the warehouse and shipping modules, and finance for Check Credit. The only real question was the Bill module. In the current process, invoices were calculated and typed in the finance department. In the new process, the invoices would be produced automatically, so there

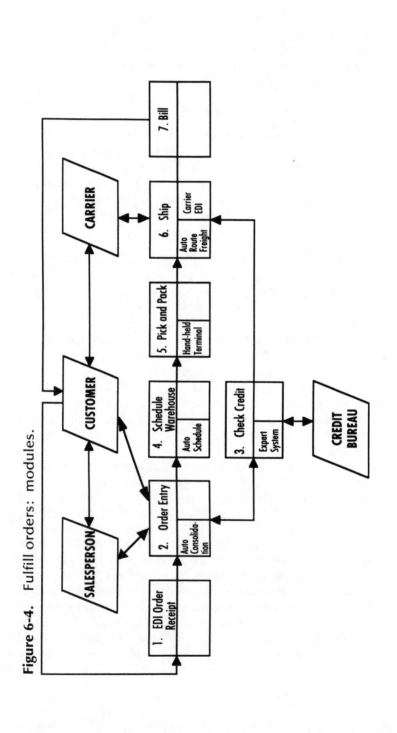

Figure 6-4. Fulfill orders: modules.

Figure 6-5. Fulfill orders: deployment options.

MODULE	Organizational Deployment			SubVision			OTHER
	OP	MKT	F&A	1	2	3	
1. EDI Order Receipt		X		X	X		If Order Entry centralized, receipt should be centralized. If Order Entry decentralized, can use service bureau to distribute.
2A. Order Entry - Basic		X		X			Can be centralized or decentralized by region.
2B. Auto Consolidation		X		X	X		
3A. Check Credit - Basic			X	X			Align with Order Entry.
3B. Expert System			X	X	X	X	
4A. Schedule Warehouse - Basic	X			X			Align with Manufacturing.
4B. Auto Schedule	X			X	X		
5A. Pick and Pack - Basic	X			X			Align with Schedule
5B. Hand-held Terminal	X			X	X	X	
6A. Ship - Basic	X			X			Align with Schedule
6B. Auto route and freight	X			X	X		
6C. Carrier EDI	X			X	X	X	
7. Bill		X	X	X			Align with Order Entry.

seemed to be no work left for the Billing section to do, except perhaps to mail the invoices. The invoices could be printed there or anywhere else for that matter. At first, the reengineering team planned to produce invoices in the Order Processing unit. Then it realized that the accounts payable section was already mailing out checks to vendors, so it decided that invoices should be mailed from there as well. Whether the invoices should actually be printed in accounts payable, however, was deferred to the Transformation stage.

Although the ABC Toy Company was currently centralized, it had a number of regional sales offices, and the reengineering team considered whether parts of the Fulfill Orders process should be decentralized as well. In particular, order entry could be decentralized to the regional offices. It seemed clear that EDI order receipt, credit checking, and billing should be centralized or decentralized along with order entry so that the customer service representative could handle the entire transaction with the customers. If it were decided to decentralize order entry, a service bureau could be contracted to distribute the EDI orders to the regional offices. The reengineering team weighed the advantages in speed and responsiveness of decentralized order entry against the cost and decided to keep it centralized.

With regard to the warehouse and shipping modules, it was clear that they should remain wherever manufacturing was, and ABC had no plans to expand beyond its current single plant.

Task 4A.9—Apply Technology

Technology is one of the key enablers of business process reengineering (the others being information and human potential). The new process vision developed in Stage 3 will certainly have been informed by a knowledge of the current capabilities, uses, and limitations of technology. But in this task specific applications of technology will be made to the process.

The major applications of technology to business process reengineering are to:

- ❏ Analyze, e.g., simulations, correlations, trends, spreadsheets, budget, or standard versus actual.
- ❏ Capture and document, e.g., image, data storage, microform.
- ❏ Communicate, e.g., data communications, telephony, video, networks.
- ❏ Control, e.g., telemetry, process control, artificial intelligence, feedback, command and control.
- ❏ Human interface, e.g., graphics, voice recognition/response, video, pen-based.
- ❏ Identify, e.g., bar codes, magnetic stripes, transponders.
- ❏ Informate, e.g., telemetry, on-line access.
- ❏ Manage, e.g., decision support, management information.
- ❏ Manufacture, e.g., computer-aided design, computer-aided or integrated manufacturing, materials handling, robotics.

❑ Provide mobility, e.g., cellular telephone, laptop or handheld computers.

❑ Share expertise, e.g., knowledge-based expert systems, bulletin boards.

❑ Share information, e.g., data bases, external information services, and networks.

In the Fulfill Orders process, management information technology was used in the order entry, check credit, pick and pack, and ship activities. Telecommunications technology was used in the EDI order receipt and ship activities. Data capture technology was used in EDI order receipt, order entry, and ship. Data storage, analysis, and presentation technologies were used in each activity from order entry onward. Automatic identification and mobile technologies were used in pick and pack. And expert systems technology was used in check credit and ship.

While the final decisions will be deferred to the Transformation stage, this task should make some preliminary decisions with respect to the application of technology. The most important of these decisions is usually whether the technology will be obtained off-the-shelf, by integrating off-the-shelf components, or by developing a custom solution. Generally, these three alternatives represent a spectrum of increasing time, cost, and risk. It is becoming less and less common for any but the largest and/or most specialized and/or most performance-critical processes to be supported by totally customized technology. To select among these alternatives, the reengineering team must look at what is commercially available. Much of this information is likely to have surfaced during the benchmarking Task 3.4. At this point, with a much firmer idea of the technical design of the process, the reengineering team will be much better prepared to talk to vendors and to appreciate demonstrations.

This task will also allow the team to quantify (if it has not already done so) or refine its estimate of the cost of implementing the reengineered process.

TASK 4A.10—PLAN IMPLEMENTATION

This task will develop preliminary plans (to be refined in Stage 5) for implementing the technical aspects of the reengineered process, including development, procurement, facilities, test, conversion, and deployment. These plans will then be time phased, along with the parallel plans for implementing the social aspects of the process, developed in Task 4B.12. The completion of this task and Task 4B.12 completes the Solution stage. At this milestone, the reengineering team usually presents to the sponsors its recommended process design, estimates of cost and time, and implementation plan.

This milestone review is the most important in the entire reengineering project. After this point, resources will be expended much more quickly than before. After this point, knowledge of the plans will spread well beyond the team and its sponsors. Whereas before the reengineered process was an opportunity and a compelling vision, now it becomes a detailed plan and a lot of hard work and difficult change. This can be intimidating. It is up to the reengineering team and its sponsors and champions to ensure that the plan is sold to everyone to whom it needs to be sold. This is both good project management and good change management.

One prerequisite for obtaining the needed support is to identify early the stakeholders and their issues and then addressing those issues. Another prerequisite is keeping the necessary people involved and revalidating their commitment to the project. Another is managing their expectations: There should be no surprises at the milestone review. And of course the business case for proceeding should be compelling.

7

Stage 4B: Solution: Social Design

Social design *must* be performed in conjunction with technical design: The social and technical components of a process must be congruent if the process is to be effective. Chapter 6 both introduces the subject of process design and provides the methodology for technical design. This chapter provides the methodology for social design. The reader will obtain the fullest understanding of the materials in this chapter by first reading at least the introductory and recap sections of Chapter 6.

The purpose of this stage is to specify the social dimension of the new process. The social design stage produces descriptions of the organization, staffing, jobs, career paths, and incentives employed by the reengineered process. Together with Stage 4A: Technical Design, it produces designs for the interaction of social and technical elements. Finally, it produces preliminary plans for recruitment, education, training, reorganization, and redeployment of personnel.

The key questions answered by this stage include:

❑ What technical and human resources will we need to reengineer? What activities will each reengineering team member be responsible for? What priorities and dependencies exist?
❑ What immediate opportunities exist? What can we accomplish in ninety days? One year? Beyond one year?
❑ What human resources will we need in the reengineered process?
❑ What targets and measures should we establish?
❑ How will responsibilities change? What training programs will be needed?

❑ Who is likely to resist the changes called for? How can they be motivated to accept these changes? What other obstacles exist?

❑ What will our new organization look like?

Please remember that Social Design is performed concurrently with Technical Design and by the same people: the reengineering team. Thus, technical and social issues are addressed concurrently.

The Social Design stage is conducted as twelve tasks:

4B.1 —Empower Customer Contact Personnel
4B.2 —Identify Job Characteristic Clusters
4B.3 —Define Jobs/Teams
4B.4 —Define Skills and Staffing Needs
4B.5 —Specify Management Structure
4B.6 —Redraw Organizational Boundaries
4B.7 —Specify Job Changes
4B.8 —Design Career Paths
4B.9 —Define Transitional Organization
4B.10—Design Change Management Program
4B.11—Design Incentives
4B.12—Plan Implementation

TASK 4B.1—EMPOWER CUSTOMER CONTACT PERSONNEL

To improve the responsiveness and quality of service provided to the customer by a process, it is necessary to empower customer contact personnel. Customer contact is the point where organizations have the greatest ability to form or change the customers' perception of the organization and its products and services. Yet the people working at the point of contact with the customer are often the lowest-paid, least-esteemed employees: order takers, sales clerks, tellers, customer service representatives, waiters, clerks, receptionists, etc.

By "empowerment," we mean the changes in responsibility, authority, knowledge, skills, and tools needed to enable customer contact personnel to get the job done the right way the first time. Some people prefer the term "enable" to "empower," feeling that the former portrays management in a more facilitative role. Some have referred to this enabling role as "the leader as servant." In this "enabling" view, "empowerment" is criticized as implying that management legitimately has the power, and hands it down to the workers whom they empower. That is inaccurate. In truth, the customer contact people have always had considerable power, namely the power to enhance or to destroy the organization's relationship with the customer.

Business process reengineering (BPR) is firmly in the Theory Y school of management. It encourages the belief that almost all workers want to work and to do a good job but the organization prevents them from doing so. One way in which the organization detracts from an individual's performance is by failing to clearly communicate what it wants the employee to do. Another way is by giving the employee incentives to do something different than what the organization really wants. Still another way is by failing to give the employee the resources to do the job right.

Social design of a business process aims to eliminate all of these dysfunctions. In particular, this task looks at the changes that are needed in the definition of customer contact jobs: the responsibility and authority assigned them and whether they are commensurate with the scope of the job. It also looks at the additional knowledge and skills needed to do the job better and any needed improvement in the tools provided to the customer contact person. Then, recognizing that customer contact personnel are themselves customers of other personnel, and so on, this task defines the changes needed for *all* personnel to improve service to their customers.

For most organizations, the term "customer" is reserved for the external customers, those that buy or consume the organization's products or services. Convincing an organization that it needs to do a better job in serving the external customers is much easier than convincing them that it needs to serve internal customers better. As a matter of fact, it is hard for many people to even think of their coworkers as "customers." Rather, they are often seen as disruptions to one's work, as unreasonable, demanding irritants, as "those guys in the X department." Such feelings are exacerbated by the legacy functional organization.

Clearly, this paradigm must be changed before an organization can achieve high levels of performance. The success of the customer contact personnel depends on the support that they receive from their internal "suppliers"; and the success of those people depends on the support that they receive, in turn, from their internal suppliers, and so on. In the reengineered organization, everyone views himself or herself as a customer contact person and believes that what they do is important to the ultimate quality of the product or service delivered to the external customer.

At the ABC Toy Company, the reengineering team defined the roles needed in the Fulfill Orders process as shown in Figure 7-1.

Task 4B.2—Identify Job Characteristic Clusters

All jobs, even the simplest, have multiple requirements: human characteristics that are important in their performance. Even the legendary screw-turner's job on an assembly line could be described in terms of such characteristics as manual dexterity, stamina, or attentiveness. The important job characteristics can be grouped into three categories: skills, knowledge, and orientation.

Skills are the abilities and competencies required in the job—how to do things. The word *skill* is synonymous with the words *trade* and *craft* because the essence of a vocation is the set of skills required in its performance. Skills are generally acquired by training and perfected by practice. *Knowledge* is information, learning, and the understanding, comprehension, judgment, and insight that stem from the information and learning how to use it. In short, knowledge provides the basis for

Figure 7-1. Fulfill orders: roles and responsibilities.

Role	Responsibility/ Authority	Knowledge	Skills	Tools
Order Processors	Take, change, and finalize orders. Take credit actions, with advice. Resolve problems with customer and salesperson. Answer order inquiries.	Credit policy. Line of goods. Warehouse operations. Customers.	Interpersonal. Keyboarding. Telephone. Negotiating.	On-line system. Expert credit system.
Warehouseperson	Pick, pack, and move orders to shipping area.	Line of goods. Warehouse operations.	Forklift operation.	On-line system. Handheld terminal.
Shippers	Select time and method of shipment. Schedule and assist carriers. Load.	Shipping methods.	Forklift operation. Interpersonal.	On-line system.
Credit Manager	Review and set credit limits. Make exceptional credit decisions.	Customers. Credit management. Credit information sources.	Credit analysis.	Account history. Expert credit system.

effective application of skills. Knowledge is generally acquired by education and expanded and modified by experience. In general, doing something well is a skill; knowing what to do next is knowledge. Both skills and knowledge comprise the *content* a worker brings to a job. The work itself is the content brought to a job by the organization. By contrast, orientation is the *context* a worker brings to a job, and culture and strategy are the context brought to a job by the organization. *Orientation* means the set of attitudes, beliefs, and preferences a person has. It has long been recognized that orientation can have a substantial impact on a person's ability to do a job. In fact, so-called aptitude tests test mostly for orientation.

Each category of job characteristics or requirements—skills, knowledge, and orientation—itself consists of a number of specific skills, areas of knowledge, or aspects of orientation. Furthermore, there is a continuum associated with each of these characteristics: the level of proficiency at the skill, the mastery of the area of knowledge, the depth of the attitude. For the purposes of social design, we may represent the "amount" of most skills or areas of knowledge or attitudes with a simple triage scheme: high, moderate, or low. Grading some aspects of orientation, however, lends itself better to a dichotomy. For example, an individual prefers to manage other people or not, they prefer activity oriented work or project oriented, they prefer to work indoors or outdoors. We use both the triage and dichotomy methods to describe job requirements and worker profiles; we rarely need to be more detailed.

This task, then, identifies the set of skills, knowledge, and orientation relevant to both the current and the reengineered process. Where do we obtain such information? For the current process jobs, we can use job descriptions and employment advertisements. When these do not exist or are inadequate, we can interview the job incumbents and their supervisors. But we must remember that we are attempting here to identify the characteristics of jobs, not of the people who hold those jobs. This distinction is important. Throughout this stage, social design deals mostly with jobs and not with jobholders. In the next stage, Transformation, we bring the social design down to individual people. Also, this task identifies those characteristics (i.e., skills, knowledge, orientation, and level of each) required to perform the job as it was designed to be done. That is, it identifies what is necessary to perform well.

The ABC Toy Company reengineering team developed the matrix shown in Figure 7-2 for the current job requirements for the Fulfill Orders and Service Customer Request processes. While we have been concentrating on the Fulfill Orders process,

Figure 7-2. Fulfill orders: current jobs assessment.

KEY: H = High, M = Moderate, L = Low, P = Project, A = Activity — Current Jobs	SKILLS						KNOWLEDGE					ORIENTATION				
	Interpersonal	Keyboarding	Telephone	Negotiating	Analytical	Forklift Operation	Line of Goods	Warehouse Operation	Credit Management	Customers	Shipping Methods	People	Production	Control	Facilitation	Activity/Project
0.1 Order Editor	M		L		L		L		M			L	M	H		A
0.2 Order Clerk			L					M					H			A
0.3 Back Order Clerk	L		L	L	L		L		M	M					L	A
C.1 Credit Manager	H		H	M	M				H	M		M		H	M	A
I.1 Inventory Supervisor				L			H	M				H	H			A
W.1 Warehouse Clerk		M		M				H				H	L	L		A
W.2 Warehouseperson						H	H	H				L	H			A
S.1 Shipping Clerk				L			L	L			H	M				A
S.2 Traffic Manager	L		L	L	M			M			L	H	M	M		A
S.3 Dockhand						M	L	M				L	M		L	A
B.1 Billing Clerk		M					L					H	M			A
Service Customer Request Process																
Customer Service Rep.	H	H	L	L			M	L	L	M	L	H			H	A

the Technical Design stage identified an opportunity to merge the Service Customer Request process with the Fulfill Orders process. In anticipation of that outcome, we will begin to show information for the one job in Service Customer Request—the customer service representative.

Figure 7-3 shows how the reengineering team redefined the job requirements. Four of the jobs (order clerk, inventory supervisor, warehouse clerk, and billing clerk) are obviated by the automation introduced with the order processing system. The order editor job is empowered by raising the level of interpersonal and telephone skills, by adding keyboarding and negotiating skills, by

Figure 7-3. Fulfill orders: redefined jobs assessment.

KEY		SKILLS						KNOWLEDGE					ORIENTATION				
H = High M = Moderate L = Low P = Project A = Activity																	
Redefined Jobs		Interpersonal	Keyboarding	Telephone	Negotiating	Analytical	Forklift Operation	Line of Goods	Warehouse Operation	Credit Management	Customers	Shipping Methods	People	Production	Control	Facilitation	Activity/Project
0.1 Order Editor		H	H	H	M			M		L	M		M	M	H	M	A
0.2 Order Clerk																	
0.3 Back Order Clerk				L						L	M					L	A
C.1 Credit Manager		L		L	M					H	M		L		H	M	A
I.1 Inventory Supervisor																	
W.1 Warehouse Clerk																	
W.2 Warehouseperson			L				H	H	H			L		H	L	L	A
S.1 Shipping Clerk																	
S.2 Traffic Manager		L		L	L	L			M		L	H		M	M		A
S.3 Dockhand							M	L	M					M		L	A
B.1 Billing Clerk																	
Service Customer Request Process																	
Customer Service Rep.		H		H	L	L		M	L	L	M	L	H			H	A

raising the level of knowledge of the line of goods, by adding knowledge of credit management, by raising the level of people orientation, and by adding a facilitation orientation.

By empowering the order editor—the primary customer contact job—the reengineering team drastically reduced the requirements for the back-order clerk and for the credit manager jobs. In the warehouse, the warehouseworker job needed to acquire some keyboarding skills to operate the handheld terminals and computer terminals. The job also needed to acquire a balanced control/facilitation orientation. Of all the remaining jobs, only the dockhand job was unchanged.

TASK 4B.3 — DEFINE JOBS/TEAMS

In the previous task, we identified the skills, knowledge, and orientation that would be needed in current jobs *as they are redefined to meet the needs of the reengineered process*. In this task, we look at the clustering of job requirements in order to determine which current job titles should be retained or upgraded, which combined, and which eliminated.

In general, reengineering replaces complex processes previously separated into simple jobs with simplified processes performed by workers with more complex jobs. In this sense, BPR is a reversal of the Industrial Revolution. Where it is possible to do so, a single job is defined to meet the needs of the reengineered process. When this is not possible, a team is defined.

Ideally, a single job should perform an entire process. This would eliminate all the nonvalue-added activities for handing off work, communicating, coordinating, controlling, etc. It would also reduce the opportunities to introduce errors into the process. Thus, the ideal situation, with a single "caseworker" handling a process from beginning to end, should be a more productive and higher quality process than one in which many jobs are involved. In the delivery of social services, an actual caseworker may play precisely this role. In other businesses, an account manager may play a very similar role.

Consider the advantages of such a model. From the organization's point of view, a single individual can be held responsible for the entire process, and productivity and quality are improved. From the customer's point of view, there is only one person with whom to deal, and quality and responsiveness are improved. Why, then, haven't more organizations adopted the caseworker model? Part of the reason is the way this model challenges our traditional ideas of organization. Part of the reason is that it is difficult or impossible to find real people with all of the skills, knowledge, and orientation requirements to do the job if it takes in the whole process.

In the latter case, organizations sometimes substitute teams for caseworkers. In this model, a number of people (the team) collectively possess all of the skills, knowledge, and orientation requirements to do the job right. And they jointly share responsibility for the process results. Emergency response teams, surgical teams, aircraft and ship crews, power plant control room teams are all examples of teams.

At the ABC Toy Company, the reengineering team decided that the three current jobs in the Fulfill Orders process (order editor, order clerk, and back-order clerk) and the current job in

the Service Customer Request process (customer service representative) could be combined into a single job. The title "customer service representative" was retained for this new job. Because only a few decisions would be left to the credit manager,
the team felt that "credit advisor" was a more descriptive title for
the revised job. The warehouseworker job would not change very
much. The shipping clerk and traffic manager jobs could be combined into a new job called Logistics. And the dockhand job was
given a new title, Shipments, to reflect the team's view that the
job was more than the physical manipulation of goods only.
Moreover, the reengineering team recognized that the new Logistics and Shipments jobs had to work together closely in order to
actually ship goods, so it designated those two jobs the Shipping
Team.

TASK 4B.4—DEFINE SKILLS AND STAFFING NEEDS

This task begins by identifying the level of each skill, area of knowledge,
and orientation requirement needed for each new job and reflects these
requirements in a matrix similar to Figure 7-3. This is a revision of the
matrix prepared in Task 4B.2. The revision is partly mechanical and
partly judgmental. The mechanical part is to make the level of each requirement in the reengineered job equal to the maximum of the levels in
any of the jobs combined into the new job.

> For example, at the ABC Toy Company, the new customer
> service representative (CSR) job was created by combining an old
> job of the same name from the Service Customer Request pro-
> cess with three old jobs from the Fulfill Orders process: order
> editor, order clerk, and back-order clerk. With respect to the skill
> Keyboarding, the order editor requirement was "high," so the
> new CSR job also has the requirement "high." With respect to
> the area of knowledge Warehouse Operations, the old CSR re-
> quirement was "low," and none of the other combined jobs had
> any requirement, so the new CSR job also has the requirement
> "low."

Once we have completed this mechanical revision, we need to apply
business judgment to the result. For example, with respect to the orientation characteristic Control, the mechanical analysis for the CSR would
assign the requirement "high," because the order editor requirement
was "high." But the reengineering team decided that the new job had to

be more facilitative and less control oriented in order to provide the desired levels of customer service, so it revised the control requirement to "medium."

This task also defines the relationship between staffing levels and volumes and identifies staffing needed at current and projected volumes. In order to define the relationship between staffing levels and volumes, we need to understand the volume drivers of labor.

> For the CSR job, the reengineering team decided that the volume drivers were the number of orders received (since each order had to be handled by the CSR) and the number of telephone calls received, for the same reason.

> For the Warehouseworker job, the volume driver is the number of order line items received, since each line item represents a different stockkeeping unit (SKU) that must be picked.

> For the Shipments job, it is again the number of orders, for each becomes a shipment.

> For the Logistics job, the reengineering team felt that the job was not volume sensitive, since one person would suffice at any foreseeable volume.

To translate the understanding of volume drivers into staffing requirements, we need to know two things: the anticipated volume and how much volume each person can handle. Since, in practice, different people can handle different volumes and the same person may handle different volumes on different days, we must make do with an average value. We usually call this average a *work standard*.

When the standard is for work already being done, we can use an average of actual performance either as is or with adjustment. However, when we are attempting to develop a standard for doing work differently than it is now done (which is the usual case in reengineering), we clearly have no data on which to base an estimate. One approach to overcome this difficulty is to use an *engineered standard*. An engineered standard is developed by breaking down a job into its most elemental components (read an instruction, lift an object, turn a screw, etc.) and then applying existing standards for each of the components. Since the elemental components are present in many jobs, there is plenty of data for them, even though there are no data for the job as a whole. This approach works fairly well for simple, highly structured, and repetitive jobs.

But those are not the kinds of jobs that BPR gives us, so another approach is needed. What we have found to be a good approach is to start with standards for the current jobs. If they exist, use them. If not, observe the performance of those jobs over a sample period and develop averages. Then consider the changes that reengineering is making to the work and to the job. Are we making the work easier or more difficult? Are we making the job more or less productive? Are we eliminating portions of the work by discarding unneeded steps or by reducing the number of errors? Based on such considerations, develop an *estimated standard*. During Stage 5: Transformation we recommend, as discussed in Chapter 8, that each reengineered process be pilot tested before it is rolled out. The pilot test period gives us an opportunity to test also whether our estimated standard is correct or not. Since we cannot make very many staffing changes, anyway, until the new process is rolled out, the only effect of inaccuracy in our estimated standard is to introduce an inaccuracy in the estimated economics of the process. Most of the time organizations can live with this inaccuracy, because the magnitude of the error is unlikely to reverse the business case for reengineering. When this is not so, for example, when a major capital investment will be required to enable reengineering to reach the pilot test stage, then other approaches are clearly needed, e.g., modeling, simulation, or in-depth benchmarking.

The final piece of information needed to estimate staffing requirements is the estimated volume for each of the volume drivers, and we need to know both the average volume and the peak volume, because our staffing scenarios must encompass both conditions. Often, we will already have developed volume estimates during the Identification stage (Task 2.8—Map Resources). Other times we must develop those estimates. Either way, we divide the volumes (average and peak) by the standard to obtain the required average and peak staffing.

We next confront the question: Given that so many people are needed on average and so many at peak volume conditions, how many positions (head count) should we create? Although this is a simple question, it has no simple answer. Clearly, we need more than the number of people needed to handle average volume, because not everyone will be at work every day: they will be sick, on vacation, away for training, and so on. Also clearly, we will usually not want to staff for the peak, because that would mean that the staff is underutilized at nonpeak times. If we staff at lower than the number required at peak, however, how do we handle the peak workload? Here are some of the solutions that organizations are using.

❑ *Load level.* This approach moves work from peak periods to non-peak periods. This is sometimes accomplished through pricing incentives, sometimes through work scheduling, and sometimes by just letting the work pile up in a backlog. An organization's ability to do these kinds of things depends on such factors as the size of the peak relative to the average, the duration of the peak period, and the price versus time elasticity of the demand.

❑ *Cross-training.* This approach trains personnel who normally work in another process to do the work in this process when needed. An organization's ability to use this approach is determined by whether all processes peak at the same time or at different times. The famous historical example of the many coal companies that sold ice in the summer is one example of this, as is the more contemporary example of swimming pool companies that sell Christmas ornaments.

❑ *Overtime.* Here we handle the peak by asking our employees to work longer hours. Again, an organization's ability to use this approach depends on the height and breadth of the peak. Experience shows that, at least with some jobs, burnout can occur, and workers begin to do the same work in more hours.

❑ *Expandable staff.* This approach is used by many retailers. They employ more people than they need to handle average volumes, but they use them on a part-time basis. Then, at peak volumes, they work those same people on a full-time or overtime basis. An important question with this approach is whether sufficient numbers of qualified people can be found to accept these conditions.

❑ *Temporary staff.* In this approach, staff are added in anticipation of the peak and dismissed when the peak has passed. An entire industry exists to provide temporary workers on demand, and some organizations have had reasonable success with temporary workers but more commonly to fill in on a spot basis than to provide peak staffing. Some companies have had excellent results using their former employees, who may have retired or chosen a domestic occupation.

❑ *Staff sharing.* In this approach, different companies that experience peaks at different times agree to trade their staff as needed. Obviously this works best when the processes are very similar in the companies. Good examples of staff sharing include the participation of fire companies from different municipalities in a major fire and the participation of line crews from different power or telephone companies in a major outage.

❑ *Outsourcing.* In this approach, the organization turns over responsibility for the process (or portions of it) to a firm that specializes in performing the outsourced activities. This approach doesn't really solve the peak staffing problem, it just makes it someone else's problem. If the outsource vendor provides the service for several organizations and the peaks for those organizations do not all occur at the same time, the vendor may be able to use several of the other approaches better than its customer could.

Organizations may use any or all of these methods of dealing with peak workloads, and their success in so doing plays a large part in their determination of the normal staffing level. The less successful an organization is in economically handling its peak workload by one or a combination of the approaches described above, the more likely it is that they will need to overstaff, that is, staff at levels above that needed to handle the average workload.

Other factors that an organization needs to consider in determining its normal staffing levels are the number of planned and unplanned absences; the extent of training, cross-training, and other developmental time it intends to provide; the variability of the "normal" workload; and the flexibility of the staff to absorb that variability.

Taking all of this into account, Figure 7-4 shows the calculations for the ABC Toy Company.

Figure 7-4. Fulfill orders: staffing needs.

Job	Volume Drivers	Estimated Standards	Staffing		
			Avg FTE	Peak FTE	Head Count
Customer Service Representative	Number of orders Number of calls	20 orders/person/day, calls included	4	10	6
Warehouse Person	Number of order line items	150 line items/person/day	3	13	8
Logistics	One person job at foreseeable volumes				1
Shipments	Number of orders	40 orders/person/day	2	5	3

TASK 4B.5—SPECIFY MANAGEMENT STRUCTURE

This task specifies how the three main components of management (work management, leadership, and personnel development) will be accomplished in the reengineered process.

Leadership is necessary to get people to work and pull together in the same direction. The job of the leader is to plan and set directions. Work management is necessary to ensure that the right work is done by the right people in the right time frame in the right way. The job of the work manager is to organize the people, direct the work, and control the results. Personnel development is necessary to perfect the skills, knowledge, and orientation of employees to ensure the supply of qualified employees. The job of the personnel developer is to assess, coach, and advise the employees.

In traditional management theory, these three roles of management are lodged in the same individual. But this ignores the fact that not all managers are equally adept at all three roles. Because BPR seeks to leverage human potential, it ought to encourage us to design the social aspects of processes to take advantage of people's strengths rather than to overcome people's weaknesses. It should encourage us to assign responsibility for the three management roles to the individuals best suited to perform them well. These are not always the same person, and they are often not even the person to whom one reports. In many jobs (perhaps most) the person who knows how to do the work best is the worker, not the worker's boss. Leadership can come from anywhere in the organization. And personnel development is usually best accomplished by a more senior person with whom one has a good personal relationship. Some companies have institutionalized such relationships in formal mentoring programs. In most companies, there is an informal organizational structure that implicitly recognizes the divisibility of the management role and assigns management responsibilities to those individuals better able to perform them than those officially recognized in the formal organizational structure. If we reengineer correctly, the differences between the formal and informal organizations ought to vanish!

The object of this task, then, is to identify the process owner and responsibilities for work management and personnel development; to define team leadership; and to assess the need for first- and second-level management. In order to make these decisions, the task structures and analyzes feasible alternatives.

The *process owner* is the lowest level manager responsible for the entire process. In the unreengineered organization, the process owner is, by this definition, the CEO or COO, since most processes are cross-functional. In an unreengineered organization, there is no process owner, because no one takes responsibility for the process: No one is held accountable for process results. In fact, the process may not even be recognized as such. In the reengineered organization, however, there is a single manager both responsible and accountable for the process: the process owner. This does not necessarily mean that all of the people involved in the process report to the process owner. Although the number of organizational boundaries traversed by the reengineered process will be reduced, the process may still cross into other managerial domains. What this does mean is that one manager is responsible and accountable for the process; that manager's performance evaluation and incentive compensation depend on the success of the process. The process owner is expected to negotiate with and coordinate with the managers whose domain the process crosses. The advantages of having a single process owner for each process are obvious.

Usually, the candidates for process ownership are the most senior managers responsible for a portion of the process.

At the ABC Toy Company, the candidates for ownership of the Fulfill Orders process were the materials management director and the vice president of marketing.

The reengineering team felt that the materials management director was a good candidate for process ownership because he was already managing the majority of the people affected by reengineering the process, and because he had technical expertise in logistics, which was a key discipline in the process. On the other hand, the materials management director had always been a control-oriented, rather than a facilitative type of person, and the team was concerned that he might not give appropriate emphasis to customer service. Also, he lacked customer contact experience.

The vice president of marketing was a good candidate for process ownership, the team felt, because she was highly service oriented, was customer focused, and already had a high level of customer contact. The team also felt that she had enough of a control orientation for the Fulfill Orders process because she was, after all, responsible for the sales and promotions budgets. On the other hand, she lacked any experience or expertise with logistics.

Weighing these pros and cons, the reengineering team decided to recommend that the vice president of marketing be appointed owner of the Fulfill Orders process.

Figure 7-5 shows, in tabular form, what the reengineering team recommended for the management structure of the Fulfill Orders process. Notice that leadership comes sometimes from the people doing the work, sometimes from a team leader, and sometimes from a managerial position. Work management comes from the same sources, but often sources different than those for leadership. Personnel development comes from sources different than the sources for leadership and work management and, in three cases out of four, from someone not in (or no longer in) the process. Finally, please notice that the title of the vice president of marketing has been changed to vice president of marketing and distribution to reflect the team's recommendation that she be made process owner.

BPR often designs organizations that are "flatter" than they were before. That is, they contain fewer management levels. Since all employees are empowered, more of them are responsible for managing their own work or are part of self-managed teams, so their managers have less responsibility for work management. As a result, each manager can supervise more people. In a reengineered organization, it is not uncommon to see managers with ten to twenty direct reports, as compared with the three to seven common in unreengineered organizations. In an unreengineered organization, with an average of five direct reports for each manager, three management levels containing thirty-one managers

Figure 7-5.   Fulfill orders: management structure.

Team	Job	Work Management	Personnel Development	Team Leadership	Reporting Relationships
Customer Service	Customer Service Rep.	Self	Sales Manager	Rotating	VP Marketing and Distribution
Credit	Credit Advisor	Self	Self	Self	Part-time responsibility of Treasurer
Warehouse	Warehouseperson	Team Leader	Materials Management Director	Lead Warehouseperson	Logistics Supervisor
Shipping	Logistics & Shipping	Logistics Supervisor	Materials Management Director	Logistics Supervisor	VP Marketing and Distribution

could support 125 nonmanagement personnel. This is a staff to management ratio of about four to one. By contrast, in a reengineered organization, with an average of ten direct reports for each manager, three management levels containing 111 managers could support 1,000 nonmanagement personnel. This is a staff to management ratio of about nine to one. Viewed another way, the organization with 125 nonmanagement personnel might have only two management levels after reengineering; an entire level of management will have been eliminated.

When one looks at the organizational structure of a large organization, with many management levels and numerous staff administrative and professional support personnel, one quickly realizes that the entire structure between the first level managers (who actually manage people) and senior managers (who actually manage the enterprise by setting its direction and allocating its resources)—that is, middle managers—are primarily dedicated to relaying information between the former and the latter. In the upward direction, they analyze, interpret, synthesize, and perform special studies to inform senior managers. In the downward direction, they translate senior managers' strategies into tactics, policies, and operational procedures. And, in performing these roles, middle managers both add and subtract value. They add value by reducing the risk that a wrong decision will be made or that a strategy is incorrectly implemented. But they subtract value by reducing the organization's flexibility and by slowing down its response time. Any organization that is reengineering its processes must explicitly consider the trade-offs between the value adds and value subtracts that middle managers represent. And many have concluded that the minuses outweigh the pluses, which is another reason that organizations are becoming flatter.

In the reengineered organization, we can see clearly how the three enablers of BPR—technology, information, and human potential—have contributed to the flattening of the organization. Technology lets managers be more efficient and expand the span of their control in both space and time. Information enables them to be in touch with what is happening in the organization and its environment. And human potential enables workers to be more autonomous, reducing the need for management.

TASK 4B.6—REDRAW ORGANIZATIONAL BOUNDARIES

This task considers changing the organizational structure to ensure that each team resides within a single organization and to reduce the number of organizational boundaries traversed by the process.

The teams defined for reengineered processes are essentially different from teams selected for projects, such as the reengineering team. The latter are assembled for specific purposes for a specific period of time. Then the team members return to their home organizations. We often choose these teams specifically to bring together people from different organizations, as we did with the reengineering team.

The teams in reengineered processes, by contrast, are permanent features of the process (at least of the current subVision of the process). They are usually designed to perform activities, subprocesses, or the entire process, that is, repetitive work, rather than a project. Because of the team's durability and the repetitive nature of its work, the members of the team must be located within the same organization, have the same leadership, and ideally, have their personnel development provided from the same source. Some organizations have attempted to use process teams whose members continued to reside in their former functional areas, but this has all of the disadvantages and ambiguities of other forms of "matrix management."

When the design for a reengineered process places all of the teams and individuals within one, or at most a few, organizations, it reduces the number of organizational boundaries that the process must traverse. This automatically improves the efficiency and quality of the process. Why? Because each boundary crossed by the process creates a need for additional effort: effort to hand off work, communicate, coordinate, synchronize, explain, control, record, reconcile, protect oneself, etc. Similarly, each boundary crossed by the process creates additional opportunities for error: opportunities to disagree, misunderstand, misinterpret, miscommunicate, mistranscribe, etc. The fewer the boundaries, the less the effort and the higher the quality. In short, the greater the efficiency. In the political realm, this is the idea behind the European Community and the North American Free Trade Agreement.

At the ABC Toy Company, the team's decisions about management structure, reflected in Figure 7-5, were also decisions about organizational structure: Virtually all of the people involved in the Fulfill Orders process were to reside in the marketing and distribution department. One exception to this was the treasurer, who would occasionally be called upon to make credit decisions. The other exception was the people who mailed out invoices. When the reengineering team decided to automate order processing, it eliminated most of the need for the billing department, since invoices would now be produced automatically. The remaining work of the billing department, mailing the invoices to the customers, would have to be done by someone else.

Since the accounts payable department was already doing a lot of mailing, in this case to vendors, the reengineering team thought that accounts payable could mail invoices as well.

TASK 4B.7 — SPECIFY JOB CHANGES

This task prepares a new matrix of skills, knowledge, and orientation requirements versus transitions from old jobs to new jobs. The elements of the matrix consists of the number of degrees of change required by the transition. For example, if job A requires a low level of skill X and job B requires a high level of that skill, then the element at the intersection of "transition job A to job B" and "skill X" will be $+2$ (from low to high).

This task also assigns weights to each skill, knowledge, and orientation requirement, representing the relative difficulty of acquiring that characteristic. The weighted changes are then summed, producing a measure of the difficulty of making the transition from old to new jobs. The transition difficulty measure is used to preplan the reorganization and a curriculum for training and education of process personnel, which will take place in stage 5.

The relative difficulty weights for each job requirement represent the relative difficulty of increasing one level in the required characteristic (e.g., from none to low or low to moderate). For example, the weights might represent the estimated number of weeks of training required to increase proficiency by one level.

We recognize that this approach is based on several simplifying assumptions: (1) The difficulty of acquiring a basic level of a skill, knowledge, or orientation when one has none is the same as the difficulty of developing from the basic level to the moderate level and the same as from the moderate level to the advanced level. (2) It is primarily training that is required to develop skills, knowledge, and orientation; or, if it is a combination of training and experience, these can be combined into a single measure. (3) The difficulty of making a job transition is a linear function of the difficulties in acquiring the skill, knowledge, and orientation requirements of the job.

Nevertheless, we believe that this approach provides a reasonable way of measuring the difficulty of job transitions. Many readers will find this approach similar to that used in numeric job evaluation systems (e.g., the Hay system).

At the ABC Toy Company, the reengineering team decided to use a 10-point scale for measuring the relative difficulty of each job requirement. They then compared the job requirements for current jobs (developed in Task 4B.2) with the requirements for new jobs (developed in Task 4B.4) and prepared the table shown in Figure 7-6. The table does not contain all forty-eight current job to new job pairings because many are clearly infeasible.

Notice two things in particular about this table. First, although the team started out with the intention of using a 10-point scale for difficulty, they decided that analytical skills were much more difficult to acquire if one lacked them. It might take a college-level course to increase one degree of proficiency in this area. So the team assigned analytical skills a weight of 15. Second, it is usually necessary to train someone only when he or she has a level of skill, knowledge, or orientation below that required by the job. Sometimes, however, more is less. The reengineering team recognized that the current order editor job had a higher level of control orientation than was wanted in the customer service representative job. And they recognized that training would be needed to reorient the order editors to be less control oriented. They indicated this need by placing a " – " in the appropriate row and column. The minus counts as one degree of change.

The transition to the new customer service representative job would be moderately hard from the current CSR job (38 points) and difficult from either the order-editor (94 points) or order clerk job (95 points). The transition to the new warehouseworker job would be easy from the current warehouseworker job (23 points), moderate from the dockhand job (30 points), and fairly hard from the traffic manager (54 points) and inventory supervisor (54 points) jobs. The transition to the new logistics supervisor job would be easy from the traffic manager job (0 points) and moderate from the current CSR job (43 points) and the warehouse supervisor job (25 points). Finally, the transition to the new shipments job would be easy from the current warehouseworker job (5 points), dockhand job (0 points) and warehouse supervisor job (0 points); it would be moderate from the traffic manager job (25 points) and the inventory supervisor job (35 points).

TASK 4B.8—DESIGN CAREER PATHS

This task is similar to the preceding one, except that now the matrix is of transitions from one new job to another new job. This task provides a formal solution to one of the vexing problems of reengineering. In reengineered processes, job distinctions (such as compensation) based

Figure 7-6. Fulfill orders: job changes.

From	To	SKILLS						KNOWLEDGE					ORIENTATION					Weighted Change Points
		Interpersonal	Keyboarding	Telephone	Negotiating	Analytical	Forklift Operation	Line of Goods	Warehouse Operation	Credit Management	Customers	Shipping Methods	People	Production	Control	Facilitation	Activity/Project	
Weights		8	5	3	5	15	10	2	4	5	5	10	8	4	3	5	5	
Order Editor	Customer Service Rep	+	+++	++	++			+	+	+		+	++		-	+++		94
Order Editor	Logistics Supervisor	++		++	+				++	+		+++	+	++	++	++		43
Back Order Clerk	Customer Service Rep	++	+++	++	+			+	++	+		+	+		+	+		95
Warehouseperson	Warehouseperson		+															13
Warehouseperson	Shipments															+		5
Traffic Manager	Warehouseperson		+				+++	+++	+							+		54
Traffic Manager	Logistics Supervisor																	0
Traffic Manager	Shipments						++	++										25
Dockhand	Warehouseperson		+				+	++	+					+	+	+		30
Dockhand	Shipments																	0
Inventory Supervisor	Warehouseperson		+				+++		+			+				+		54
Inventory Supervisor	Shipments						++					+				+		35
Customer Service Rep	Customer Service Rep		+++										+++	+++	++			38
Customer Service Rep	Logistics Supervisor				+				+			++	++	++	++			38
Warehouse Supervisor	Warehouseperson																	0
Warehouse Supervisor	Logistics Supervisor		+		+						+	+						25
Warehouse Supervisor	Shipments																	0

KEY

+++ Large change   – or + Small change

++ Moderate change   (blank) No change

on hierarchical position and reporting relationships tend to be replaced by distinctions based on knowledge and skill. But since most jobs are enriched, they are multidimensional, so that it is difficult to compare them directly.

This task develops measures of the difficulty of making transitions from job A to job B and from job B to job A. If A to B is more difficult than B to A, then clearly job B is the "bigger" job. This task considers all such transitions and determines which transitions are feasible. This leads directly to the career path.

Some jobs (the "biggest") will have no career path within the process. In this case, it is necessary to identify feasible transitions into other processes. Since the question "How will this all affect me?" underlies most of the resistance to change, successful completion of this task and communication of its results is one of the most important components of the change management program.

Figure 7-7 shows all twelve of the transitions among the four jobs of the reengineered Fulfill Orders process at the ABC Toy Company. It was obtained by comparing the rows of the matrix developed in Task 4B.4.

Figure 7-8 shows the career paths extracted from the matrix. Since the number of change points to transition from the shipments job to any other job is greater than the number of points from them to shipments, shipments is the lowest level job in the process. The logistics supervisor job and warehouseworker job are most accessible from the shipments job, at 25 and 62 points, respectively. The warehouseworker and logistics supervisor jobs are about the same level, with 59 points required to transition from warehouseworker to logistics supervisor and 45 points in the reverse direction. To transition from logistics supervisor to customer service representative 95 points are required. While this is a difficult transition, the transition from warehouseworker (120 points) or shipments (130) would be even more difficult.

Since transitions to the CSR job are more difficult than transitions from it, the CSR is the "biggest" job in the process. Therefore promotion opportunities for the CSR must be outside the Fulfill Orders process. Looking at the skills, knowledge, and orientation requirements for the CSR, the reengineering team felt that the most likely next step for the CSR would be into the sales organization. Such a move would be facilitated by the decision, already made in Task 4B.5, to make the sales manager responsible for the personnel development of CSRs.

Figure 7-7. Fulfill orders: job transitions.

From	To	SKILLS					KNOWLEDGE						ORIENTATION					Weighted Change Points
Weights →		Interpersonal 8	Keyboarding 5	Telephone 3	Negotiating 5	Analytical 15	Forklift Operation 10	Line of Goods 2	Warehouse Operation 4	Credit Management 5	Customers 5	Shipping Methods 10	People 8	Production 4	Control 3	Facilitation 5	Activity/Project 5	
Customer Service Rep	Logistics Supervisor								+			++						24
Customer Service Rep	Warehouseperson						+++	+	++					+				44
Customer Service Rep	Shipments						++		+									24
Logistics Supervisor	Customer Service Rep	++	+++	++	+			++		+	+		+++			+++		95
Logistics Supervisor	Warehouseperson						+++	+++	+							+		45
Logistics Supervisor	Shipments						++	+								+		27
Warehouseperson	Customer Service Rep	+++	++	+++	++	+				+	++		+++		+	++		120
Warehouseperson	Logistics Supervisor	+		+	+	+					+	++			+			59
Warehouseperson	Shipments																	0
Shipments	Customer Service Rep	+++	+++	+++	++			+			++	++	+++		++	++		130
Shipments	Logistics Supervisor	+		+	+	+					+	++			++			62
Shipments	Warehouseperson						+	++	+					+				25

KEY

+++ Large change   – or + Small change

++ Moderate change   (blank) No change

Figure 7-8.   Fulfill orders: career paths.

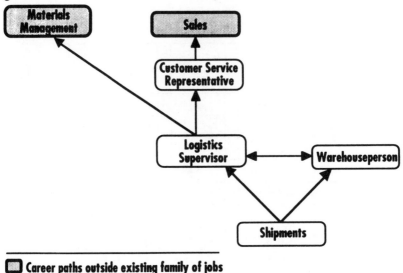

◼ **Career paths outside existing family of jobs**

Because of the difficulty of the transition from logistics supervisor to CSR, the reengineering team thought that it ought to
design another promotional opportunity for the logistics supervisor. Again looking at the skills, knowledge, and orientation requirements for the logistics supervisor, the team felt that a likely
next step would be into the materials management organization.
Of course, actual opportunities would have to await the reengineering of other processes.

Several things are worth observing about this example. First, by
considering the feasible transitions among the jobs, we have effectively
rank ordered them with respect to their requirements. That is, we have
put the jobs in order from "smallest" to "largest." In those compensation schemes where salaries and/or wages are determined by job content
and responsibilities, most of the work of job evaluation has already been
done.

Second, we have taken the unprecedented step (for many organizations) of saying that a nonmanagement job (the CSR) is bigger than a
management job (the logistics supervisor). What a revolutionary idea!
While organizations may have become accustomed to the fact that some
individual contributors (especially salespeople) may earn more than line
managers when their contribution can be measured easily, it is quite

another thing to accept the idea that individual workers may contribute more than managers as a matter of course. Managers of most organizations have come to expect that their positions carry esteem, if not economic rewards, and they can be expected to resist any suggestions that aim to overturn the established order.

Finally, the example illustrates the way in which customer contact jobs tend to become much more empowered, rich, and more complex in a reengineered organization.

TASK 4B.9—DEFINE TRANSITIONAL ORGANIZATION

To this point, Stage 4B has focused on the social design needed to realize the final process Vision. This task addresses the social design for the subVisions, if any. It is conducted in parallel with Task 4A.8—Specify Deployment, so that the social and technical elements of the process will be congruent.

Usually, the need to reach the final vision through a series of subVisions is forced by the technical design, since it can take a long time to develop a new system, for example. But sometimes the social design forces the phasing, for example, when a major education and training program is needed.

This task describes the jobs, management methods, and organization structures at points intermediate between the current situation and the final process design. It also identifies the changes needed to effect the transitions. At this point also the reengineering team has sufficient information about the shape of the new process design to begin work on any near-term opportunities for process improvement.

The pursuit of near-term opportunities often poses a dilemma for a reengineering team. On the one hand, the sponsors and other stakeholders are understandably impatient for results, and the reengineering team is understandably reluctant to ignore an obvious improvement opportunity. On the other hand, it is all too easy to fall into the trap of pursuing easy wins and thereby losing momentum for the more significant gains. Some organizations have dealt with this issue by chartering two teams: one to work on longer-term projects and one on shorter-term.

Figure 7-9 shows the transitional organizations for the Fulfill Orders process.

TASK 4B.10—DESIGN CHANGE MANAGEMENT PROGRAM

This is the *single most important task in Rapid Re,* because far more reengineering projects fail for lack of effective change management than be-

Figure 7-9.   Fulfill orders: transitional organization.

	SubVision One	SubVision Two	SubVision Three
Jobs	Customer Service Rep	Customer Service Rep	Customer Service Rep
	Warehouse Supervisor	Logistics Supervisor	Logistics Supervisor
	Traffic Manager	Warehouseperson	Warehouseperson
	Warehouseperson	Warehouse Clerk	Shipments
	Warehouse Clerk	Shipping Clerk	Credit Advisor
	Shipping Clerk	Dockhand	
	Dockhand	Credit Manager	
	Credit Manager		
Organization	Customer Service Team	Customer Service Team	Customer Service Team
	Shipping Clerk, Dockhand report to Traffic Manager	Shipping Clerk, Shipments report to Logistics Supervisor	Shipping Team
	Warehouseperson, Warehouse Clerk report to Warehouse Supervisor	Warehouse Team	Warehouse Team
	Credit Manager reports to Treasurer	Credit Manager reports to Treasurer	Treasurer is Credit Advisor

cause their technical or social designs are flawed. This task refines and expands on the change management plan drafted in Task 1.4. At that time, in the Preparation stage, the reengineering team should begin to think who the stakeholders are who will be affected by reengineering, what their issues are likely to be, and how the team should manage communications with them. From that point until this, the primary purpose of communication is to keep things under control until the question, "What will reengineering mean to me?" can be answered.

By this point in the reengineering project, the major dimensions of that question will have been settled: job definitions, organization structure, and head count. The only major question not yet settled will be what names go with what jobs: That question will be settled in Stage 5. However, for those jobs with a head count of only one or two (such as some management jobs), the name and the job may be synonymous.

Even if we don't yet know all of the details of how the reengineering will affect all of the stakeholders, we must begin to anticipate and act on our understanding, in order to be proactive. Remember that the most marketable employees are likely to leave first, and they may be the very ones you least want to lose. Nonemployee stakeholders may also take actions we would prefer they didn't. So continual communication is essential.

The Design Change Management task begins with identification of the stakeholders and their likely issues. Some stakeholders are people holding the same jobs; they usually have common interests so the job can be treated as the stakeholder. Other stakeholders (typically managers) hold unique jobs, so the stakeholder is the individual. When the program is executed, however, each person must be treated as an individual, regardless of his or her job.

While the employees are an obvious class of stakeholder, there are many others. Depending on the organization, these may include distributors and sales representatives, suppliers, shareholders, regulators, and directors.

One reason for performing this task at this time is that in order to assess the stakeholders' attitudes we may need to do a baseline assessment, that is, survey the stakeholders' attitude both before and after we announce the changes. For each stakeholder, this task also identifies their expected avenues of resistance and defines measures of the level of resistance or buy-in. It then plans a communications program, a program to assess buy-in and intervene, if necessary, and a general education and training program for all personnel.

At the ABC Toy Company, the reengineering team identified all of the employees involved in the Fulfill Orders process as stakeholders. The salespersons were also stakeholders, as were the customers.

The first stakeholder analyzed was the credit manager. His issue was that his position was being eliminated: he would no longer be required to come to work on Monday, Wednesday, and Friday. The team felt that he was most likely to resist this change by being uncooperative on the development of the expert credit system, so it decided to measure his buy-in through his cooperation. Since the credit manager was the person whose knowledge would be engineered into the system, his cooperation was essential. The team recommended that the credit manager be given a sweetened pension and a consulting contract to participate in the development.

The second stakeholder was the treasurer. With the elimination of the credit manager job, the treasurer would have one less direct report. Additionally, he would sometimes have to make credit decisions; this was additional work for him. The reengineering team anticipated that the treasurer would resist by opposing the expert credit system, so the team proposed to thoroughly pilot test the system and validate it. During this process, the team would monitor the treasurer's skepticism or support for the new way of doing things. It also recommended that the treasurer be given a nominal monetary incentive for the new work.

The controller was the third stakeholder. His issue was the elimination of the billing department. The team anticipated that he would resist by claiming that a loss of control would occur from automatic printing of invoices that are inserted and mailed by accounts payable. So the team planned to get approval from the ABC Toy Company's public accountants and use that approval to convince the controller. The team would measure his buy-in by his acceptance of the change.

The materials management director was the fourth stakeholder. He had had responsibility for the entire warehouse, and now it was to be taken away from him. The team felt that he would be demoralized and demotivated. He had always received good performance evaluations, and now he was losing responsibility through no fault of his own. The team felt strongly that he was a person the company could ill afford to lose, its resident authority on logistics. The purchasing and inventory control functions for which he was still responsible were important, but he would have far fewer people and functions reporting to him. The team members recommended that he be appointed head of the reengineering team for Stage 5. They felt that, first, he could make a significant contribution to the project and second, they hoped that a more challenging job might emerge from the reengineering of other business processes. The team recommended that the president and vice president of operations speak with the materials management director, and it planned to assess his buy-in through his enthusiasm at his new assignment.

The fifth stakeholder was the personnel currently holding jobs as CSRs, order editors, or back-order clerks. The team thought that they would have two issues: the reduction in the number of positions and the difficulty of making the transition to the new CSR job. The team anticipated that these people would resist with fear, uncertainty, lower productivity, and lack of cooperation with the reengineering project. The team's strategy for overcoming resistance included heavy communication and training, a promise of a fair evaluation for the open positions, upgrading the CSR position's pay and status, and extensive coaching and support as the personnel eased into their first day on the job. The team planned to assess the buy-in of this group through several means: monitoring attendance and illness trends, group discussions, and, when the training began, feedback from the instructors on their attitude and participation.

The sixth stakeholder was the personnel currently holding jobs as order clerks, shipping clerks, or billing clerks. Their issue was that those positions were being eliminated. Their resistance could be expected to mirror that of the CSRs, order.editors, and back-order clerks. The team's strategy for ensuring their cooperation throughout implementation of the reengineered process was to give them a fair evaluation for all open positions, to provide outplacement assistance if none could be found, and to promise them a bonus for working to the implementation. Assessment of their buy-in would be primarily through attendance records.

The seventh stakeholder was the salespeople. Their issues were three. First, they would have to solicit the customers to submit reorders directly from the stores. This was not only more work for them, but it made them ask the customers for something other than an order—a change in procedure. Second, they would lose some control over the reorders, because they would no longer be in the loop. And third, and most important, the salespeople were worried that the reengineered process would perform worse, not better, than the current process. The team's strategy for ensuring their cooperation was to present the business case and plan for reengineering the Fulfill Orders process at a sales meeting, emphasizing the careful pilot testing before full implementation and the fact that store-level reorders would not be implemented until the second year. The team planned to assess the salespeople's buy-in in the first year by a periodic survey and during the second year by the percentage of customers signed up for store level reorders.

The eighth and last stakeholder was the customers. Their issue was whether the change would make things better or worse. The team decided to invite several of the most important customers to serve as an advisory panel during the implementation. The ABC Toy Company would pay their expenses. The team also decided to include all customers in the distribution of information on the purpose and progress of the reengineering project. The team felt that the best measure of customers' buy-in to the project would be their orders as compared with the prior year.

TASK 4B.11—DESIGN INCENTIVES

The purpose of this task is to align individual, organizational, and process goals by defining incentives to motivate people to make the transition to the new process, achieve the planned levels of process performance, and commit to continuous improvement.

The subject of incentives is one that can be and has been the subject of books in its own right. For our purposes, we refer only to two of the most important scholars of motivation, Maslow and Herzberg.

The psychiatrist Abraham Maslow, in his book *Motivation and Personality* (New York: Harper & Row, 1954), identified a five-level hierarchy of human needs. At the lowest level are the *physiological needs* such as food, clothing, shelter, oxygen, sleep. On the second level are the *safety needs*, which include physical and emotional security. The third level is *social needs*, such as love, affection, affiliation, friendship, and belonging. On the fourth level are the *esteem needs*, such as power, achievement, and status. Finally, on the fifth and highest level, are the *self-actualization needs* such as self-fulfillment—the use of whatever special skills and aptitudes one possesses.

Maslow observed that only an unfulfilled need can be a motivator and that the lowest level unfulfilled need was the effective motivator. Following are some examples. A person who is hungry will risk danger. A person who feels unsafe will reject companionship. A person who feels unloved will abase himself. A person with low self-esteem will not develop his aptitudes. In each case, an unfulfilled need at the lower level effectively blocks the person from pursuing fulfillment of a need at the higher level.

By the same token, fulfilled needs are not motivators. Once a person has "enough" material things to satisfy his physiological needs, more of the same is not a motivator. The same is true on the other levels as well, although it becomes increasingly difficult to define "enough" as we move up the hierarchy. In the final analysis, the determination of whether a need is fulfilled or unfulfilled is subjective.

To complicate matters further, consider money. Money is the most common incentive used in business, and money can contribute to any or all of the five levels of the hierarchy. It can buy the material objects needed to satisfy the physiological needs. It can buy some of the things needed to provide physical security (a home in a good neighborhood, security devices, bodyguard) and just having it gives some people emotional security. It can buy the material possessions and experiences helpful in attracting friends and lovers. And money is often the way we keep score of our status; sometimes by how much we have, sometimes by how much we spend. Finally, money can pay for the education or leisure time needed for self-actualization.

However, money is both a dubious and an ambiguous motivator. It is dubious because, in the amounts that we typically use to motivate people, it makes a marginal contribution to the satisfaction of unfulfilled needs. Most of the people with whom we deal in North American business have fulfilled their physiological needs. They are not hungry, and they have adequate clothing and shelter. Any desires they have for better food, more stylish clothing, or more spacious shelter comes from the esteem level, not the physiological level.

On the safety level, the greatest unfulfilled need today is job security. And, unfortunately, BPR may have contributed to the lack of job security in the short term. In the long term, reengineering will contribute to job security by making our organizations stronger and increasing the value contributed by workers, but in the short term it has created a period of adjustment that is unsettling to many. Money cannot replace job security or significantly improve people's perception of their physical security, at least not in the amounts we typically provide as incentives.

Similarly, monetary incentives are not likely to contribute much to the fulfillment of social needs. Only at the esteem level can money make much of a difference, and then only if it is the amount of money one has from which one draws his or her esteem. Ironically, it is at the self-actualization level that money may have its greatest impact, when one achieves financial independence. But money can motivate at this level also only if all of the lower levels are filled.

Money is an ambiguous motivator because, first, we are usually unsure if it is what money can buy that people value or the recognition that it implies. And second, we are usually unsure which unfilled need at which level the money is aimed.

Maslow's theories and the conclusions we have drawn from them are entirely consistent with the studies of the industrial psychologist Frederick Herzberg in his book *Work and the Nature of Man* (New York: T.Y. Crowell, 1966). Herzberg formulated a two-factor theory of motivation in the workplace that divided all of the many variables associated with a job into two classes. The first class, which he called "hygienic factors," included pay, benefits, office space, equipment, and information. In other words, the *job context*. The second class, the *job content*, includes the challenge and variety of the work, the degree of autonomy experienced by the worker, the opportunity the work provides for learning and for recognition, and the sense of completion experienced by the worker.

Herzberg's studies showed that the first factors could not motivate, they could only demotivate, so he called them "job dissatisfiers." According to Herzberg, these factors provide the necessary but not sufficient condition for motivation: enough of them and the worker will not be dissatisfied. But more of them will not make the worker satisfied. The only job satisfiers, according to Herzberg, are the contents of the job itself, so he called them "motivators."

Herzberg's theory coincides with our experience. Most of us know people who are happy and energized by work that pays little and provides unattractive working conditions, and most of us know people who are unhappy and drained by jobs they dislike that remunerate them very well. It is ironic, and perhaps telling, that our organizations have invested and continue to invest huge quantities of time, effort, and resources in getting the compensation, benefits, and working conditions "right" and very little in getting the work itself right.

BPR utilizes the work of Maslow and Herzberg by attempting to design jobs that are intrinsically satisfying and motivating. Remember that we began Social Design by empowering all jobs in the organization. This usually resulted in jobs that were considerably broader than the jobs in the unreengineered process. By broadening and empowering jobs, we enhanced process performance by improving productivity, accuracy, and responsiveness and by enabling customer contact personnel to satisfy the customer with "one-stop shopping." But at the same time, by broadening jobs we also enriched them. We provided jobs with greater challenge and variety and made workers responsible for the results of their efforts. In so doing, we created jobs rich in motivation and fulfillment of esteem and self-actualization needs.

Then when a single caseworker was infeasible, we organized teams. In so doing, we empowered the work group, we enriched the work, and provided cross-training. Thereby we fulfilled the social and esteem levels of needs. Then we explicitly assigned management responsibility for the development of personnel and designed career paths for each job. Now we are designing incentives, both economic and noneconomic. In the Technical Design of the process in Stage 4A, we designed measures of process performance and informated the process so that the workers would have ongoing feedback on the status and performance of their process.

In Maslow's terminology, we are attempting to create a process design that satisfies the workers' needs at all levels. In Herzberg's terminology, we are attempting to create a process design that is rich in job motivators. Both intuitively and experientially, if we succeed we will truly have leveraged human potential into breakthrough performance.

This task also defines the measurements and feedback mechanisms needed to support the administration of the incentives. This is another example of Instrument and Informate. The principle followed is that incentives are most effective when the party being monitored is always aware of his or her current performance.

Incentives are usually monetary and nonmonetary awards and recognition. They should not be promotions since promotions should be based on capability, not performance. That is, we follow the 4-P rule of personnel management: Pay for Performance, Promote for Potential. Paying for performance uses economic awards as incentives. These motivators may be dubious and ambiguous, but they are expected and relatively easy to administer. Promoting for potential, however, is a marked departure for many organizations. They most often promote for performance. In fact, many organizations promote because, within their compensation systems, promotion is the only means available for paying people more money. In the reengineered organization, however, there is no intrinsic reason why pay should depend upon organizational level.

By following the principle of promote for potential, organizations can avoid the trap of the Peter Principle (coincidentally, two more Ps). J. Laurence Peter, in his book *The Peter Principle: Why Things Always Go Wrong* (New York: Morrocco, 1969), observed that most organizations promote for performance. Although this may seem like an innocuous or even benign practice, its logical conclusions are chilling. As long as an individual continues to perform well, he or she will be promoted. When promotions stop is when the person reaches his or her "level of incompetence." The implications of this are that over time, most positions in an organization will be filled with incompetent people! The reality is that many positions are. But are these really "incompetent people" or only people whose potential is not exploited by the organization?

In the reengineered organization, we may misjudge a person's potential for a promotion. But we would never knowingly promote him or her from a position in which they were competent into a position in which they were likely to be incompetent. Nor need we. Compensation systems in the reengineered organization ought to reward current performance and the acquisition of new skills and knowledge that make the employee more valuable. And since we design processes for continuous improvement (see Task 5.9 in Chapter 8), the organization should benefit from the development of personnel in their *present* position.

There are three areas in which we may wish to provide incentives. The first is to encourage people to make the transition to the reengineered process. The second is to encourage people to optimize the performance of the reengineered process. And the third is to encourage people to continually improve the reengineered process. Each incentive program needs to be structured to specify what measures of performance will be used; what economic and noneconomic incentives will be provided; and for the economic incentives, the basis and structure of the award and how it will be paid.

Figure 7-10 shows typical incentive structures.

Figure 7-11 shows the incentive program for the ABC Toy Company's Fulfill Orders process.

TASK 4B.12—PLAN IMPLEMENTATION

This task will develop preliminary plans (to be refined in Stage 5) for implementing the social aspects of the reengineered process, including

Figure 7-10. Typical incentive structure.

	Facilitate Transition	Optimize Performance	Continuous Improvement
Measures	Time, Quality	Performance	Innovation
Non-Economic Incentives	Recognition, Process Status	Recognition, Process Status	Recognition, Process Status
Economic Incentives	Bonus	Base Salary, Bonus	Base Salary, Bonus
Award Basis	Group or Individual Performance		
Award Structure	Lump Sum, Percentage of Salary, Scaled		
Payout	One-Time or Periodic		

Figure 7-11. Fulfill orders: ongoing incentives.

	Customer Service		Warehouse	

Performance Measures	• Customer Satisfaction
	• Order throughput
	  – to release
	• Order entry accuracy
			• Customer Satisfaction
			• Order throughput
			  – to ship
			• Order fill accuracy	

Employee Recognition	CSR of the month		Warehouse Employee of the Month	
Award Basis	Group Performance		Group Performance	
Award Structure	Flat Amounts	% of Salary	Flat Amounts	% of Salary
Payout Schedule	Annual	Monthly	Annual	Monthly

recruitment, education, training, reorganization, and redeployment. These plans will then be time phased, along with the parallel plans for implementing the technical aspects of the process, developed in Task 4A.10.

This task also defines the "governance structure" for Stage 5, that is, the roles and responsibilities of the reengineering sponsor, the process owner, the reengineering project manager, and other individuals and organizations. Typically, the information services and human resources functions play major roles in Stage 5.

Figure 7-12 shows the Transformation stage reengineering project team at the ABC Toy Company. This team is different from

Figure 7-12. Fulfill orders: reengineering team transformation stage.

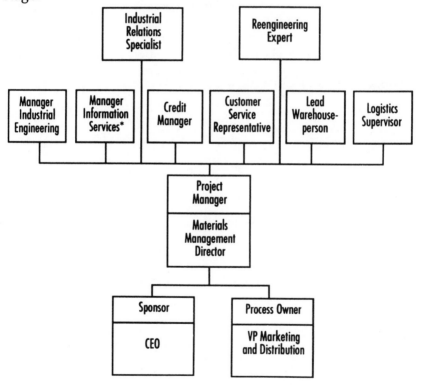

*New Position

the team that develops the process design. First, the materials management director has been appointed project manager, as decided in the change management plan. Second, a newly hired manager of information services has been added to the team. And third, some lower-level people, the people whose jobs are going to change dramatically, have been added to the team.

When we show this organization chart to people, many remark "It's upside down!" We respond, "Who says so?"

The traditional organization chart, with senior management on top and the workers on the bottom, is representative of the command and control paradigm that has all information flowing to the top, where decisions are made, and all directions flowing downward. The inverted organization chart, Figure 7-12, with the workers at the top and senior management at the bottom, is representative of an alternative paradigm. In this paradigm workers are empowered and the role of management is to support those empowered workers. Because the reengineering team was proposing to implement the latter paradigm with its social design of the Fulfill Orders process, the team members seized on this organization chart as a way of communicating the change to their fellow employees and stakeholders.

8

Stage 5:
Transformation

The purpose of this stage is to realize the process vision by implementing the process design produced in Stage 4. The Transformation stage produces pilot and full production versions of the reengineered process and continual changes throughout the production version's life.

The key questions answered by this stage include:

- ❏ When should we begin to monitor progress? How do we know if we're on the right track?
- ❏ What mechanism should we develop for solving unanticipated problems?
- ❏ How do we ensure the transition period goes smoothly?
- ❏ How do we continue to build momentum for ongoing change?
- ❏ What technique should we use to realign the organization?

If the reengineering project has been successful thus far, the designs and plans produced in previous stages will almost completely specify the work of the Transformation stage. We say "almost" because implementation never goes quite as planned. As anyone who has ever managed a project knows, it is the implementation details and how they are handled that spells the difference between success and failure. It has been repeatedly shown that project overruns and failures stem less often from our misjudging the activities we have planned than they do from the activities that we have failed to plan. That is why we place emphasis on planning the reengineering project from the outset. Without a plan, you can't be sure of where the project is going, how well it is going, or whether indeed it has arrived at its destination.

The Transformation Stage consists of nine tasks:

5.1—Complete Business System Design.
5.2—Perform Technical Design.
5.3—Develop Test and Rollout Plans.
5.4—Evaluate Personnel.
5.5—Construct System.
5.6—Train Staff.
5.7—Pilot New Process.
5.8—Refine and Transition.
5.9—Continuous Improvement.

Tasks 5.1 and 5.2 are devoted to completion of the business system design. Task 5.3 is devoted to planning for the testing and rollout of the new process. Task 5.4 is devoted to evaluation and selection of the personnel who will staff the new process. Task 5.5 is devoted to construction of the new system. Task 5.6 provides training to the process staff and others who may need it. Tasks 5.7 and 5.8 are devoted to pilot testing the new process, making adjustments based on the pilot test experience, and, finally, deploying the reengineered process throughout the organization. Task 5.9 is devoted to continuous improvement of the process after deployment.

Remember that, as in the other stages of reengineering, these tasks are not designed for strictly serial performance. Tasks 5.1, 5.2, 5.3, and 5.5 form one partially ordered set of tasks concerning implementation of the technical design. Tasks 5.4 and 5.6 form another partially ordered set of tasks concerning implementation of the social design. Then Tasks 5.7 and 5.8 form another partially ordered set that must follow the first two sets. However, Task 5.8 (Refine and Transition) may well involve repetition of parts of any of the earlier tasks.

The following discussion assumes that the primary technology employed in the technical design of the process is *information technology*. In most processes, particularly those performed in offices, that will be the case. But in other processes, particularly those performed in industrial settings, the technical design of the process may well employ *physical technologies*, such as materials handling, mining and machining, and process control. If this is the case, you should make the appropriate translation. For example, when we speak of the choice between a custom-developed application and an off-the-shelf application package, translate this into the choice between a custom-engineered physical system and one purchased off the shelf. Even in those processes performed in offices, there will most often be physical changes. These are usually the facilities changes necessitated by new information technologies (e.g., the installation of computers and networks) and the facilities changes necessitated by new job, team, and organization relationships (e.g., moves or rearrangements of work space).

The participants in the Transformation stage include the reengineering team (which was selected in Task 4B.12) and supporting organizations such as information services, human resources, office administration, facilities, industrial engineering, process stakeholders, the process owner, the sponsor, and other senior management. As with earlier stages, a facilitator may also participate. Unlike the earlier stages, where the roles and responsibilities of the reengineering team are relatively clear cut, the position of the reengineering team in the Transformation stage will be determined by the role(s) assigned them in the implementation plan (Tasks 4A.10 and 4B.12).

In some reengineering projects, the reengineering team acts as a steering committee, with primary responsibility for implementation assigned to the functional organizations. In other projects, the reengineering team acts as a general contractor, doing the things it can itself and subcontracting the things it can't do to the functional organizations or outside vendors. Yet other reengineering projects have the reengineering team as an advisor to the process owner, who has primary responsibility for implementation. The latter role is most common when the bulk of the development work is delegated to outside vendors.

Recap

This recap is for those readers referring to this chapter without having read Section Two, Chapters 2 through 7.

At this point in the reengineering project, an organization will have selected the business process or processes it wishes to reengineer and will have developed a vision of what results are expected from reengineering. The vision will incorporate both the estimated gains from reengineering and a sense of how the technical and social aspects of the reengineered process will differ from those of the current process. The organization will also have developed a design to realize the process vision and developed a plan for implementing that design. That plan is implemented in the Transformation stage.

The ABC Toy Company developed a vision for its Fulfill Orders process that it thought would help it expand its market share. The technical design for Fulfill Orders included an on-line order processing system and expert systems for credit decisions, warehouse optimization, and routing. The social design for the process included combining eight jobs into four empowered jobs, self-managed work teams, new career paths, new responsibilities for personnel development, and an organization restructured to keep almost all of the process within one department.

Task 5.1—Complete Business System Design

In this and subsequent tasks, Rapid Re uses the nomenclature of information engineering. However, any proven method of system development is equally valid.

This task is concerned with the "external" design of the new or revised system supporting the reengineered process. It includes modeling subprocesses, modeling data, defining applications, and designing dialogs and screens. Alternatively, this task could involve the selection of a commercially available application package and the external design of any modifications.

The design and development of automated application systems is an enterprise fraught with risk and difficulty. Notwithstanding the fact that larger organizations have been building such systems for thirty years or more, the success rate is considerably lower than other similar organizational undertakings. Studies have shown that about 30 percent of all application development projects are abandoned before completion, and of those that are completed, the average project overruns 100 percent in time and 100 percent in budget.

The primary cause of this unsatisfactory performance is that most organizations have not reengineered their systems development process. This is a topic worthy of its own book, and many books have been written on software engineering, systems development methodologies, and project management. The topic is addressed in our American Management Association seminar "Reengineering the Information Systems Organization," however, it is not our purpose to reproduce that work here. Rather, it is to make the point that the development of customized application systems to implement the technical design of a reengineered process should be avoided if at all possible. Such development not only increases the risk of failure, it invariably lengthens the time for implementation.

Fortunately, there is now a rich variety of off-the-shelf application packages available for most business applications. And many packages contain built-in options that permit different organizations to customize the application to their needs. Even when a single application package lacks all of the required features and functions, an organization still has several options for using the package. One option is to *modify* the package, that is, to change some of the package vendor's code. This option is the least desirable because it increases both the risk and the difficulty of maintaining the system. A second option is to *extend* the package, that is, to leave the vendor's code unchanged but to write additional code that works with the package. Sometimes the vendor provides supported Application Programming Interfaces (API) to facilitate extending the package. Other times, the organization will write code that "surrounds" the vendor's package. Either way, this option of extending the package is less risky than the first. A third option is to *integrate* the package, that is, to make the package work with another package or custom program by using the integration features of the operating environment. Especially with microcomputer operating environments such as UNIX or Microsoft Windows, the integration capabilities are extensive. This option is the least risky of the three.

Of course, these decisions are not simple. They involve such important considerations as:

- ❏ On which technical platforms is the package available and which does my organization support?
- ❏ What data structures does the package use and are these structures we can work with?
- ❏ Is there any need to interface this application with preexisting applications, and if so, how can this be accomplished?
- ❏ What is our level of confidence that the package will perform as advertised?
- ❏ What is our level of confidence that the package vendor will remain viable and provide adequate support?

Discussion of these issues is beyond the scope of this book. They are included only to illustrate that, while the use of commercially available application packages is an attractive option that should be considered by every reengineering team, it is a complex decision requiring careful analysis.

This task, then, begins by modeling subprocesses, that is, by extending the level of detail of the technical design of the process.

Next is the modeling of data. This, too, is an expansion of the level of detail in the technical design. Specifically, this involves defining the attributes of each entity modeled in Task 4A.1 and defining the permissible values for each attribute. For example, an attribute of the entity "employee" is "date of birth," which consists of the attributes "month of birth," "day of birth," and "year of birth." Permissible values for "month of birth" are "1" through "12," etc.

Once the subprocesses and data are modeled, the next step is to define the application. This consists of specifying the *business rules* associated with each activity and step of the process design.

In the ABC Toy Company's Fulfill Orders process, the activity Enter Order has a step called Identify Customer. The business rules for this step might be:

1. Accept customer name from terminal.
2. Search customer file for instances with customer name similar to that accepted from terminal.
3. If an exact match with the customer name is found in file, retrieve associated customer information and exit this step.
4. If an exact match with the customer name is not found in file, display the filed customer names in order of decreasing similarity to the entered name. Also display a message on the terminal giving the operator the option of selecting one of the displayed names, of reentering the customer name, or of indicating that this is a new customer. If the operator chooses to reenter the name, go to 1.
5. If the operator selects one of the displayed names, retrieve the associated customer information and exit this step.
6. Otherwise go to the step Enter New Customer.

There are many ways of representing the business rules. The specific system development methodology that the reengineering team adopts will generally include a standard. Some of the common standards include input-process-output (IPO), hierarchical input-process-output (HIPO) and structured English (pseudo-code). Once the application has been defined, the reengineering team may investigate the availability of commercially available packages for that application. If a package solution appears to be feasible, then the remaining work of this task is to evaluate and select the package, to demonstrate it, and to decide what modifications or extensions to make or how to integrate it with other software. If a package solution is infeasible, then the remaining work of this task is to design the human interface and a prototype of the system.

The human interface consists of the dialogs between the system and its human users and the individual screen displays that comprise the dialog. With a package, the package vendor has designed the human interface already, hopefully with a good understanding of human factors. Indeed, the quality of the human interface and its congruence with the social design of the process will be one of the most important package evaluation criteria.

Organizations designing their own applications should use similar considerations in designing the human interface. The term *user friendly* has been misused and overused, but it captures the essence of interface design. We want the interactions between the technology and its human users to be intuitively easy for anyone who understands the application. This emphatically does *not* mean that the human interface should mimic the interface of the system it is replacing, because the human interfaces of most of the legacy systems are terrible! Rather, the reengineered human interface should make it easy to learn the system and easy to use it. Ideally, it should incorporate graphic features rather than arcane codes and commands, and it should provide help for the novice and shortcuts for the experienced user.

Organizations designing their own applications should develop a prototype because it has been shown to be a more effective communication tool than a paper-based design. Remember that the time and cost of repairing an error in a system goes up exponentially as the error is promulgated through requirements, design, development, and implementation. The purpose of the prototype is for the developers and their clients to both understand the essential features of the new system and to experiment with modifications before making a heavy investment in system construction. Some system development environments permit expansion of the prototype into the production system, but most do not. Even so, the development of a prototype may well be worth the effort.

This task, then, is where the prototype will be designed by organizations designing their own applications. The next task is where the prototype will be developed.

At the ABC Toy Company the reengineering project team for the Fulfill Orders process decided that it had no choice but to select a package for the order processing application. Up to now, ABC Toy Company had had no information services organization at all. It had just hired a manager of information services and the reengineering team was his first assignment. The team was able to find several order processing packages that appeared to meet all of its requirements. One of the requirements was that the package be able to provide data to the existing PC-based Peachtree accounting package because there was no plan to replace it. Another requirement was that the order processing package be

able to accept batch input of orders conforming to industry standard electronic data interchange (EDI) formats.

The team was also able to find an off-the-shelf expert system
for warehouse optimization and routing of shipments, although
its implementation would require substantial assistance from the
vendor.

For the expert credit system, the team decided to build its
own application, using an off-the-shelf "tool set." It recognized
that the company would have to retain a knowledge engineer to
work with the credit manager to extract his expertise and represent it as a set of rules for the expert system's knowledge base.
The team also recognized that it would need to build an interface
between the accounts receivable system and the expert system so
that the latter would have access to a customer's credit history.

TASK 5.2—PERFORM TECHNICAL DESIGN

This task is concerned with the "internal" design of the new or revised
system supporting the reengineered process. For packages, this task
was already performed by the vendor.

This task selects the platform or platforms on which the application
system will be mounted. For both information systems and physical systems, the platform consists of hardware and software: The primary difference is in the terminal devices. Information systems terminals provide human interface. Physical systems terminals provide interfaces
with both humans and things.

The platform selection decision should be driven by the needs and
availability of the application software. All other things being equal, a
reengineering team should first select the most suitable application
package and then select the platform that package best runs on. That is
why we place the selection of the package in the previous task. But often
a reengineering team will not have a completely free choice in the selection of the platform. Sometimes this is because the system must interact
with other systems and the best way to do this is to mount the new
system on the same platform as the old. Other times this is because the
organization has made a strategic decision to mount all new development on the same platform.

Once the platform has been selected, the remaining work of the task
depends on whether the application will be based on a package or will
be custom developed. If the application is based on a package, the next
step involves selecting the package options to be used and/or designing
extensions or modifications to the package or to the interfaces between

the package and other system. If the application is custom developed, the next step is to design the physical data structure. This means mapping the attributes of an entry into data fields, deciding which data fields should reside in which records or tables, and specifying how the relationships among entities should be represented. It also means specifying the media on which the data will reside and the methods of assessing the data. The choices here are limited by the capabilities of the data management subsystem of the selected platform.

Another part of this task is the detail design of the system, including further refinement of the business rules developed in Task 5.1, segregation of the business rules into system components or modules, and extension of the business rules to include interactions among the modules and with the users of the system.

With the completion of these activities, the system structure will be completely specified. The remaining work of this task is to finalize definitions and plans for the pilot implementation and for the project deliverables.

TASK 5.3—DEVELOP TEST AND ROLLOUT PLANS

This task determines the methods to be used for system validation, that is, it determines how to verify the correctness and quality of the project deliverables. The two main tools of verification are *standards* and *independent review*. Standards are important for several reasons. First, they provide direction to the developers; second, they provide a benchmark for the reviewers; and third, they help to condition the expectations of the clients. Independent review means that people other than the developers review the deliverables. "Review" may include system, stress, parallel or pilot testing, inspection or observation, "walk throughs," demonstrations, etc.

The task also determines the methods to be used for conversion and transition and develops a time-phased deployment plan. Several issues are involved in conversion. First, the new system may be replacing (partially or completely) an existing system, often called the *legacy system*. The plan must identify legacy system roles and interfaces in the process and determine how these will change. It must also decide how to dispose of the legacy data: will it be converted, allowed to "run off," or be ignored? How will the new system results be reconciled with the legacy system results? The reengineering team must assess and document conversion requirements. The time and resources involved in conversion can be substantial and are often underestimated.

There are also several issues involved in deployment, or *fielding*, of the system, particularly in a geographically dispersed organization. The personnel who will be involved in fielding the system "on site" should be involved in planning. The deployment plan should address such issues as What training will be required at each site? What documentation? How will each site get help with their problems? How can the impact of the new system on each site be coordinated with that site's business cycle?

Finally, the task assesses the impacts of the new system and defines fallback and contingency plans. These are especially important in view of Murphy's law: If anything can go wrong, it will. The last thing we want to have happen is to discover that the new system doesn't work and we have no way to revert to the old system.

There was a small electrical parts distributor that was changing its order fulfillment system. The key technological innovation was to replace a labor-intensive manual order processing system with a sophisticated on-line service. After some modification to the system and a reasonable amount of testing and training of the operators of the new system, cut-over was scheduled for Monday morning. That Friday afternoon, the company president fired all of the order processors who had not been trained to operate the new system (75 percent of them) without notice. And on Monday morning, the new system didn't work! It took the on-line service vendor nearly a month to fix the problem. Meanwhile, the remaining order processors and whoever else could be pressed into service were unable to keep up with the flow of orders. The warehouse was underutilized. The customers were unhappy. And cash flow slowed down. It took the company months to recover from this misfortune and all because they failed to develop a contingency and fallback plan.

In building systems, it is always appropriate to hope for the best and plan for the worst.

Task 5.4—Evaluate Personnel

This task assesses current personnel in terms of their skills, knowledge, orientation, the extent of their "buy-in" to the change, and their aptitude.

The assessment of aptitude is very important, because determination of the disposition of each person should be based on them and not on the job they hold. Some people are underqualified for their jobs, other people are overqualified. And some people possess skills, knowledge, and orientation unrelated to their present job but very desirable in another job. The assessment of each person is then matched against the job requirements and staffing levels developed in Task 4B.4 in order to identify personnel shortages or excesses and training needs.

Inasmuch as business process reengineering (BPR) usually improves the efficiency and effectiveness of a process and the productivity of the people involved in the process, in a reengineered process it is usually true that fewer people can handle the same amount of work. This means that, all else being equal, there will be too many people for the amount of work. The question then becomes what to do with those people.

One of the difficulties in reengineering an organization one process at a time is that we don't get a comprehensive picture of the staffing needs of the organization. We may find that we sever competent employees from one process and then have to recruit outside the organization to staff another process. Also, since reengineering improves the operational effectiveness of an organization, we often find that the amount of work goes up, not down, as the organization becomes more successful in the marketplace. In these scenarios we may find that we sever employees only to have to hire new ones for the *same* process.

For these reasons, an organization undertaking reengineering should think long and hard about severing competent employees. And in our experience, this is what is being done in organizations that begin with reengineering. Those organizations that begin with downsizing (or "rightsizing," as the current euphemism calls it) sometimes reengineer after the fact to try to restore the effectiveness lost with the personnel cuts. (And to keep the staff lean: There is considerable evidence that the organizations that cut staff without changing the way work is done find their staff levels creeping upward toward their previous levels.)

But if an organization decides to retain employees beyond the level needed by the process, what does it do with them? The answer to this question depends to a great extent on the company's business strategy. If the strategy is to retrench, downsize, surrender market share, exit certain businesses, then it may well be appropriate to reduce staff. On the other hand, if the strategy is expansive, to grow, enter new markets, expand market share, then it is possibly inappropriate to reduce staff. Even if it appears more profitable in the short term to shed certain employees while hiring others, this may be an anomaly of our accounting systems.

Our accounting systems treat people as expenses when they are really assets. The job experiences, training, and education that we provide our employees are really investments, not expenses. That is why most employees become more productive as they age. And that is why we pay more to more senior people. If we had to treat employees as assets on the organization's books, we would be far less ready to write them off. But what do we do with them while we are waiting for the level of business to increase? There is no single answer, but here are several suggestions:

- ❑ *Transitioning.* Often, when a process is first reengineered, the performance measures move in the opposite direction from that expected. In other words, productivity goes down, as does quality, while costs go up. The reason is that a period of transition is generally necessary after any significant change, before the new process stabilizes. During this period, we may need more people, not fewer.
- ❑ *Promotion.* Use the free employees to stimulate more or new business.
- ❑ *Job sharing.* Instead of reducing head count, reduce full-time equivalent head count by having people share their jobs. Many people will welcome the additional leisure time, particularly if it is not accompanied by a proportionate decrease in pay.
- ❑ *Cross-training.* Train people to perform more than one job.
- ❑ *Intrapreneurship.* Encourage the employees to find new business opportunities for the organization.
- ❑ *Reengineering acceleration.* Use the free employees to staff reengineering teams.

In spite of all these tactics, it is often necessary to reduce staff, and the question then becomes which staff to retain. The first criterion should be the person's aptitude for the reengineered job. The second criterion should be the person's buy-in to the change, whether they approach it with enthusiasm or fear. Once we know who will staff the reengineered process and how their current skills, knowledge, and orientation compare with the job requirements, we can prescribe the training needs of each person. The training needs from this task are then used to finalize the components of the education and training curriculum and to assign individuals to specific courses.

At the ABC Toy Company the reengineering team assessed the current skills and aptitude of each of the affected staff against the requirements of the Fulfill Orders process. Figure 8-1 shows the result of its assessment for the Customer Service Representative (CSR) position.

In evaluating the staff, the team used a simple triage system for disposition: keep, let go, or not sure. The first group would

Figure 8-1. Fulfill orders: personnel evaluation for CSR position.

Requirements	Interpersonal	Keyboarding	Telephone	Negotiating	Analytical	Forklift Operation	Line of Goods	Warehouse Operation	Credit Management	Customers	Shipping Methods	People	Production	Control	Facilitation	Activity/Project	Evaluation
(Requirements)	H	H	H	M	L		M	L	L	M	L	H	M	M	H	A	
M. Smith –current	M	H	L	M	L		L			M		M	M	H	A	A	
–aptitude	A	A	A	A			G	G	G		G	A		G	L	A	Train
T. Jones –current	H	L	M	L	L		M			M		H	L	L	L	A	
–aptitude		G	G	G				A	A		L				G	A	Train
L. Brown –current	P		L		A		H			L		L	A	A		A	
–aptitude	H	A		P	M			L	L	A	G	P	H	H	P	A	Reassign or outplace
V. Williams –current	H	G	P	L	L		M	L	L	M	L	H		A	H	A	
–aptitude	M		H	G								M		L			Train
S. Henderson –current	M	L	M		M		H	M		L		M	L	L	M	A	
–aptitude	A	G	A	A					G	G	A	A	G	G	A		Train
W. Clinton –current	H	L	H	M	L		M	L	L	A	A	G	A	A	P	A	
–aptitude	P	A															Train and reevaluate

KEY

H = High   P = Poor
M = Moderate   G = Good
L = Low   A = Average

be trained. The second group would be reassigned to another process or outplaced. And the third group would be trained, reevaluated, and then placed in one or another of the first two groups.

If the first group contained more than enough people to staff the process, some of them would be let go as well. In this case, the primary criteria for retention would be the extent to which they met the job requirements and their buy-in to the change.

Based on the assessment of training needs, the reengineering team identified a curriculum consisting of the following courses:

❑ *An Introduction to the ABC Toy Company.* Covering the products, the customers, the history, and providing overviews of manufacturing and distribution.
❑ *Serving the Customer.* Covering customers' needs, interpersonal skills, telephone skills, negotiation skills, facilitation, and an introduction to credit management.
❑ *Basic Keyboarding.*
❑ *Intermediate Keyboarding.*
❑ *Preventing and Solving Problems.* Covering analytical methods and controls.
❑ *Working as a Team.*

TASK 5.5—CONSTRUCT SYSTEM

This task produces an operations-ready version of the new process. When the process is based on a custom-developed system, this task includes development and testing of databases, development and testing of systems and procedures, and documentation. When the process is based on a package, this task includes installation and modification or extension of the package, and its testing. In either case, the task also includes conversion of data.

Testing is usually a multistep, multilevel procedure, proceeding from the testing of the smallest system units, through larger and larger aggregates of system units, until the entire system is tested as a unit. Even then, additional testing is usually performed to determine the behavior of the system under stress, to compare the results of the new system with that of the old, and to develop client comfort with the system.

All of the activities included in this task should have been planned in earlier tasks.

TASK 5.6—TRAIN STAFF

This task provides training in the operation, administration, and maintenance of the new process, just in time for the staff to assume their new responsibilities. It also includes coaching as they assume those responsibilities. We want to train personnel just in time because too early means that they will forget what they've been taught and too late means that they are unprepared for their responsibilities.

Sometimes we train personnel to work with the system while it is still being tested. This gives the staff additional time to develop their comfort and proficiency with the system before they have to use it "live," and it gives the system developers additional and unplanned test cases to evaluate. But the system should be in a reasonably good state before we allow people to work with it, otherwise we run the risk of alienating them.

TASK 5.7—PILOT NEW PROCESSES

This task operates the new process in a limited area in order to identify any needed improvements or corrections, without incurring the risk of a full deployment.

TASK 5.8—REFINE AND TRANSITION

This task corrects the flaws discovered during pilot operation and deploys the new process in a controlled manner, in accordance with the roll-out plan developed in Task 5.3.

TASK 5.9—CONTINUOUS IMPROVEMENT

Grammatically speaking, the improvement of a business process cannot be *continuous*, for improvements are not made at every moment of time, but rather *continual*, for improvements are made in every interval of time. But the term "continuous improvement" is the term used in the literature, so we shall honor it.

People often ask us whether reengineering is an ongoing program for organizations. Certainly, some writers would have you believe that it is. But we disagree. We believe that reengineering is too difficult and painful a process to engage in without good reason. If an organization correctly identifies its business objectives and its business processes, correctly assesses the impact of each process on the business objectives and the consequent opportunity to contribute to the business by reengineering the strategic value-added processes and then develops and realizes a vision for breakthrough performance of the process, the only thing left for it to do is to build continuous improvement into the process. Then the organization should not have to re-reengineer unless it again encounters a change in its business strategy or environment.

Reengineering may become an ongoing program for some organizations because they have many different processes to reengineer, for example when the enterprise consists of many diverse units. And some organizations may have to repeatedly reengineer because they are in an industry encountering frequent changes, for example in technology, regulation, or competition. But most companies should not have to reengineer very often. For them, continuous improvement should suffice.

Robert B. Reich, Secretary of Labor in the Clinton administration, wrote an interesting article entitled "Entrepreneurship Reconsidered— The Team as Hero," in the May/June 1987 issue of *Harvard Business Review*. In it, Reich considered the question of why many products invented by Americans had been taken over by other countries. The products included transistors, color television, robots, videocassette recorders, basic oxygen furnaces, continuous steel casters, microwave ovens, automobile stamping machines, computerized machine tools, and integrated circuits. Reich attributed this to the fact that our foreign competitors, particularly Japan, were better than we in quickly and effectively transforming ideas into incrementally better products, in other words, continuous improvement. And the reason, according to Reich:

❑ "The older and still dominant American myth involves two kinds of actors: entrepreneurial heroes and industrial drones— the inspired and the perspired.

❑ "At best, they [the workers] put in a decent effort in executing the entrepreneurial hero's grand design. At worst, they demand more wages and benefits for less work, do the minimum expected of them, or function as bland bureaucrats mired in standard operating procedures."

In other words, American companies reserve the right and obligation to improve products and services to relatively few workers, while our foreign competitors enlist the participation of all of their employees. In other words, they make better use of their human potential.

The reader should recognize that the paradigm that Reich is proposing is the paradigm represented by the social design of BPR. From this perspective, we can see that the reason that Japanese business has been so successful is that it has been engineered. Whether by luck, culture, or more careful attention to American quality proponents like J.M. Juran and W.E. Deming, the Japanese have come very close to the kinds of processes that American companies have been seeking to attain through reengineering.

In North America, continuous improvement is an unnatural act. Left to their own devices, organizations often mindlessly follow the practices of the past, never questioning whether there is a better way. That is why there are such rich opportunities in BPR. But just because we have reengineered a process, we have not automatically overcome the tendency to let things be as they are. Rather, if we want continuous improvement, we must design it into the process.

In order that continuous process improvement take place, three requirements must be met:

1. Process personnel must be given clear performance goals, measures of goal attainment, and information on the current and past values of those measures.
2. Process personnel must be given the tools necessary to effect changes in performance.
3. Process personnel must be given the responsibility, authority, and incentives for improving performance.

The first two requirements were addressed by Task 4A.3—Instrument and Informate. The last two requirements were addressed by Task 4B.1—Empower Customer Contact Personnel. And the third requirement was also addressed by Task 4B.11—Design Incentives.

BPR provides the technical and social context for continuous improvement. On the social side, it provides empowered and motivated employees with the capability of contributing all that their human potential contains. On the technical side, it provides the information and tools to assess current performance and improve upon it.

One final note on the technical design. Since one of the levers of process performance is the use of technology, continuous improvement means the implementation of successively better systems. A prerequisite for this is a systems testing environment that provides a vehicle for progressive improvement. Such a vehicle would, ideally, include:

❑ The capability to accumulate test cases and interesting scenarios to exercise the system
❑ Regression testing to ensure that previously corrected problems do not recur

❑ Establishment of base defect rates and tracking of changes
❑ Automatic application of test cases and comparison of test results

These capabilities are common in commercial software development companies and in aerospace and defense contractors, but they are lacking in most other organizations.

Section III

Resources

9

Selecting Reengineering Tools

Business Process Reengineering (BPR) is an exercise in the management of detail—the kind of activity that benefits from the use of automated tools. But be careful in selecting reengineering tools. Pick wrong and suddenly the team is doing more attending to the tool than reengineering. Pick well and the team is freed from the tedious, thankless task of handling the large amount of detail on which your project depends. The right way to pick reengineering tools is to consider the choice as a careful investment from which you expect a return. Notice though that the normal rules of investing in tools must be revised to make the right reengineering tool choices.

Selecting reengineering tools is different from the normal software acquisition decision. In a nonreengineering project setting, we expect to see the same tool applied by the same staff over and over through the years. Therefore, we can justify considerable investment in training staff, installing the tool, and having consultants in to get things started off on the right foot. Most tools, even relatively simple end-user tools like spreadsheets, assume that a new user will need time to become initially capable and some longer period to become fully capable with the tool. For most tools that longer period is 90–120 days. For sophisticated tools the longer period is six months to a year. In reengineering projects, only the most extraordinary tool benefit could justify devoting a quarter or more of the whole project schedule to preparing tool users. And because the reengineering project is an infrequent occurrence, the period within which the tool investment must be recovered is quite short. So selecting reengineering tools is different.

This chapter discusses selecting reengineering tools in light of the special needs of reengineering projects. Remember the right tool selections may be anything from pencils, papers, and chalkboards through big-ticket fully integrated BPR toolsets or Computer-Aided Software Engineering (CASE) tools.

Benefits and Requirements of Tools

If we look at buying tools as an investment, then the expected benefits of the choice must exceed the expected costs within the investment period. As we have seen, the short, nonrepeating nature of reengineering projects makes us look at tool benefits and tool requirements from a new point of view. Those viewpoints on tool benefits and requirements are the topic of this section.

New Viewpoint: Reengineering Tool Benefits

The categories of benefits expected from reengineering tools are not much different from those of nonreengineering tools. They include:

❑ Improved productivity
❑ Faster projects
❑ Higher quality levels
❑ Elimination of tedious work, allowing focus on value-added work

However, note that these benefits come only after first learning the tool. If your staff does not already know the tool, then they must learn it and will not achieve any benefit until they do.

> Reengineering tool benefits differ in that we must steeply discount their value if the tool skills are not already in-house. We should strongly question any expected benefit from a tool we have yet to learn.

Many sophisticated toolsets and CASE tools require a year for a new user to master. Even mundane office tools such as spreadsheets require several months before full comfort with the tool's advanced features is achieved. If the expected benefits of the tool (minus the training cost) are less than if doing the work manually, then the right tools for that task are pencil, paper, and whiteboards.

If the time required to learn a tool is six months or more, ask yourself if you must have that tool to do the BPR project. If not, drop it.

If the time to fully learn the tool is measured in months, then discount the expected benefit severely. Is the steeply discounted benefit still worth the expected cost?

If the tool is supposed to be "easy" to learn, then get reliable references who can confirm that ease of learning.

If the tool is already in-house, how hard will it be to train the rest of the reengineering team to use it?

This last point about training the rest of the team to use existing in-house tools brings us to the special business requirements for reengineering tools.

New Viewpoint: Reengineering Tool Requirements

Reengineering tools must:

- ❏ Be usable by business people
- ❏ Generate a return on investment (ROI)
- ❏ Enhance vision clarity
- ❏ Enforce design consistency
- ❏ Provide top-down refinement from corporate goals to working system

All but the first of these requirements might apply to tools for any project, BPR or otherwise. The requirement to "be usable by business people" most distinguishes the reengineering tool selection. Most reengineering team members are not technical people. Business people will be responsible for analyzing the needs of the business and envisioning a new business process for meeting those needs. Tools that enhance the clarity of "their" vision, that enforce consistency of "their" design, and that keep "their" design aligned with the original goals of the system will be of value. All others should check their technology at the door.

This viewpoint further refines our focus on "learnability" in the tool selection process by specifying who must be able to learn the tool. If the time required for "business people" to learn a tool is six months or more, ask yourself if you must have that tool to do the BPR project. If the tool is judged to be essential, then reconsider the BPR project scope.

Some strategies for equipping reengineering teams call for a technical specialist to enter all of the inputs into the tool so that the rest of the team can suggest further refinements, which the technician then enters. One example of this approach is the joint application development (JAD) methodology. But, even with JAD, the business people looking at tool outputs must be trained to understand the output screens before the tool can contribute to their "clarity of vision." It will take time before the business people and technical people on the team learn to work together in this way.

Platforms

Any automated reengineering tool choice also implies the choice of computers, operating systems, and local area networks (LANs) that will run the tools. We call these tool-enabling choices the tool's *platform*. Unlike the reengineering project team, the platform associated with reengineering tools, and probably the tools themselves, will be around for a long time. While they are around, even during the BPR project, the reengineering team platform should at least be able to interact with the rest of the company's platform. So after finding tools that deliver the benefits needed by the team and that comply with the requirements of BPR, we must also consider the platform on which the tools are available. Again the cost implications of the tool platform choice must be factored into the comparison between tool expected benefits and expected costs.

> If the desired tools do not run on a platform already available in the company, then the reengineering team will need to acquire and operate the platform themselves. At best this would be a distraction from the work of the team—at worst it would be a major burden.
> If the desired tools do not run on a platform already available in the company, then how will the tools be supported after the BPR project, for example, to make later enhancements to the system?
> What will happen to the platform after the reengineering project?

These considerations point out a major difference between the reengineering tool decision and the platform decision. While the reengineering tool decision is concerned about a one-year ROI window, the platform decision is concerned with a three-to-five–year ROI window. Obviously, the reengineering tools must run on something, so any conflict between platform and BPR tool choices must be resolved. As with the BPR tool choice, relevant issues guide the development of a platform selection strategy.

New Viewpoint: Integration as Overriding Platform Issue

The issues in making the reengineering platform selection include:

❑ Productivity
❑ Cost-Benefit
❑ Compatibility with present standards
❑ Compatibility with future standards
❑ Wide availability of alternative tools

A larger issue underlies all of these platform selection issues. That larger issue is "integration," the ability of different tools and different users to interact and interchange results across the platform. The platform choice has a lot to do with how easily integration may be achieved.

Integration directly affects productivity by expediting linkages between users and tool processes. These improved linkages directly improve processing times and information availability. While productivity enhancements can be achieved in many ways, integration enhances productivity through standards that ensure that several tools all operate in the same compatible way. The result of such standards is a wide variety of tools that can interact across the platform. Understanding the role of integration as a platform productivity vehicle leads us to prefer platforms that are compatible with both existing and future standards.

New Viewpoint: Platform Selection Strategy

At some point the conflicts between platform selection and reengineering tool selection must be resolved and that resolution will often be a compromise. The following reengineering platform selection strategy helps put that compromise in context:

> The tool software is the driver for both benefit and cost in tools. Choose the tool software first, then pick the platform to maximize software investment leverage.

First, the benefit that you seek from reengineering tools comes from the software. Second, except for mainframe/minicomputer environments, the software choice will be the cost-driver in the tool selection decision. Presumably a reengineering group will not select a mainframe platform unless it were already owned by the company, so even in that case the software investment in reengineering tools may exceed any incremental investment for the hardware.

Therefore, choose the right tool software first. The hardware choice, operating system choice, and LAN choice only make sense after the reengineering tool software has been chosen.

> If the best platform for the software is not otherwise available in the company, then what additional expense is involved in acquiring, supporting, and operating the platform?
> Does the tool selection still make sense in light of that platform expense?
> If the best platform is too expensive, consider less capable (but more widely available in the company) platforms. Does the now discounted benefit still make sense versus the costs?

Ultimately, the added platform expense may force the reengineering team to go back and reconsider its reengineering tool choice because the benefit from the tool does not warrant the overall expense.

Platform Alternatives

The platform options available to a BPR team are actually much more restricted than they would appear at first. Several types of platforms, which would otherwise be acceptable, are usually eliminated by the nature of those platforms' technology. First, it is extremely unlikely that any expected tool benefits could be great enough to warrant the purchase of mainframe or minicomputer hosts. Only organizations that already use that technology would consider it as the platform for reengineering tools. Second, because engineering workstations generally run the Unix operating system, business people will usually require significant retraining before they can use those systems. More importantly, a Unix reengineering environment will require major investment in Unix systems management/support skills. Since Unix-literate business people and Unix-literate systems managers are uncommon in business, it will be uncommon to see reengineering teams selecting Unix workstations as their tools platform. Exceptions to this observation will occur in companies that have standardized on Unix and are already using Unix in support of their business staff. Such Unix standardization is more common in European, Asian, and South American companies than it is in the United States.

By a process of elimination we are left with a much reduced set of candidate platforms. Not coincidentally, this reduced set is where most of the business tools in common use today run—*personal computers*. That observation still leaves us with several platform details to be decided, including:

- [ ] Personal Computer host type
- [ ] Operating systems—DOS, Windows, OS/2
- [ ] LAN—Novell, Banyan Vines, LanManager

These decisions are usually decided based on local preferences and existing infrastructure. In general, choices that conform with that local platform preference will improve the integration between the reengineering team and the balance of the company. If the local platform does not run your BPR tools or does not run them well, then you must go with a platform that does run them well.

Global Tool Cost Issues

As stated above, tool choice is first and foremost about the benefits that the tool is to deliver for a given expected cost. Major influences on expected cost for almost any tool choice include:

- [ ] Learning curve
- [ ] Integration
- [ ] Lifetime tool cost expectation

Each of these influences is summarized here to contribute to an understanding of the tool selection process.

Learning Curve

Realistic expectations about how much it will cost to learn a new tool are essential to assessing the tool's expected cost. The experiences of others, hopefully with the same tool you are considering, can tell you a lot about what to expect. If other users of the same tools cannot be found, then users of similar tools should be sought out.

Some general guidance emerges from the literature of tool adoption, including:

- [ ] Recovery of the cost of learning a toolset during one project is unlikely.[1]

1. Christopher F. Kemerer, "How the Learning Curve Affects CASE Tool Adoption," *IEEE Software*, May 1992.

❑ Learning time to master a sophisticated tool averages from six months to one year.[2]
❑ Productivity of tool users drops during the period of initial fielding and early use of a new tool.
❑ For large toolsets, that productivity drop may be for six months or more.
❑ The cost of learning the tool may be over twice the cost of the tool.[3]

In addition to the experiences of others, asking yourself a few questions about the tool can tell you a lot about how easy it will be for your team to learn.

Does the tool call for you to learn a new way of thinking?
Is the tool arbitrarily different from what the staff already knows?
Does the tool share a common "look-and-feel" with other tools that the staff uses or will use?

If a tool calls for your staff to learn a new way of thinking about its problem, then it is probably not appropriate for supporting a BPR project. First staff members will need to learn the new way of thinking, and then they will know what to do with the tool. Those who are able to learn the new approach will master it in six months or less; the rest may never get it. These timescales are inconsistent with the needs of a BPR project.

If a new tool arbitrarily differs in syntax, or format, or procedure from the staff's old tools, then the staff will be moderately less productive for a month while it "unlearns" the old tool. We experience this effect in our own lives when we change from one word processor to another. The activity to be performed is about the same in each tool, but all the arbitrary details we learned on the old tool don't work anymore. We must "unlearn" them.

If a new tool shares a "look-and-feel" with other tools that the staff uses, then learning the new tool will be significantly easier than if it does not. For example, under an ad hoc Graphic User Interface (GUI) standard like Microsoft Windows℠ many things work the same way across applications. Regardless of which software I use, the choices for saving a file are in the same menu and have a common name. Learning one

2. Ibid.
3. Clifford C. Huff, "Elements of a Realistic CASE Tool Adoption Budget," *Communications of the ACM,* April 1992, p. 53.

application teaches me a lot about the others. Standard user interfaces as in Windows or OS/2 Presentation Manager are important because they speed learning.

Integration

Automating BPR requires more than one tool. Tools are specialty oriented. But reengineering is inherently a multispecialty activity. Because multiple tools are involved, some way to integrate the several tools must be provided. By "integrate" we mean using the output of one tool as the input of another—having the output of the business process analysis tool serve as the input of the modeling tool. The output from the reengineering tools must also be integrated into word processing documents, for example reports or plans.

Without a single tool to support all BPR automation needs, there is no way to avoid the need for integration solutions. But there is a lot of difference between the cost of alternative integration approaches. Three major tool integration approaches are shown as the following: Figure 9-1 Minimal Integration, Figure 9-2 Common Format Integration, and Figure 9-3 Partially Integrated Toolkit.

In Minimal Integration, the tools and the operating system give no help for integrating the toolset. It is often easier to just rekey the data from one tool to another than it is to automate integration in such cases. The situation is often seen with standalone DOS tools, which were never intended to generate any outputs except screens and printed reports. The only way to get at the tool's data is by redirecting the tool's printer output. That redirected output is sent to another program, which will put the print job back into data record format and subsequently pass those records to the other tools for input. But then there is no way to get the newly captured batch data into the receiving tool. So another workaround program is needed to input the data. It literally becomes

Figure 9-1. Minimal integration.

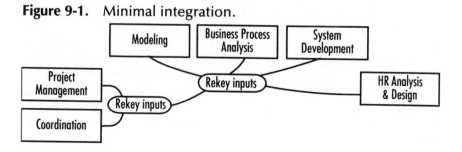

Figure 9-2. Common format integration.

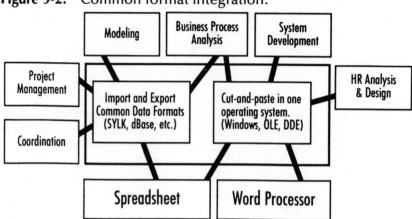

easier to rekey the data than it is to get these workaround programs to work. This scenario is surprisingly common.

The Common Format Integration solution eliminates the need to rekey data from one tool to another. The Common Format solution operates at two levels: tool level and operating system level.

At the tool level, tools themselves are written to accept inputs from other programs. The data exchange between programs is made by passing a file between the programs. A family of standard file formats has been agreed upon to facilitate this exchange. Those commonly accepted standards include Sylk, RTF, and dBase formats.

At the operating system level, operating system vendors (Microsoft Windows and IBM OS/2) have provided facilities to allow data to be "cut-and-pasted" from one tool session to another. These mechanisms have been standardized and widely disseminated so that the tool buyer has a right to expect that such cut-and-paste facilities will exist for tools sold on those two operating systems.

Although fully integrated BPR toolsets are not available, it is possible to meet the needs of several major BPR activities by using a partially integrated BPR toolset or CASE toolset to do modeling, business process analysis, and system development. In that case, many of the necessary flows of data among tools are directly supported by the CASE product itself, usually by allowing the several subsystems to share the same database instead of passing data copies around as in the Common Format solution. Obviously, the other data flows not directly supported in the CASE tool may be implemented either by rekeying and/or "common format" solutions when possible.

Figure 9-3. Partially integrated toolsets.

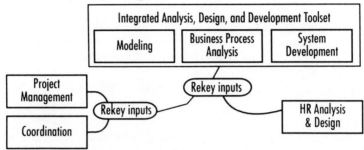

Unfortunately, integrated toolsets that make the Partially Integrated Toolkit solution possible are also the toolsets that take six months to a year to learn. So if your organization does not already have the toolsets in place, then the Partially Integrated Toolkit approach will not be an option.

Most BPR teams will need to either rekey data, copy files from tool-to-tool, or cut-and-paste data from tool-to-tool. Of the three options, copying files offers the best opportunity for the BPR team to integrate the tools while controlling and protecting the project's critical data. This is because file transfer is a more controllable and disciplined method than cut-and-paste, ensuring that all team members share the same data. Plan and budget someone to manage and implement file transfers, backups, and synchronization among tools.

Tool Cost Expectations

Setting realistic expectations about the cost of reengineering tools is largely a matter of looking at other people's experiences and asking yourself if there is any rational basis to believe that your tools experience will be any different.

> Expect project productivity to drop for a period after initial tool introduction—a six-month drop for new integrated toolsets, three to four weeks for a spreadsheet/project-management-tool approach.
> Expect initial tool purchase price to be the tip of the iceberg.
> Expect to spend money and time on training staff to use tools.

Categories of Tools

There are many types of tools applicable to a BPR project. In order to ensure a systematic review of tools for reengineering, the following categories are offered as a reference model of reengineering tools:

Project Management:	Plan, schedule, budget, report, and track projects.
Coordination:	Distribute plans and communicate updated details of plans.
Modeling:	Make a model of something to understand its structure and workings (often a working model).
Business Process Analysis:	Systematically reduce the business to its parts and their interactions.
HR Analysis and Design:	Analyze, design, and establish the human part of the system.
System Development:	Transform analyses into an automated business process.

Although this list clumps tools into neat categories, the reality is that many real world tools combine several of these categories. The list simply reflects the kinds of activities done in a reengineering project, so that tools to automate those activities can be considered. Any real world reengineering project will probably need to combine several different tools in order to meet the automation needs of the project. *Note:* It is not always the case that a specialized tool is required to perform a specialized activity. For example, we will later show that many BPR activities may be performed well by using general purpose tools such as spreadsheets and project management tools.

> If a given BPR project's needs can be met with general purpose tools, the team can get on with the project without buying and learning special purpose tools. These tools are typically well supported by file-exchange Common-Format integration.

This observation is very important because these are the tools with which business people will already be most familiar.

Each category of tools plays a major role in more than one reengineering stage. Figure 9-4 shows the applicability of tool categories by reengineering stage.

A summary discussion of each of the tool categories is provided in

Figure 9-4. Applicability of tool categories by reengineering stage.

Tool Category	Preparation	Identification	Vision	Solution	Transformation
Project Management	X	X	X	X	X
Coordination	X	X	X	X	X
Modeling		X	X	X	X
Business Process Analysis		X	X	X	
System Development				X	X
Human Resources Analysis & Design		X	X	X	X

the following sections. For each tool category the major uses of the tool are listed, the issues relevant to that tool category are discussed, and representative samples of that tool category are described. Discussion of specific tools is not meant to list all of the tools in a given category but rather to show examples.

Project Management Tools

Project Management (PM) tools have two major roles in BPR automation. The obvious role is in support of planning and running the BPR project. But a nonobvious role for PM tools is in Business Process Analysis and Modeling. This use of PM tools as an inexpensive CASE tool is important because it is an inexpensive but effective response to the high learning cost of CASE. Figure 9-5 summarizes the uses of PM tools for BPR project planning and management. An example of the use of PM tools for Business Process Analysis and Modeling follows Figure 9-5. As shown in Figure 9-5, PM tools can be used in many planning and management

Figure 9-5. Specific uses of PM tools for project planning and management.

Project Management Tools versus Rapid Re™ Steps		Project Planning	Schedule	Allocate Resource	Plan Budget	Schedule Tracking & Adjust	Budget Tracking & Adjust
1.	Preparation	X	X	X	X		
1.4	Plan Change	X	X	X	X		
2.	Identification					X	X
3.	Vision					X	X
4.	Solution	X	X	X	X	X	X
4A.	Technical Design	X	X	X	X	X	X
4A.10	Plan Implementation	X	X	X	X		
4B.	Social Design	X	X	X	X	X	X
4B.12	Plan Implementation	X	X	X	X		
5.	Transformation	X	X	X	X	X	X
5.3	Develop Test & Roll-Out Plans	X	X	X	X		
5.5	Construct System					X	X
5.7	Pilot New Processes					X	X
5.8	Refine and Transition					X	X
5.9	Continuous Improvement	X	X	X	X	X	X

roles in a BPR project. Since these roles are widely understood they will receive no further discussion here.

New Viewpoint: PM Tools for Analysis and Modeling

The use of a Project Management tool as a CASE tool substitute to conduct analyses and modeling is a new idea for most readers. So we illustrate that usage with an example of such use.

CASE tools and PM tools both address the same problem—designing an optimum process by arranging the sequence of its steps. Both types of tool do rather well at representing processes and subprocesses. Where they begin to differ is that the PM tools do not represent the data's internal structure as CASE tools can—PM tools can only give name to data items. Of course CASE tools can do many things that PM tools cannot, such as code generation and screen generation. But, for analysis and modeling purposes, PM tools have distinct advantages over CASE:

❑ PM tools are comprehensible by business people, CASE is not.
❑ The learning time for PM tools is low.
❑ The common-format integration support for PM tools is high.
❑ PM tools work in processes, the natural media of reengineering. CASE works in functions and data.
❑ PM tool activity-based costing (ABC) support is better than CASE tools.

To see how a PM tool can parallel a CASE tool's analyses we have to make sure that the PM tool can represent the same sorts of things that the CASE tool can. Figure 9-6 shows elements represented within a CASE tool and the corresponding elements as represented in a PM tool. As you can see the correspondence between CASE analysis tools and PM tools is not complete. CASE tools do provide support for representing the structure of data, PM tools do not. The best a PM tool can do is to represent the name of an input or an output by calling it a milestone. However, a spreadsheet can be used to supplement the PM tool to refine descriptions of those named data with a spreadsheet table per data type table. The deficiencies of the PM tool in this respect are not too discouraging.

The combination of a PM tool and spreadsheets make an effective tool for BPR. While the PM tools are not as powerful as the CASE tools, the price is right and the BPR team can use them right away. Given the long learning time for CASE tools or specialized BPR toolkits, a PM tool

Figure 9-6.   Correspondence between CASE and PM.

Mapping CASE Into Project Management Tool	
CASE Tools	PM Tools
Processes	Project
Subprocesses	Subprojects/Tasks
Input/Output Data	Milestones
Data Structure	Supplement PM with Spreadsheet Tables
Activity-Based Costing	Resources/Cashflow

approach will often offer the best solution for BPR analysis and modeling.

To illustrate the use of PM tools for BPR we show analyses of the Fulfill Orders process of the ABC Toy Company example. The figures show actual output from a PM tool (MacProject II). Other tools support similar features. The standard reports provided with the PM tool meet many BPR needs without requiring any modification.

In Figure 9-7 we show the sequence of activities by which Fulfill Orders is conducted. The Fulfill Orders process is represented in the PM tool as a "subproject" of the "project" named "ABC Toy Company." The activities of Fulfill Orders are represented in the PM tool as "tasks" (the square cornered boxes in Figure 9-7). The rounded corner boxes are activity inputs and outputs. Figure 9-8 summarizes these mappings.

In Figure 9-9, we see the distribution of Fulfill Orders activities over time. PM tools allows us to capture this process time and expense information. Knowing the time and expense distribution within a process is an important part of BPR. CASE tools seldom support time and expense capture. Figure 9-10 shows a similar time distribution, but this time showing worker distribution over time. Note that both of these time distribution charts show the progress of fulfilling a single order.

Figures 9-11 and 9-12 show the cost and income entry screens. In Figure 9-11 we capture cost and income data for each activity of the process (referred to in the PM tool as tasks). For example, one could imagine that Pack Order would have a fixed cost for the crate and any dispos-

Figure 9-7. Model processes for ABC Toys.

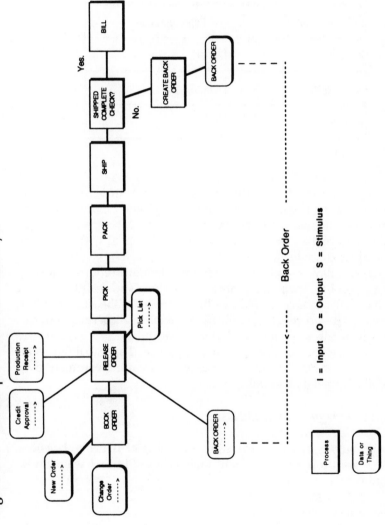

Figure 9-8. Mapping between BPR terms and PM tool terms.

Mapping Between BPR and PM Tools	
BPR Representation	PM Representation
Process	Project
Subprocesses	Subprojects
Activities	Tasks

able dunnage associated with the order. Similarly, in Figure 9-12 we capture unit cost information for resources consumed by process activities. In this case the resources shown are all labor.

Finally, Figure 9-13 shows the cash flow associated with the act of fulfilling that single order.

In short, we have seen that by using the standard reports of an off-the-shelf PM tool we have automated the capture and maintenance of much of the analysis data needed in a BPR project. At the same time we have modeled the process structure in a way that all participants can clearly envision the sequence of activities within the process and the time and expense consequences of that sequence. This capability is an impressive amount of value for the price and a great improvement over handling all of this data manually.

Project Management Tools Issues

As with buying any tool, there are a number of issues to consider as you compare project management tools. These PM tool selection issues include:

❑ Multiuser access
❑ Subproject support
❑ Alternative project views
❑ Resource planning
❑ Resource leveling
❑ Capacity

Figure 9-9. Fulfill orders: task timeline.

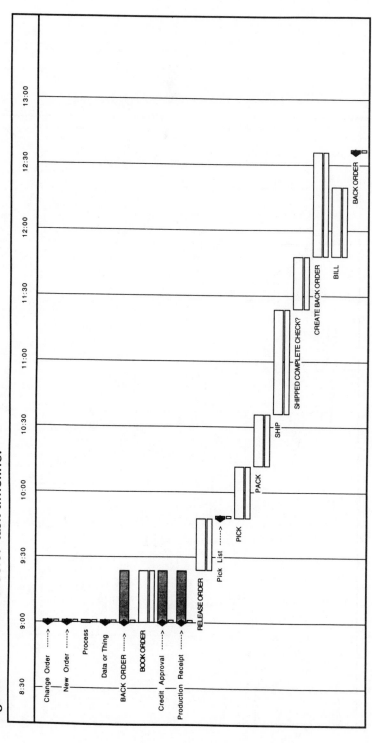

Figure 9-10. Fulfill orders: resource timeline.

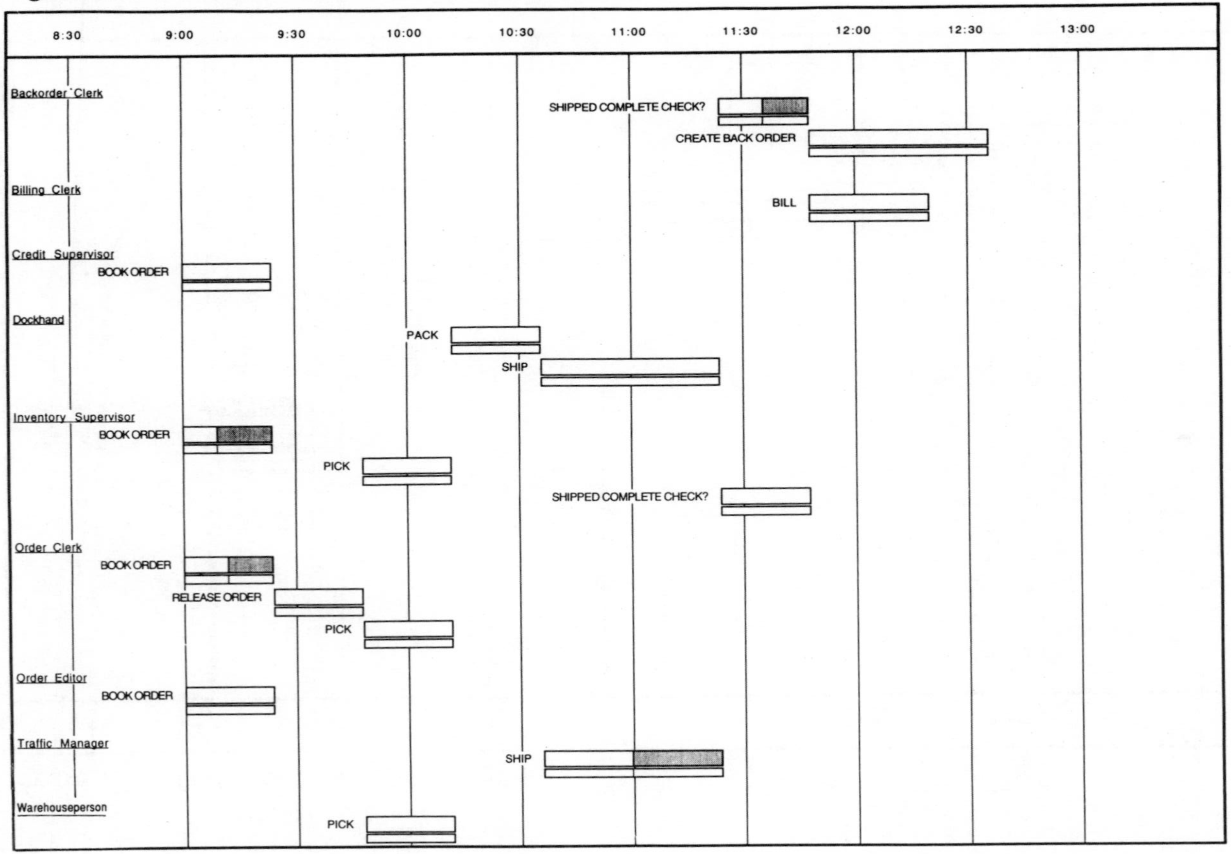

Figure 9-11. Fixed cost/income entries by task from MacProject II.

Name	Fixed Cost	Fixed Income
Change Order ------>	2.00	0.00
New Order ------>	2.00	0.00
Process	0.00	0.00
Data or Thing	0.00	0.00
BACK ORDER ------>	2.00	0.00
BOOK ORDER	10.00	0.00
Credit Approval ------>	2.00	0.00
Production Receipt ------>	2.00	0.00
RELEASE ORDER	10.00	0.00
Pick List ------>	2.00	0.00
PICK	100.00	0.00
PACK	100.00	0.00
SHIP	500.00	0.00
SHIPPED COMPLETE CHECK?	10.00	0.00
CREATE BACK ORDER	10.00	0.00
BACK ORDER	10.00	0.00
BILL	10.00	7000.00

Each of these issues is summarized in the following list:

Does the tool support multiple user access to the same project data? If not, then the synchronization of distributed analysis document versions will need to be addressed as a specific management challenge.

Does the tool support subprojects? Subproject support allows the analysis of subprocesses to be conducted independently once they have been identified as distinct processes. This allows the BPR project to be conducted by "peeling-the-onion"—analyze and model the processes, then proceed in the next level to its subprocesses.

Does the tool provide alternative views of the project? When looking at process interdependency, a bubble-and-line drawing contributes to clarity. But that same drawing is confusing when we want to see the process in terms of time. The tool should provide a set of alternative views of the problem including Critical Path Method (CPM) bubble-and-line graphs, Gantt charts, Work breakdown structure drawings, schedule, and cash flow.

Figure 9-12. Resource entry by worker type.

Resource Name	Cost/Day	# Available	Calendar Name	Accrual Method
Back Order Clerk	64.00	1.00	Project Calendar	Multiple
Billing Clerk	64.00	2.00	Project Calendar	Multiple
Credit Supervisor	160.00	1.00	Project Calendar	Multiple
Dockhand	160.00	4.00	Project Calendar	Multiple
Inventory Supervisor	160.00	1.00	Project Calendar	Multiple
Order Clerk	64.00	2.00	Project Calendar	Multiple
Order Editor	50.00	2.00	Project Calendar	Multiple
Traffic Manager	200.00	1.00	Project Calendar	Multiple
Warehouseperson	160.00	4.00	Project Calendar	Multiple

> Do tools help in resource requirement planning? Highlight resource bottlenecks? Highlight excess resources?
>
> Do the tools support resource leveling? Can the tool move resources from an activity with excess resources to an activity which is resource constrained?
>
> Can the tool handle as large a set of processes, subprocesses, activities, and resources as your project will require?

Representative Project Management Tools

Some representative Project Management tools are listed in Figure 9-14. The tool subcategories are organized according to how the tool is packaged. The tool subcategory Integrated Project Managers means that tool comes with or is an add-on module to a larger tool. Integrated Project Managers are usually associated with high-end (expensive) CASE tools. "Sophisticated Standalone PM's" imply rich functionality usually hosted on a personal computer. The category "Entry Level Standalone PMs" has no entries because the limitations seen in that category of tools prevent their being worth serious consideration. Figure 9-14 shows representative Project Management tools in these three subcategories.

Coordination Tools

The members of the BPR team come from different organizations and disciplines. Building and maintaining the team focus is a major communication and coordination challenge. Coordination tools facilitate the communication by enhancing information flow, dissemination of plans/schedules, and BPR team workflow. Figure 9-15 summarizes the types of Coordination tools and their uses in a BPR project.

Figure 9-13. Cash flow for fulfill orders.

Starting	Plan Costs	Plan Income	Actual Costs	Actual Income	Ending	Plan Cumulative	Actual Cumulative
9:00	48.50	0.00	0.00	0.00	9:30	-48.50	0.00
9:30	120.40	0.00	0.00	0.00	10:00	-168.90	0.00
10:00	125.60	0.00	0.00	0.00	10:30	-294.50	0.00
10:30	530.00	0.00	0.00	0.00	11:00	-824.50	0.00
11:00	29.60	0.00	0.00	0.00	11:30	-854.10	0.00
11:30	35.60	7000.00	0.00	0.00	12:00	6110.30	0.00
12:00	16.00	0.00	0.00	0.00	12:30	6094.30	0.00
12:30	11.60	0.00	0.00	0.00	13:00	6082.70	0.00

Figure 9-14.   Representative PM tools.

Typical Application Packaging	Typical Vendor Packages (Vendor: Product)
Integrated Project Managers (PMs)	
• PM integrated into modeling, analysis, and system development tools	TI: IEF/Project Manager
Sophisticated Standalone PMs	
• Views: (Gantt, Critical Path, WBS, PERT, Budget, Resource Histograms)	Harvard: Project Manager
• Subprojects	Microsoft: Project for Windows
• Time-scaled graphics	
• Custom-icons supported	Primavera: Suretrak
• Cross-project resource leveling	
• Capacity limited only by HW	CA: Superproject for Windows
Entry-Level Standalone PMs	
• Critical Path, Gantt Charts, Calendar	Not seriously recommended
• Limited capacity	
• No resource leveling	
• No subprojects	

Coordination Tool Issues

There are many issues to consider in buying Coordination tools because these tools are shared by so many members of the organization that the impact of a choice is widely felt. Coordination tool issues include:

❑ Integration
❑ Platform
❑ User features

Figure 9-15. Applicability of coordination tools.

Coordination Tools versus Rapid Re™ Steps	E-Mail	Scheduler Applications	Shared Calendar	Shared Spreadsheets	Bulletin Boards	Groupware
1. Preparation	X	X	X			
1.4 Plan Change	X	X	X	X	X	
2. Identification	X	X	X	X	X	X
3. Vision	X	X	X	X	X	X
4. Solution	X	X	X	X	X	X
4A. Technical Design	X	X	X	X	X	X
4A.10 Plan Implementation	X	X	X	X	X	X
4B. Social Design	X	X	X	X	X	X
4B.1 Empower Customer Contact Personnel	X				X	
4B.12 Plan Implementation	X	X	X			
5. Transformation	X	X	X	X	X	X
5.3 Develop Test & Roll-Out Plans		X	X			
5.5 Construct System	X	X	X		X	
5.7 Pilot New Processes	X	X	X		X	
5.8 Refine and Transition	X	X	X		X	
5.9 Continuous Improvement	X				X	

❑ Administration features
❑ Standards

Integration is an important Coordination tool issue because so much of coordination involves exchanging documents through the tool. If we cannot easily pass a word processing document over the E-Mail system, then the only recourse is to retype important passages into the E-Mail message. The same concern applies to embedding graphics, for example PM tool drawings or spreadsheet pie-charts, in an E-Mail message.

The Coordination tools selected should be compatible with the platform choices of all of the different parties among whom coordination is needed. This requirement includes the organizations outside of the reengineering team.

As with all other tool selections, ease of use is critical. Can we easily message one another? Can we easily exchange the various types of desired documents? Can we easily save copies of mail? Can we access the mail from the road?

Administering Coordination tools such as E-Mail Systems is notoriously difficult. What features are provided to make it easy to manage disk space, add/change user accounts, and set up gateways to other E-Mail systems?

Standards are the key to many of the other Coordination tool issues, for example Integration and supporting multiple platforms. Standards that must be considered in selecting Coordination tools include:

❑ International—X.400 (XAPI), X.500 (Name Management).
❑ De facto—Novell (MHS), Microsoft (MAPI), Lotus/Borland (VIM), Apple (OCE).
❑ Is the choice compatible with other existing company E-Mail systems?

Coordination Tool Examples

There are several categories of Coordination tools, including:

❑ E-Mail
❑ Scheduling Applications
❑ Shared Calendars
❑ Shared Spreadsheets
❑ Bulletin Boards
❑ Groupware

Some of these solutions, such as shared spreadsheets, seem quite trivial. They are on the list to remind us that not all Coordination tools need to be complicated to be effective. If one department keeps up a budget spreadsheet and everyone else has read-only rights to that budget over the LAN, then we have a simple, effective Coordination tool. Other tools such as Groupware are sophisticated and often complex. Such complex tools will not be BPR tool options unless they are already in place. Figure 9-16 shows specific tools in each Coordination subcategory. The examples shown are only representative. There are many other such tools in each subcategory.

Modeling Tool

The variety of tools in the Modeling category is very large partially because so many different disciplines do modeling. Each of these specialties has developed its own tool, which applies to one small facet of the BPR project. Care must be taken to find some general tools that can meet many modeling needs, instead of populating the project with a raft of specialized tools that must all be learned and applied in the right way at the right time. One such general modeling toolset is the combination of PM tools and spreadsheets (see the example of such application under the previous discussion New Viewpoint: PM Tools for Analysis and Modeling). Such a general tool approach may be appropriate to an organization not having modeling tools in place. Figure 9-17 shows the major points where modeling tools apply in the BPR project. The ALT. entries indicate that a general toolset of PM tool/spreadsheet may suffice for that activity.

Modeling Tool Issues

Modeling tool selection issues reflect the great variety of tools available. The issues in modeling tool selection include:

- ❏ Methodology used
- ❏ Alternative views
- ❏ Input form
- ❏ Generality
- ❏ Simulation
- ❏ Standards

(Text continues on page 242.)

Figure 9-16.   Representative coordination tools.

Typical Application Packaging	Typical Vendor Packages (Vendor: Product)
Electronic-Mail (E-Mail)	
• Exchange, save, & find messages.	Microsoft: Mail for PC Networks
	Lotus: cc:Mail
	Wordperfect: Office
Scheduling Applications	
• Find a mutually available time and set up meetings.	Microsoft: Schedule+
	Lotus: cc:Mail (3rd party Option)
• Individual & group schedules.	WordPerfect: Office (bundled)
	CA: UpToDate
Shared Spreadsheets	
• Users submit update values to a central project spreadsheet.	Microsoft: Excel
• Link subproject sheets to parent.	Lotus: 1-2-3
Bulletin Boards	
• A common message board for all to log in to read.	Galacticomm: The Major BBS
• Online facility for new system users to report comments to development/ reengineering team.	All E-Mail packages
	CompuServe, et al
Groupware	
• Software supports building applications with enterprisewide database sharing and service sharing.	Lotus: Notes

Figure 9-17. Applicability of modeling tools.

Modeling Tools versus Rapid Re™ Steps	Dataflow Diagram	Process Modeling	Information Modeling	Project Management Tools	Spreadsheets	Prototype Tools	Simulation	Performance Modeling
1. Preparation								
2. Identification								
2.1 Model Customers	X	X						
2.2 Define & Measure Performance					X			
2.3 Define Entities	X		X	ALT				
2.4 Model Processes	X	X						
2.5 Identify Activities	X	X			ALT			
2.6 Extend Process Model	X	X		ALT				
2.9 Prioritize Processes								
3. Vision								
3.1 Understand Process Structure	X	X		ALT	ALT		X	
3.2 Understand Process Flow	X	X		ALT	ALT		X	
3.3 Identify Value-Adding Activities								
3.4 Benchmark Performance								
3.5 Determine Performance Drivers							X	
3.6 Estimate Opportunity		X			ALT		X	
4. Solution								
4A. Technical Design								
4A.1 Model Entity Relationships	X		X	ALT				
4A.2 Reexamine Process Linkages		X					X	
4A.3 Instrument and Informate	X	X	X	ALT	ALT			
4A.4 Consolidate Interfaces & Information	X	X	X	ALT				
4A.5 Redefine Alternatives		X						
4A.6 Relocate & Retime Controls		X		ALT	ALT			
4A.7 Modularize		X		ALT	ALT			
4A.8 Specify Deployment							X	X
5. Transformation								
5.1 Complete Business System Design		X	X	ALT			X	X
5.2 Perform Technical Design		X	X	ALT			X	

Note: ALT indicates use of Project Management Tools & Spreadsheets as alternative to CASE toolset.

It is important to remember where modeling tools come from. Most modeling tools are nothing more than the automation of a specific modeling methodology. To determine if the modeling tool is appropriate to your needs you must examine the methodology that it automates. Has the methodology been used successfully in your type of business or on the type of problem you are solving? If not, what are the limitations of the methodology? Every methodology has its limits.

Does the tool easily allow you to view the problem from an alternative perspective? Examples of some desirable alternative points of view include:

❏ Process view (CPM chart)
❏ Functional view (work breakdown structure)
❏ Data view

As with PM tools, it will be important to have modeling tools that allow you to easily see the problem from alternative points of view.

What input notation is used to describe the thing being modeled? One of the principal directions that modeling tool makers have explored is how to create better ways to unambiguously describe a problem. Several types of notation have been proposed including:

❏ Graphic-based iconic languages
❏ Stylized natural language (pseudo-English)

Look hard at whether you feel comfortable with describing your problem in the input language of the tool. Some of the input languages are cryptic and take a long time to learn. One iconic language has over twenty variously different arrow-shaped icons just for describing different kinds of inputs.

Different modeling techniques will be needed at different times in the BPR project. Does the tool's technique cover the range of needs you have? Some of the techniques applicable to each BPR stage (and the names of their authors) include:

❏ *Identification.* Data Flow Diagrams (e.g., Yourdon, GaneSarson), Entity-Relationship (Chen), Object-Oriented Modeling (Rumbaugh, Jacobson).
❏ *Vision.* Spreadsheets, Matrixes, Activity-Based-Costing, Process Modeling (e.g., Constantine, Jackson), Information Modeling (e.g., Chen).
❏ *Solution.* Entity-Relationship, Prototyping.
❏ *Transformation.* Performance Modeling.

Can the model actually be "run" or is it static? Many phenomena such as timing problems and scaling problems only show up when the model is animated in a dynamic simulation.

Does the Modeling Tool comply with relevant Modeling standards? Depending on the industry and nationality involved, modeling tools are expected to adhere to several standards, for example:

❑ Portable Common Tool Environment (European Community Standard 149)
❑ ISO 9000 Series Standards
❑ SAA (IBM)
❑ AD/Cycle (IBM)
❑ Mil. Std. 2167A
❑ IDEF (Aerospace/Manufacturing)

Modeling Tool Examples

There are many ways to categorize modeling tools: by specialty, by industry, or by methodology. Here we choose to categorize modeling tools by their scope (which also corresponds to their price). Integrated BPR toolkits have recently arrived on the market and generally cover both modeling and business process analysis. Big-shop CASE modeling tools are part of a large tool intended for supporting an enterprise-wide scope. Project CASE modeling tools are part of a CASE toolset for supporting a project-wide scope. Useful partial solutions are stand-alone packages, whose scope is some specialized aspect of modeling. Figure 9-18 shows specific tools in each Modeling tool subcategory. The examples shown are only representative. There are many other such tools in each subcategory.

Business Process Analysis

As with Modeling tools, there are many different Business Process Analysis tools, each reflecting its own favorite methodology. Here again, a general purpose toolset, like a PM tool combined with a spreadsheet, may be an effective alternative to buying and learning a specialized toolset. Figure 9-19 shows the points where BP Analysis tools apply in the BPR project. The ALT entries indicate that a general toolset of PM tool/ spreadsheet may suffice for that activity.

(Text continues on page 246.)

Figure 9-18. Representative BPR modeling tools.

Typical Application Packaging	Typical Vendor Packages (Vendor: Product)
Big Shop CASE	
• CASE plus Project Management	Texas Instruments: IEF
• Big Staffs > 50	CADRE: Teamwork/SA
• Mainframe heritage	Knowledgeware: IEW
• Client-Server available	Intersolv: Excelerator
• Project management	CGI Systems: Pacdesign
• Configuration management	
• One modeling methodology	
• Big Ticket	
Project CASE	
• All CASE, less management	Popkin: System Architect
• Staffs (5-30)	
• Client-Server heritage	S/Cubed: DAISYS
• Many modeling methodologies	
• Rich CASE at lower price	Evergreen: Evergreen
• Capacity limited only by HW	
Useful Partial Solutions	
	Spreadsheets
	Market Engineering Inc: Crystal Ball
	(Sensitivity Analyses)
	CADRE: Teamwork/SIM
	(Simulation running models)

Figure 9-19. Applicability of business process analysis tools.

Business Process Analysis Tools versus Rapid Re™ Steps		Structured Analysis Dataflow Diagrams	Structured Design (Process Design)	Project Management Tools	Spreadsheets	Organization Charts	Simulation & Sensitivity Analysis	Activity-Based Costing
2.2	Define & Measure Performance			X	X			
2.5	Identify Activities		X	ALT	ALT			
2.7	Map Organization	X	X	ALT	ALT	X		X
2.8	Map Resources			ALT	ALT	X		X
2.9	Prioritize Processes			ALT	ALT		X	X
3.1	Understand Process Structure		X	ALT	ALT	X		X
3.2	Understand Process Flow	X	X	ALT	ALT		X	
3.3	Identify Value-Adding Activities		X		X			
3.4	Benchmark Performance				X		X	X
3.5	Determine Performance Drivers				X		X	X
3.6	Estimate Opportunity				X		X	X
3.7	EnVision the Ideal (External)		X	ALT	X		X	X
3.8	EnVision the Ideal (Internal)		X	ALT	X		X	X
3.9	Integrate Visions		X	ALT	X		X	X
3.1	Define SubVisions		X	ALT	X		X	X
4A.2	Reexamine Process Linkages		X	ALT	X		X	
4A.3	Instrument and Informate	X	X	ALT	ALT			
4A.4	Consolidate Interfaces & Information	X	X	ALT			X	
4A.5	Redefine Alternatives		X	ALT	ALT		X	
4A.6	Relocate & Retime Controls		X	ALT	ALT		X	X
4B.2	Identify Job Characteristic Clusters			X	X		X	X
4B.3	Define Jobs/Teams			ALT	X			X
4B.4	Define Skills & Staffing Needs		X	ALT	X		X	X
4B.5	Specify Management Structure		X	ALT	X	X		
4B.6	Redraw Organizational Boundaries		X	ALT	ALT	X	X	X
4B.7	Specify Job Changes			X	X			
4B.8	Design Career Paths			X	X			
4B.9	Define Transitional Organization				X			
4B.10	Design Change Management Program				X			

Note: ALT indicates use of Project Management Tools and Spreadsheets as alternative to CASE toolset.

Business Process (BP) Analysis Tool Issues

The issues for choosing Business Process Analysis Tools are much the same as those described earlier for modeling tools:

❑ Methodology used
❑ Alternative views
❑ Input format used
❑ Generality of the tool
❑ Standards

The appropriateness of the methodology used by the BP Analysis tool is crucial, since this is the primary tool to be used by business people to enter and view their inputs. A methodology that appears arbitrary and inflexible, or is in any way not supportive of that dialogue with business people, will be a major hindrance to the project. Methodologies are a particular concern in the crop of BPR toolsets emerging in the market because they tend to offer only one methodology. Make sure the methodology of your BP Analysis tool matches the needs of the project's business people.

As with modeling tools, BP analysis tools must provide alternate views of the results they have collected. To a procurement person, a process is mainly a flow of materials from raw stock to finished goods. But to a Human Resources (HR) person, the same process is mainly the expenditure of labor according to specialty type. These and other points of view should be visible in the BP analysis tool. In that sense, the generality of the chosen tool is important because the tool must be used by all of the specialists on the team.

BP Analysis Tool Examples

There are many ways to categorize BP Analysis tools: by specialty, by industry, or by methodology. Since so many BP analysis tools are packaged together with modeling tools, we use the same categories for BP Analysis tools that we used for modeling tools. Integrated BPR toolkits have recently arrived on the market and generally cover both modeling and business process analysis. Big-shop CASE modeling tools are part of a large tool intended for supporting an enterprise-wide scope. Project CASE modeling tools are part of a CASE toolset for supporting a project-wide scope. Figure 9-20 shows specific tools in each BP Analysis tool subcategory. The examples shown are only representative. There are many other such tools in each subcategory.

Figure 9-20. Representative modeling tools.

Typical Application Packaging	Typical Vendor Packages (Vendor: Product)
Big Shop CASE	
• CASE plus Project Management	Texas Instruments: IEF
• Big Staffs > 50	CADRE: Teamwork/SD
• Mainframe heritage	Knowledgeware: IEW
• Client-Server available	Intersolv: Excelerator
• Project management	CGI Systems: Pacdesign
• Configuration management	
• One modeling methodology	
• Big Ticket	
Project CASE	
• All CASE, less management	Popkin: System Architect
• Staffs (5-50)	
• Client-Server heritage	S/Cubed: DAISYS
• Many modeling methodologies	
• Rich CASE at lower price	Evergreen: Evergreen
Useful Partial Solutions	
	Spreadsheets
	Project Management Tools
	Market Engineering Inc: Crystal Ball
	(Sensitivity Analyses)

HR Analysis and Design

Human resources tools is a much less well-developed category that were some of the previous categories. Figure 9-21 indicates where in the methodology automated HR support tools may apply. As in previous tool applicability tables, ALT. indicates use of Project Management Tools and Spreadsheets as alternative to dedicated HR toolsets.

Figure 9-21. Applicability of HR analysis and design tools.

HR Analysis & Design Tools versus Rapid Re™ Steps	Project Management Tool and Spreadsheet	Organization Chart Tools	Activity-Based Costing	Team Building	Job Skills Elicitor	Salary Planning	Candidate/Requisition Tracking & History	Position History
1. Preparation								
1.3 Train Team		X		X				
1.4 Plan Change	X			X				
2. Identification								
2.5 Identify Activities	ALT		X					
2.7 Map Organization	ALT	X	X					
2.8 Map Resources	ALT	X	X					
3. Vision								
3.1 Understand Process Structure	ALT		X					
3.2 Understand Process Flow	ALT		X					
4A. Technical Design								
4A.2 Reexamine Process Linkages	ALT	X	X					X
4A.6 Relocate & Retime Controls	ALT		X					X
4A.7 Modularize	ALT		X					X
4B. Social Design								
4B.1 Empower Customer Contact Personnel	ALT		X		X			X
4B.2 Identify Job Characteristic Clusters	ALT	X	X		X			X
4B.3 Define Jobs/Teams	ALT	X				X	X	X
4B.4 Define Skills & Staffing Needs	ALT		X		X	X	X	X
4B.5 Specify Management Structure	ALT	X			X			
4B.6 Redraw Organizational Boundaries		X						
4B.7 Specify Job Changes	X				X	X	X	X
4B.8 Design Career Paths	X				X	X	X	X
4B.9 Define Transitional Organization	X	X						X
4B.10 Design Change Management Program	X							X
4B.11 Design Incentives	X					X	X	X
5. Transformation								
5.4 Evaluate Personnel	X				X	X	X	X
5.6 Train Staff					X	X		X

Note: ALT indicates use of Project Management Tools &/or Spreadsheets as alternative to HR toolset.

Human Relations Analysis and Design Tool Issues

The issues for choosing HR tools reflect the fragmentation in that marketplace. Those issues include:

❏ Target audience
❏ Job vision
❏ Accountability and security

The target audience an HR tool was designed for will heavily influence its acceptability in your organization. Small companies can often live within the constraints of a toolset that imposes structure on the HR process because they have fewer regulations in place. Big companies, on the other hand, have many HR procedures in place and usually require that any HR tools that they use be customizable:

❏ Off-the-shelf tool leverage is best in small companies—if the price is right.
❏ Big companies need more tool-tailoring to conform to existing practices.
❏ Big company tools reflect the greater support needs in their price.

Will using the tool help envision and add value to the task of describing jobs, roles, tasks, and skills? Can the tool be customized to support local preferences? For example:

❏ Can skill and performance evaluation categories be tailored?
❏ Can evaluation criteria be weighted?
❏ Can several people contribute to one vision of the job (or is it single user)?

From the point of view of accountability and security, personnel decisions are sensitive and may be subject to external review. Personnel transactions often require special handling. For example:

❏ Can personnel decisions be shown to be rational by supporting evidence?
❏ Can the tool ensure there is enough information to support a decision?
❏ Can a chain of evidence supporting decisions be maintained?
❏ Is decision process consistent in all cases?
❏ Is the level of security offered by the tool consistent with data sensitivity?

HR Analysis and Design Tool Examples

Figure 9-22 shows representative examples of HR Analysis and Design tools. The tools are categorized as big company tools, small company tools, and organization chart drawing tools.

System Development Tools

System development tools are sometimes packaged with Integrated BPR toolsets and CASE toolsets. In other cases, these tools are separately

Figure 9-22. Representative HR analysis and design tools.

Typical Application Packaging	Typical Vendor Packages (Vendor: Product)	Stand Alone	LAN	Integrated
Big Shop HR Tools -------------	----------------	----	----	----
• More bookkeeping automation, less decision automation	**Requisition/Candidate Tracking & Position History**			
• Many HR practices in place, to be conformed to by tool	Revelation: HR-Applicant Track			
	Spectrum HR: AM/2000		X	
• Extensive tailoring available	Greentree Sys: Retrieve/Tracking		X	
• Consulting support available	Abra Cadabra: AbraTrak		X	
	MicroTrac: Restrac		X	
Small Shop HR Tools -----------	----------------			
• More decision automation	**Job Skill Elicitation,**			
• Less practices to conform to	**Compensation Planning, Team**			
• Less HR expertise on staff	Hi Tech: Employee Evaluator and			
• "Expertise-in-a-box" systems	Salary Manager	X		
• Elicit jobs and skill sets, and	Performance Mentor: Mentor 2.0			
selection criteria	(Skills assessment)	X		
	Performance Mentor: Supersynch			
	(Team Building)	X		
	Roosand: SPARTA			
	(Salary Projection and Rating)	X		
Org. Chart Drawing Tools -------	----------------			
	Corel Draw	X		
	Harvard Graphics	X		

packaged as software development environments. These tools are usually most heavily involved in the Technical Solution phase of a project as shown in Figure 9-23.

System Development Tools Issues

System development tool issues is a large topic area. Some common issues relevant to choosing system development tools include:

❑ How well the tools support change
❑ Control of the work products
❑ Productivity
❑ Integration
❑ Platforms targeted
❑ Standards supported

How well a tool supports changes is often more important than how well it supports fast initial development. Once the system is developed, it is critical that the completed version of the system be protected from unauthorized changes:

❑ Is there good support for controlling change to the system?
❑ Are changes incorporated into design and analysis documents?
❑ Does the tool help find the places affected by changes?

The company's investment in the system must be protected:

❑ Are configuration management and control features automatic?
❑ Is developer access restricted to selected modules?

Standards ensure availability, flexibility, and portability of enabling technology:

❑ Languages: ANSI SQL, COBOL, C
❑ Look-and-Feel: Windows, Presentation Manager
❑ Portable Common Tool Environment - Euro Std 149
❑ MIL STD 2167A
❑ OS: SAA (IBM), Windows (defacto), OS/2 (defacto), POSIX (Unix)
❑ Distributed: Open Systems Forum (OSF)

Figure 9-23. Applicability of system development tools.

System Development Tools versus Rapid Re™ Steps		Visual Programming Toolsets	Application Frameworks	Integrated Code Generators	Integrated Development Workbenches	Object-Oriented Libraries (Reuse)	Test Harnesses
2.	Identification						
3.	Vision						
4.	Solution						
4A.	Technical Design						
4A.1	Model Entity Relationships	X		X			
4A.2	Reexamine Process Linkages	X		X			X
4A.3	Instrument and Informate	X		X			
4A.4	Consolidate Interfaces & Information	X		X	X		
4A.6	Relocate & Retime Controls	X		X			X
4A.7	Modularize	X	X	X	X	X	X
4A.8	Specify Deployment	X	X	X	X	X	X
4A.9	Apply Technology	X	X	X	X	X	X
4A.10	Plan Implementation						
4B.	Social Design						
5.	Transformation						
5.1	Complete Business System Design	X	X	X	X	X	X
5.2	Perform Technical Design	X	X	X	X	X	X
5.3	Develop Test & Roll-Out Plans						X
5.5	Construct System	X	X	X	X	X	X
5.7	Pilot New Processes	X	X	X	X		
5.8	Refine and Transition	X	X	X	X	X	X
5.9	Continuous Improvement	X	X	X	X	X	X

Figure 9-24. Representative system development tools.

Typical Application Packaging	Typical Vendor Packages (Vendor: Product)	Stand Alone	LAN	Integ- rated
Visual Programming				
• Code Windows, OS/2 PM, or SQL by graphically linking icons	Microsoft: Visual Basic	X		
	Borland: ObjectVision	X		
	Powersoft: Power Builder	X	X	X
Application Frameworks				
• Partially completed application, that developers complete	Borland: Application Frameworks	X		
	Micro Focus: Cobol/2 System		X	
	Gupta: SQLBase, SQLWindows		X	
Integrated (CASE) Code Generation				
• CASE tool outputs system code	S/Cubed: Supre/Daisys	X	X	X
	AAI: Metavision Code Generation	X	X	X
	Texas Instruments: IEF Construction	X	X	X
Code Workbenches				
• Developer's set of integrated edit- compile-debug-test tools	Micro Focus: Cobol/2 Workbench	X	X	
	Digitalk: Smalltalk V	X	X	
	IBM: OS/2 WorkFrame/2	X	X	
OO Reuse Libraries				
• Components ready to assemble into an application using OO paradigm to interconnect them	Digitalk: Smalltalk V	X	X	
	Borland: ObjectVision	X		
	Microsoft: Visual Basic Third Parties	X		
Test Harnesses				
• Plan, store, and automatically administer test suites	McCabe & Assoc: Codebreaker	X	X	
	Software Research: M-Test	X	X	
	Micro Focus: Cobol/2 Workbench	X	X	

System Development Tool Examples

Figure 9-24 shows representative samples of system development tools organized by the category of technology that they represent. Categories include Visual Programming environments, Application frameworks that provide partial solutions to be tailored to local needs, Integrated Code Generation tools, Code Workbenches, reusable component libraries, and automated test harnesses. There are many more tools in each of these categories.

10

Hints

Ten Precepts for Success

To counter the most common reengineering mistakes, organizations should consider the following guidelines:

1. Begin with strategic, value-added processes, i.e., processes that are critical to your customers and your business strategy, as GM Saturn did when it built and staffed its Saturn manufacturing plants in the U.S.
2. Address support processes, too, as AT&T did when it reengineered its software development process, a process that the customer never sees but that has a positive impact on customer service.
3. Consider incorporating information technology (IT) in core, value-added services as Agway did when it recreated the IT function as a profit center instead of a cost center.
4. Rethink the boundaries between your processes and those of your suppliers and customers as Citibank did when it revolutionized banking with its Citiphone Banking program, which allows the customer to perform banking and investment transactions directly. In essence, Citibank moved the boundary between financial markets and their customers one step closer to the customer.
5. Analyze in-house versus third-party options as Continental Bank did when it decided to outsource its nonstrategic activities. This decision enabled the bank to concentrate on its core competency: providing financial services to its customers.
6. Rethink the benefit of centralization versus decentralization as IBM is currently doing in its efforts to stem the recent tide of

red ink by reconsidering breaking down a highly centralized operation into smaller business units.

7. Consider segmenting process inputs and creating parallel process flows as Federal Express did when it created several categories of service: standard overnight, priority overnight, and economy two-day in order to better meet differing customer needs.

8. Resequence activities where possible to eliminate the need for separate subprocesses as Disney did when it introduced preordering and prepaying procedures for its food services and other amenities to decrease the time that patrons spent waiting in line.

9. Rethink and relocate controls as Southern Pacific did when it centralized control points for ordering, tracking, and receiving. This enabled customers to access service information from one source rather than many separate control points.

10. Simplify interfaces and information flows as Loews did when it introduced TeleFilm and TeleTicket, which allow customers to find out what movies are playing and their show times. The systems also allow customers to order by phone, pay with a credit card, and pick tickets up at an ATM or at a special call line in the theater lobby. An added benefit to Loews is access to valuable marketing transaction data that enables it to select films for a specifically defined audience.

Why Reengineering Projects Fail

Fatal Mistake #1: Unclear Definitions

Figure 10-1 shows the answers to the question "What is BPR?" given by the same executives surveyed in Figure 1-11. While 88 percent said they were doing reengineering, fewer than half (46 percent) could successfully define business process reengineering (BPR) as process redesign (Gateway Strategic Initiative Survey, 1992).

❑ BPR is not just automation, although it often uses technology in creative and innovative ways.
❑ BPR is not just reorganization, although it almost always requires organizational change.
❑ BPR is not just downsizing, although it usually improves productivity.

Figure 10-1. Senior executives' definitions of reengineering (from 1992 survey of senior executives).

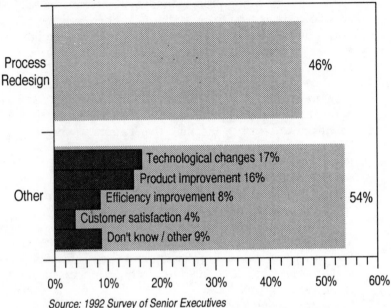

Source: 1992 Survey of Senior Executives

❏ BPR is not just quality, although it is almost always focused on customer satisfaction and the processes that support it.

❏ BPR is a balanced approach that may contain elements of these traditional improvement programs with which it is often confused (and others such as outsourcing, broad banding, continuous improvement). But BPR is more.

First, BPR seeks *breakthroughs* in important measures of performance, rather than incremental improvements. Second, BPR pursues multifaceted improvement goals—including quality, cost, flexibility, speed, accuracy, and customer satisfaction—*concurrently,* while the other programs focus on fewer goals or trade off among them.

In order to accomplish these results, BPR adopts a *process perspective* of the business whereas the other programs retain function or organizational perspectives. (TQM does examine processes, but to improve them, not reengineer them.) BPR also involves a *willingness to rethink* how work should be done, even to totally discard current practices if that should prove necessary. Finally, BPR takes a *holistic* approach to business improvement, encompassing both the technical aspects of processes (technology, standards, procedures, systems, and controls) and the social aspects (organization, staffing, policies, jobs, career paths, and incentives). In other words, *BPR leverages technology and empowers people.* The definition of BPR is:

> The rapid and radical redesign of strategic, value-added business processes—and the systems, policies, and organizational structures that support them—to optimize the work flows and productivity in an organization.

Fatal Mistake #2: Unrealistic Expectations

Perhaps because of the unclear definitions of what BPR is and perhaps because of overenthusiastic promotion of BPR's benefits, many senior executives have unrealistic expectations of what a reengineering project can accomplish. Although there are examples of 3,000 percent improvements in performance as a result of reengineering, these are exceptions. In some aspects of business processes, tenfold gains may indeed be readily attainable with BPR. But in other aspects, 30 percent improvement may well represent a breakthrough, particularly if it involves a broad aggregate measure of performance such as profitability. The point is that BPR can produce performance breakthroughs (of whatever magnitude) whereas more traditional improvement programs produce only incremental gains.

Certainly one should undertake a BPR project with a willingness—even a hope—for order of magnitude gains. But goals should be set and expectations conditioned on the basis of realistic analysis performed during the project. In addition to unrealistic expectations about the size of the gains from BPR, some executives are mistaken about the domain of its applicability. BPR is applicable to the operational level of a business, not the strategic or even the tactical. It can show you how to do things right, but only in a limited way the right things to do.

BPR will not identify the markets you should be in or the products you should develop. But it can give you effective processes for making those decisions.

Fatal Mistake #3: Inadequate Resources

As with many other corporate projects, BPR projects face the common dilemma that the people best suited to perform the work of the project are usually the ones who can least be spared from their normal duties. It helps to understand that there is no good solution to this problem and that any accommodation will be a compromise.

Hiring consultants may be a good idea, but they can't replace your own people on the BPR project. Employees bring to the reengineering team an understanding of current processes, key individuals, and culture that is difficult for an outsider to obtain. They also bring a personal stake in the project outcome. Outsiders—whether they be consultants, employees from a different division, or new hires—play an invaluable role in BPR. They bring a fresh perspective and the creative naïveté to ask, "Why do we do things this way?" Consultants can play another role as well: They can bring methods for BPR and experience it doing it (see Fatal Mistake #9). So the first requirement for adequately resourcing a BPR project is to provide a balanced mix of insiders to outsiders (say 5 or 6 to 1) on the reengineering team. The second requirement is to give the people on the reengineering team enough time to do their work. Some of the people in our reengineering seminars have told us that their reengineering team assignments were for as little as 10 percent of their time! That's barely enough to account for the loss of productivity from switching tasks.

Full-time assignments are probably neither feasible nor desirable at most companies, because we want team members to stay involved in the processes they will be reengineering. But something on the order of half-time is necessary for meaningful contribution and progress.

The third resource requirement is an adequate budget: for the insiders' salaries, for the outsiders' fees, for expenses. This should be self-evident, but nearly two-thirds (65 percent) of companies do not have budgets for programs like BPR (Gateway Reengineering Survey, 1993).

Finally, and most importantly, it is often not enough to simply assign employees, send them to seminars, and turn them loose. They must be trained and supported.

Overall, slightly more than half of companies (54 percent) are using outside resources to assist their BPR projects. Of those who aren't using outside resources, the most common reason given (by 70 percent of the executives surveyed) was "We have the knowledge and expertise to handle the project in-house." Interestingly, the larger the company, the more likely they are to use outside consultants (ranging from 43 percent for companies under $100 million to 71 percent for companies over $1 billion). This is just the opposite of what one would expect, for the larger companies should have more in-house knowledge and expertise. This is probably a case of the larger companies knowing what they don't know.

Fatal Mistake #4: Taking Too Long

Many BPR practitioners believe that reengineering projects should take three to five years. Yet few executives have that kind of patience. Figure 1-9 gives their answer to our question, "How soon do you need to see results?"

To a certain extent, management's impatience with BPR projects lasting more than one year reflects their pressing need for the performance improvements that BPR can bring. This also reflects, to a certain extent, the absence of budgets for the reengineering projects. These projects need to become self-funding quickly. These results could mean favoring low-risk projects with near-term payback over projects with more substantive returns, but it need not. Rapid Re methodology, for example, divides a BPR project into phases, each aimed at realizing a subvision with specific, tangible results.

Fatal Mistake #5: Lack of Sponsorship

Meeting senior executives' expectations for results (Fatal Mistake #2) and their tolerance of delay (Fatal Mistake #4) are certainly necessary to *retain* their sponsorship, as is satisfying their appetites for cost and risk, but one must *obtain* that sponsorship in the first place. As much as information systems, industrial engineering, and internal consulting professionals might wish it, BPR cannot be driven from the supply side. Senior management must sponsor BPR for several reasons. First, the impact of BPR is so broad that only senior management can sanction it. Second, BPR usually involves a shift in culture, and it is uniquely senior management's role to set the culture. And third, BPR requires leadership of the most visible sort.

How to obtain that sponsorship? An executive generally must go through four stages—awareness, curiosity, interest, and belief—before he or she will commit to sponsorship. Most senior executives are already at the awareness or curiosity stages, at least. According to Gateway's 1993 survey, as of January 1993, 80 percent of CEOs and COOs (but only 50 percent of human resources executives) were familiar with BPR, and the numbers are certainly higher now. To move to the interest stage, an executive must have credible evidence that BPR has worked for others and recognition of a need that BPR might satisfy.

Companies don't undertake BPR because it is trendy or because it is elegant. They do so (often as a last resort) because they need to. This need is, in our experience, driven by one of three things: pain, fear, or ambition. Companies feeling pain (e.g., low profits, shrinking market share) have to do something now. Companies feeling fear (e.g., aggressive competition, changing markets) have to do something soon. Companies feeling ambition (e.g., expand market share, enter new markets) have to do something now to realize their ambition soon. If an executive doesn't feel the need for BPR, he or she won't be interested in it.

To convert that interest into belief, the executive must be convinced that BPR will help meet the need. One way of accomplishing this is by showing the executive a demonstrated success within the company. Another way is by showing the executive exactly how you propose to carry out the BPR project. For it is not so much whether BPR can work that executives question, but whether "we" can make it work.

Fatal Mistake #6: Wrong Scope

Sometimes we hear, "We're reengineering the company" or "We're reengineering the department." Actually, you can't reengineer an organization, you can only reengineer its processes. And many processes are interorganizational and cross-functional. In fact, one of the main ways that BPR improves performance is by reducing or eliminating the errors and inefficiencies that inevitably arise when processes cross organizational boundaries.

When the scope that is chosen for a BPR project is one that includes only part of a process, the opportunity for success is diminished. By the same token, you need to select the right process to reengineer. Not all processes are equal in importance or in their contribution to organizational goals. That is why our definition of BPR focuses on strategic, value-added processes. Strategic processes support the organization's business strategy. Value-added processes deliver value to the organization's customers.

The question of scope is intimately connected with the question of sponsorship. In the ideal situation, the BPR project would be sponsored by the CEO or COO. In that case, the entire company may be examined to find the most strategic and most value-adding processes to reengineer. Sometimes, however, the sponsor is a business unit head, a general manager, or even a department head such as a CIO. In that case, the project scope must be made congruent with the sponsor's span of effective influence, and the processes selected for reengineering should be:

- ❑ Most strategic for the mission of the sponsor
- ❑ Most value-adding for the sponsor's customers
- ❑ Wholly, or mostly, within the sponsor's scope of control

Fatal Mistake #7: Technocentricism

Another thing we hear said is "We're reengineering; we've acquired image processing" or "We're reengineering; we're moving to client/server platforms." Certainly technology is a key enabler of BPR. But technology is not BPR. BPR changes the business processes—the way the work is done. Applying technology to current processes has been rightly called "paving the cow path."

This mistake is often associated with Fatal Mistake #4: Taking Too Long. Although some technology—like desktop computers for personal productivity or mobile telephony—are quick and easy to install, technologies that support and enhance a process as a whole are often more complex and difficult to implement. By contrast, the social side of processes—empowerment—usually can be implemented faster, and often provides the majority of the benefits. Many of the most successful BPR projects have been ones in which new technology was delayed to later phases. This is not to say that the social changes are easy, just that they are faster to implement. In fact, the opposite is true—the social change is almost always harder than the technical change.

Fatal Mistake #8: Mysticism

Inasmuch as BPR requires a willingness to rethink how business processes should be performed, a lot of attention has been paid to the process of "rethinking." A student of BPR reads, hears, and even sees (there are actually training films on the subject) a lot about "paradigm shifts," "breaking frame," "out of the box thinking," etc. The trouble is, one can't shift paradigms; one can only experience a paradigm shift.

By the same token, some of the published materials on BPR could lead one to believe that BPR is entirely a creative act, requiring an intuitive jump or some kind of transcendental experience. This is simply not so. BPR is an engineering discipline, although a new one. It can be practiced by the average intelligent manager or business professional.

Just as the human potential movement of the 1970s taught many ordinary people how to transform their personal lives, BPR can enable people to transform their business lives. And although both movements sometimes use mystical terminology, both are based on a discipline and specific methods for achieving the breakthrough.

Fatal Mistake #9: Lack of an Effective Methodology

A BPR methodology provides the discipline and specific methods needed to break out of the old narrow way of thinking about the business, envision a better way, and realize that vision. For example, the Rapid Re methodology consists of five stages:

1. *Preparation:* Mobilize, organize, and energize the people who will perform the reengineering project.
2. *Identification:* Develop a customer-oriented process model of the business.
3. *Vision:* Select the processes to reengineer and formulate redesign options capable of achieving breakthrough performance.
4. *Solution:* Define the technical and social requirements for the new processes and develop detailed implementation plans.
5. *Transformation:* Implement your reengineering plans.

These five stages consist of fifty-four specific tasks that lead the reengineering team from original recognition of the need to reengineer all the way to obtaining the performance breakthrough.

A good methodology provides a road map for reengineering. That is, it enables an organization to select the most appropriate destination and then to find the best route to get there. There are many ways to use the methodology, and each organization will have to select the approach that best fits its needs. Some will resequence the tasks or omit some entirely. Others will adapt tasks to their own style and culture. But without a good BPR methodology, organizations are left with the "what" but not the "how to." Without a methodology, reengineering projects run the risk of deteriorating into, on the one hand, brainstorming sessions and quality circles, or, on the other hand, more of the same old automation or operations improvement projects.

BPR projects are no more risky than other types of corporate projects with similar ambitions. Indeed, BPR may be the *only* way, in the long run, to achieve really ambitious operational goals. Failures in BPR projects have usually come from mistakes in defining, organizing, or conducting the project. To avoid these mistakes, follow the nine "commandments" of BPR:

1. Be clear.
2. Be realistic.
3. Be prepared.
4. Hurry up.
5. Have a champion.
6. Focus.
7. Technology yes, but people first.
8. Don't get snowed.
9. Follow a methodology.

Appendixes

Appendixes

Appendix A

Summary Outline of the Methodology for Business Process Reengineering

Rapid Re consists of five stages: Preparation, Identification, Vision, Solution, and Transformation. The Solution stage is further divided into Technical Design and Social Design, which are performed concurrently. The stages are designed to be performed consecutively. The end of each stage represents a major milestone in the reengineering project.

Stages are further divided into tasks—fifty-four in all. Although the limitations of written language make it appear that each task is performed sequentially, the ordering is only partial. Some tasks may be moved ahead of other tasks, some may be performed concurrently, some may be performed more than once, and others not at all. Some tasks may even be moved between stages.

Stage 1: Preparation

The purpose of this stage is to mobilize, organize, and energize the people who will perform reengineering. The Preparation stage produces a mandate for change; an organization structure and charter for the reengineering team; and a game plan.

The key questions answered by this stage include:

❏ What are senior executives' objectives and expectations? What is their level of commitment to this project?

❏ What should the goals for this project be? How aggressive can we make them without sacrificing realism?

❏ Who should be on the team? What mix of skills/capabilities should be represented on the team?

❏ What skills/capabilities are not available to team members? How can they be developed or acquired?

❏ What specific reengineering skills will team members need to learn?

❏ What will we need to communicate to employees to earn their support and trust?

TASK 1.1—RECOGNIZE NEED

The need for reengineering is usually recognized as a result of a change: a market change, a technology change, an environmental change. As a result of this change, a senior manager (the "sponsor")—motivated by pain, fear, or ambition—resolves to do something: reengineer. At this point the sponsor often recruits a facilitator.

TASK 1.2—DEVELOP EXECUTIVE CONSENSUS

This takes the form of a one-day working meeting that includes the sponsor, the process owners, and the facilitator. Its purposes are to educate the management group in the methodology and terminology to be used; secure leadership and support for the project; define the issues to be addressed; identify other stakeholders; and set goals and priorities for the project.

This task also organizes the reengineering team and develops its mandate.

TASK 1.3—TRAIN TEAM

This task equips the reengineering team members to undertake their mission. It includes defining management's expectations of them; building teamwork; learning the approach; selecting the manual and/or automated tools to be used in the project; adopting a common terminology; working through reengineering examples; and, finally, assuming responsibility for the project.

TASK 1.4—PLAN CHANGE

This task explicitly recognizes that there will be resistance to the changes that the reengineering project will introduce and that the change must be managed if the project is to be successful. It initiates change management by identifying the stakeholders and their interests. It defines how communications will be managed to ensure that the stakeholders are kept informed in a constructive way. It identifies methods of assessing the extent of buy-in by various stakeholders and methods of intervening if buy-in is found to be inadequate.

This task also develops the project plan and schedule and defines project management methods, if these have not been specified already.

Stage 2: Identification

The purpose of this stage is to develop and understand a customer-oriented process model of the business. The identification stage produces definitions of customers, processes, as well as measures of performance, and success; identification of value-adding activities; a process map of organization, resources, volumes, and frequency; and the selection of the processes to reengineer.

The key questions answered by this stage include:

- ❏ What are our major business processes?
- ❏ How do these processes interface with customer and supplier processes?
- ❏ What are our strategic processes?
- ❏ Which processes should we reengineer within ninety days, within one year, subsequently?

Task 2.1—Model Customers

This task identifies the external customers, defines their needs and wants, and identifies the various interactions between the organization and its customers.

Task 2.2—Define and Measure Performance

This task defines customer-oriented measures of performance and determines current performance levels, both averages and variances. It also examines existing standards of performance and identifies performance problems.

Task 2.3—Define Entities

This task identifies the entities, or "things" with which the organization deals. An entity is an abstraction that is realized in one or more specific instances. For example, the entity "employee" may have the instances, "Tom," "Dick," and "Harriet." Entities have attributes that describe them, e.g., Social Security number, birthdate, address. Some of the attributes relate to the state that the entity is in, e.g., employed, retired. Some entities, like employees, are long term and labeled "permanent." Other entities, like orders or checks, are "transactions."

This task also defines the states that each entity can be in and correlates state changes with interactions. That is, it identifies which interaction causes each state change.

Task 2.4—Model Processes

This task defines each process and identifies its state change sequence. It defines the process objectives and critical success factors. It identifies the process inputs and outputs.

The purpose of this task is to force the reengineering team to look at the work of the business in a new way: in terms of processes instead of functions. Processes emerge from the analysis of state change sequences; that is, a process is a series of activities that convert business inputs into business outputs by changing the state of one or more entities of interest.

Task 2.5—Identify Activities

This task identifies the major activities needed to effect each state change. It also determines the extent to which each activity adds value, that is, the extent to which the activity contributes to meeting a customer want or need.

Task 2.6—Extend Process Model

This task identifies internal and external suppliers and their interactions with the processes. At this point, the process model will begin to reveal that certain individuals and groups within the organization are both suppliers and customers. The process takes the form:

EXTERNAL SUPPLIER ➻ INTERNAL CUSTOMER/SUPPLIER ➻ INTERNAL CUSTOMER/SUPPLIER ➻ . . . ➻ INTERNAL CUSTOMER/SUPPLIER ➻ EXTERNAL CUSTOMER

The task then identifies additional measures of performance oriented toward the internal customers and incorporates these into the process model as well.

TASK 2.7—MAP ORGANIZATION

This task defines the organization(s) involved in each major activity and the type of involvement (e.g., "responsible for," "provides input to," "receives notification from"). It therefore defines the process/organizational boundaries.

TASK 2.8—MAP RESOURCES

This task estimates the head count and expense dollars in each major activity of each process. It also estimates transaction volumes and frequencies. This information is used to compute estimated annual costs per activity and process and unit costs per transaction.

TASK 2.9—PRIORITIZE PROCESSES

This task weights each process by its impact on the business goals and priorities set in Task 1.2—Develop Executive Consensus and by the resources consumed. It considers these, as well as the time, cost, difficulty, and risk of reengineering in a multidimensional approach to setting priorities for reengineering the processes.

Once the priorities are set, this task also schedules Stages 3, 4, and 5 for each selected process.

Stage 3: Vision

The purpose of this stage is to develop a process vision capable of achieving breakthrough performance. The Vision stage produces identification of current process elements such as organization, systems, and information flow, and current process problems and issues. The Vision stage also produces comparative measures of current process performance; improvement opportunities and objectives; a definition of *what* changes are required; and a statement of the new process "vision."

The key questions answered by this stage include:

❑ What are the primary subprocesses, activities, and steps that constitute our selected process(es)? In what order are they performed?

❑ How do resources, information, and work flow through each selected process?

❑ Why do we do things the way we do now? What assumptions are we making about our current work flow, policies, and procedures?

❑ Are there ways to achieve our business goals and address customer needs that seem impossible today but, if could be done, would fundamentally change our business?

❑ Consider the boundaries between our processes and our business partners, i.e., customers, suppliers, strategic allies. How might we redefine these boundaries to improve overall performance?

❑ What are the key strengths and weaknesses of each selected process?

❑ How do other companies handle the processes and associated complexities?

❑ What measures should we use when benchmarking our performance against best-in-class companies?

❑ What is causing the gap between our performance and that of best-practice companies? What can we learn from these companies?

❑ How can the results of visioning and benchmarking be used to redesign our processes?

❑ What are the specific improvement goals for our new processes?

❑ What is our vision and strategy for change? How can we communicate our vision to all employees?

TASK 3.1—UNDERSTAND PROCESS STRUCTURE

This task expands our understanding of the static aspects of the process modeled in Tasks 2.4 through 2.6 by identifying all activities and steps in the process; identifying all involved organizations and primary job functions; preparing a matrix of activities/steps versus organization/jobs; and by identifying systems and technology used and applicable policies.

TASK 3.2—UNDERSTAND PROCESS FLOW

This task expands our understanding of the dynamic aspects of the modeled process by identifying primary decision points and subprocesses; preparing a matrix of inputs/outputs and stimuli against activities/steps; and by identifying flow variations.

The objective of Tasks 3.1 and 3.2 is to develop sufficient understanding of the way current processes work to ensure that their reengineered replacements truly represent major improvement. The level of detail needed to achieve this understanding will vary but will always be less than that required to "fix" the current process. That is why we use the term "understand" rather than "analyze" in the title of these tasks.

TASK 3.3—IDENTIFY VALUE-ADDING ACTIVITIES

This task assesses the impact of each activity of the process on the external performance measures for the process, in order to identify those activities that add value, those that do not, and those that are purely for internal control.

TASK 3.4—BENCHMARK PERFORMANCE

This task compares both the performance of the organization's processes and the way those processes are conducted with those of relevant peer organizations in order to obtain ideas for improvement. The peer organizations may be within the same corporate family, they may be comparable companies, industry leaders, or best-in-class performers. The task consists of identifying relevant peers; determining their process performance and the primary differences in their processes that account for the performance differences; and assessing the applicability of those process differences to our processes.

TASK 3.5—DETERMINE PERFORMANCE DRIVERS

This task defines the factors that determine the performance of the process by identifying sources of problems and errors; enablers and inhibitors of process performance; dysfunctions and incongruities; activity or job fragmentation; or information gaps or delays.

TASK 3.6—ESTIMATE OPPORTUNITY

This task uses all of the additional information developed so far in Stage 3 to expand on the initial assessment of the opportunity for process improvement made in Task 2.9—Prioritize Processes. It estimates the degree of change needed and the difficulty of the change, the costs and benefits of the change, the level of support for the change, and the risks of making the change. It also defines the *near-term* opportunities for improvement, which can be pursued immediately.

TASK 3.7—ENVISION THE IDEAL (EXTERNAL)

This task describes how the process would operate with all of the external performance measures (defined in Task 2.2—Define and Measure Performance) optimized. In particular, it describes the behavior of those activities that interface with customers and suppliers.

TASK 3.8—ENVISION THE IDEAL (INTERNAL)

This task describes how the process would operate with all of the internal performance measures (defined in Task 2.6—Extend Process Model) optimized. It thus repeats Task 3.7, treating internal participants as customers and suppliers. This task also describes how key job functions would be performed to achieve ideal performance.

TASK 3.9—INTEGRATE VISIONS

It is possible that the internal and external visions conflict. This task identifies any such conflicts and trades off among the alternative capabilities to produce the most effective integrated vision.

TASK 3.10—DEFINE SUBVISIONS

This task examines the time frame for realization of the process vision and the possibility of defining successive subVisions between the current process and the fully integrated vision. If defined, each subVision is associated with performance goals.

Stage 4A: Solution: Technical Design

The purpose of this stage is to specify the technical dimension of the new process. The Technical Design stage produces descriptions of the technology, standards, procedures, systems, and controls employed by the reengineered process. Together with Stage 4B: Solution: Social Design it produces designs for the interaction of social and technical elements. Finally, it produces preliminary plans for systems and procedures development; procurement of hardware, software, and services; facilities enhancement, test, conversion, and deployment.

The key questions answered by this stage include:

❑ What technical resources and technologies will we need in the reengineered process?
❑ How can these resources and technologies best be acquired?
❑ How will the technical and social elements, e.g., the human interface of the system, interact?

TASK 4A.1—MODEL ENTITY RELATIONSHIPS

This task identifies the relationships among entities. It also defines the direction and cardinality of the relationships, i.e., which entity "owns" which other entity and whether the relationship is one-to-one, one-to-many, or many-to-many. Since entities are the "things" with which a process is concerned, the technical elements of the process will include collections of data about the entities. This task is a first step in modeling the data.

TASK 4A.2—REEXAMINE PROCESS LINKAGES

This task considers whether movement of steps among activities, activities among processes, or reassigned responsibility for steps would improve performance. It also identifies instances where better coordination among activities would improve performance.

TASK 4A.3—INSTRUMENT AND INFORMATE

This task identifies the information needed to measure and manage the performance of the process, defines places where the information can be stored (usually files associated with the entities), and adds steps to the process, as needed, to capture, assemble, and disseminate the needed information.

TASK 4A.4—CONSOLIDATE INTERFACES AND INFORMATION

This task defines the process changes needed to reduce or simplify interfaces, both internal and external. It identifies and eliminates duplicate information flows, and with them, reconciliation activities. More generally, this task reduces redundancy.

TASK 4A.5—REDEFINE ALTERNATIVES

This task evaluates the continued need for special cases (if any) in the process. If needed, it considers segregating the special cases in separate processes. In other words, this task seeks to replace a single complex process with one or more simpler processes.

TASK 4A.6—RELOCATE AND RETIME CONTROLS

This task seeks to reduce the number of nonvalue-added activities in the process by simplifying the control structure of the process. It accomplishes this by integrating controls into value-adding activities, by replacing error detection with error avoidance, and by moving error detection closer to the point of occurrence of the error. This task also reviews the logical relationships among activities in order to find opportunities to perform in parallel activities that are currently performed serially. Obviously this would increase the speed of the process.

TASK 4A.7—MODULARIZE

The purpose of this task is to define parts of the reengineered process that can be deployed independently. This partition of the process, if one exists, enables the process to be distributed in space (e.g., by decentralizing it) and/or in time (e.g., by substituting process parts in moving from one subVision to another).

The formal analysis of this task consists of determining the dependencies among the activities of the revised process and of determining interactions between activities and entities. This analysis allows the clustering of activities by related changes and by time/space adjacency, so that modules can be defined for movement and for implementation.

TASK 4A.8 — SPECIFY DEPLOYMENT

This task uses the modules defined in the previous task in order to evaluate structural alternatives (e.g., centralized versus decentralized) and implementation alternatives (e.g., first subVision versus second subVision). Analysis of these alternatives then leads to the selected deployment of each module in space, time, and organization. Note that this task is conducted concurrently with Task 4B.6 — Redraw Organizational Boundaries.

TASK 4A.9 — APPLY TECHNOLOGY

Technology is one of the two key enablers of business process reengineering (the other being human potential). The new process vision developed in Stage 3 will certainly have been informed by a knowledge of the current capabilities, uses, and limitations of technology. But specific applications of technology to the process will be made in this task.

The major applications of technology to business process reengineering are to:

- ❏ Analyze, e.g., simulations, statistics.
- ❏ Capture and document, e.g., image.
- ❏ Communicate, e.g., data communications.
- ❏ Control, e.g., telemetry, process control.
- ❏ Human interface, e.g., graphics, voice recognition/response.
- ❏ Identify, e.g., bar codes, magnetic strips.
- ❏ Informate, e.g., telemetry, on-line access.
- ❏ Manage, e.g., decision support, management information.
- ❏ Manufacture, e.g., CAD, CAM, CIM.
- ❏ Provide mobility, e.g., cellular telephone, laptop computers.
- ❏ Share expertise, e.g., knowledge-based expert systems.
- ❏ Share information, e.g., databases.

TASK 4A.10 — PLAN IMPLEMENTATION

In this task preliminary plans (to be refined in Stage 5) are developed for implementing the technical aspects of the reengineered process, including development, procurement, facilities, test, conversion, and deployment. These plans will then be time phased, along with the parallel plans for implementing the social aspects of the process, developed in Task 4B.12—Plan Implementation.

Stage 4B: Solution: Social Design

The purpose of this stage is to specify the social dimension of the new process. The Social Design Stage produces descriptions of the organization, staffing, jobs, career paths, and incentives employed by the reengineered process. Together with Stage 4A: Solution: Technical Design it produces designs for the interaction of social and technical elements. Finally, it produces preliminary plans for recruitment, education, training, reorganization, and redeployment of personnel.

The key questions answered by this stage include:

- ❏ What technical and human resources will we need to reengineer? What activities will each reengineering team member be responsible for? What priorities and dependencies exist?
- ❏ What immediate opportunities exist? What can we accomplish in ninety days? One year? Beyond one year?
- ❏ What human resources will we need in the reengineered process?
- ❏ What targets and measures should we establish?
- ❏ How will responsibilities change? What training programs will be needed?
- ❏ Who is likely to resist the changes called for? How can they be motivated to accept these changes? What other obstacles exist?
- ❏ What will our new organization look like?

Please remember that Stage 4B, Social Design, is performed concurrently with Stage 4A, Technical Design, and by the same people—the reengineering team. Thus, technical and social issues will be addressed concurrently.

TASK 4B.1—EMPOWER CUSTOMER CONTACT PERSONNEL

In order to improve the responsiveness and quality of service provided to the customer by a process, it is necessary to empower customer contact personnel. This task defines the changes in responsibility, authority, knowledge, skills, and tools needed to enable customer contact personnel to improve performance. Then, recognizing that customer contact personnel are themselves customers of other personnel, and so on, this task defines the changes needed for all personnel to improve service to their customers.

TASK 4B.2—IDENTIFY JOB CHARACTERISTIC CLUSTERS

This task identifies the set of skills, knowledge, and orientation (e.g., facilitation versus control, people versus things, etc.) relevant to both the current and the reengineered process. It then prepares two matrices of current jobs and redefined (i.e., empowered) jobs versus the skills, knowledge, and orientation set. Each cell of the matrix provides the level (none, low, medium, high) of the skills, knowledge, and orientation needed for the job. Using these matrices, the task then identifies clusters of job characteristics.

TASK 4B.3—DEFINE JOBS/TEAMS

This task assesses the match between the job characteristic clusters of current jobs and needed jobs and between teams of current jobs and needs. Based on this assessment, the task defines new jobs and new teams. In other words, when it is possible to do so, a single job will be defined to meet the needs of the reengineered process. When this is not possible, teams will be defined.

TASK 4B.4—DEFINE SKILLS AND STAFFING NEEDS

This task identifies the level of skills needed for each new job and revises the matrix prepared in Task 4B.2—Identify Job Characteristic Clusters. The task also defines the relationship between staffing levels and volumes and identifies staffing needed at current and projected volumes.

TASK 4B.5—SPECIFY MANAGEMENT STRUCTURE

This task specifies how the three main components of management (work management, leadership, and personnel development) will be accomplished in the reengineered process. The task identifies the process owner and responsibilities for work management and personnel development. It defines team leadership, and it assesses the need for first- and second-level management. In order to make these decisions, the task structures and analyzes feasible alternatives.

TASK 4B.6—REDRAW ORGANIZATIONAL BOUNDARIES

This task considers changing the organizational structure in order to ensure that each team resides within a single organization and to reduce the number of organizational boundaries traversed by the process. Note that this task is conducted concurrently with Task 4A.8—Specify Deployment.

TASK 4B.7—SPECIFY JOB CHANGES

This task prepares a new matrix of skills, knowledge, and orientation requirements versus transitions from old jobs to new jobs. The elements of the matrix consist of the number of degrees of change required by the transition. For example, if job A requires a low level of skill X and job B requires a high level of that skill, then the element at the intersection of "transition job A to job B" and "skill X" will be +2 (from low to high). This task also assigns weights to each skill, knowledge, and orientation requirement, representing the relative difficulty of acquiring that characteristic. The weighted changes are then summed, producing a measure of the difficulty of making the transition from old to new jobs. The transition difficulty measure is used to preplan the reorganization and a curriculum for training and education of process personnel, which will take place in Stage 5.

TASK 4B.8—DESIGN CAREER PATHS

This task is similar to the preceding one, except that now the matrix is of transitions from one new job to another new job. This task provides a formal solution to one of the vexing problems of reengineering. In reengineered processes, job distinctions (such as compensation) based on hierarchical position and reporting relationships tend to be replaced by distinctions based on knowledge and skill. But since most jobs are enriched, they are multidimensional, so that it is difficult to compare them directly.

This task develops measures of the difficulty of making transitions from job A to job B and from job B to job A. If A to B is more difficult than B to A, then clearly job B is the "bigger" job. This task considers all such transitions and determines which transitions are feasible, which leads directly to the career path. Some jobs (the "biggest") will have no career path within the process. In this case, it is necessary to identify feasible transitions into other processes. Since the question "How will this all affect me?" underlies most of the resistance to change, successful completion of this task and communication of its results are the most important components of the change management program.

TASK 4B.9—DEFINE TRANSITIONAL ORGANIZATION

To this point, Stage 4B has focused on the social design needed to realize the final process Vision. This task addresses the social design for the subVisions, if any. It is conducted in parallel with Task 4A.8—Specify Deployment, so that the social and technical elements of the process will be congruent. Usually, the need to reach the final vision through a series of subVisions is forced by the technical design, since it can take a long time to develop a new system, for example. But sometimes it is the social design that forces the phasing, for example, when a major education and training program is needed.

This task describes the jobs, management methods, and organization structures at points intermediate between the current situation and the final process design. It also identifies the changes needed to effect the transitions.

TASK 4B.10—DESIGN CHANGE MANAGEMENT PROGRAM

This is the single most important task in Rapid Re, for far more reengineering projects fail for lack of effective change management than because their technical or social designs are flawed. This task refines and expands upon the Plan Change drafted in Task 1.4.

The task begins with identification of the stakeholders and their likely issues. Some stakeholders are people holding the same jobs; they usually have common interests so the job can be treated as the stakeholder. Other stakeholders (typically managers) hold unique jobs, so the stakeholder is the individual. When the program is executed, however, each person must be treated as an individual, regardless of his or her job. For each stakeholder, this task identifies expected avenues of resistance and defines measures of the level of resistance or buy-in. It then plans a communications program, a program to assess buy-in and intervene if necessary, and a general education and training program for all personnel.

TASK 4B.11—DESIGN INCENTIVES

The purpose of this task is to align individual, organizational, and process goals by defining incentives to motivate people to make the transition to the new process; achieve the planned levels of process performance; and commit to continuous improvement. The task also defines the measurements and feedback mechanisms needed to support the administration of the incentives. This is another example of Instrument and Informate. The principle followed is that incentives are most effective when the party being monitored is always aware of his/her current performance.

Incentives are usually monetary and nonmonetary awards and recognition. They should not be promotions since promotions should be based on capability, not performance.

Task 4B.12—Plan Implementation

This task will develop preliminary plans (to be refined in Stage 5) for implementing the social aspects of the reengineered process, including recruitment, education, training, reorganization, and redeployment. These plans will then be time phased, along with the parallel plans for implementing the technical aspects of the process, developed in Task 4A.10.

This task also defines the "governance structure" for Stage 5, that is, the roles and responsibilities of the reengineering sponsor, the process owner, the reengineering project manager, and other individuals and organizations. Typically, the information services and human resources functions play major roles in Stage 5.

Stage 5: Transformation

The purpose of this stage is to realize the process vision by implementing the process design produced in Stage 4. The Transformation stage produces pilot and full production versions of the reengineered process and continual change mechanisms.

Depending on the specifics of the process design and on the number and nature of its subVisions, some tasks in Stage 5 may be repeated. In other cases, the continual change mechanisms will be used to move from subVision to subVision.

The key questions answered by this stage include:

- ❏ When should we begin to monitor progress? How do we know if we're on the right track?
- ❏ What mechanism should we develop for solving unanticipated problems?
- ❏ How do we ensure the transition period goes smoothly?
- ❏ How do we continue to build momentum for ongoing change?
- ❏ What technique should we use to realign the organization?

Task 5.1—Complete Business System Design

In this and subsequent tasks, Rapid Re uses the nomenclature of information engineering. However, any proven method of system development is equally valid.

This task is concerned with the "external" design of the new or revised system supporting the reengineered process. It includes modeling subprocesses, modeling data, defining applications, and designing dialogs and screens. Alternatively, this task could involve the selection of a commercially available application package and the external design of any modifications.

TASK 5.2—PERFORM TECHNICAL DESIGN

The task selects the platform or platforms on which the system will be mounted. It designs the data and system structures, and it defines any prototypes required to validate the design. This task is concerned with the "internal" design of the new or revised system supporting the reengineered process. For packages, this task was already performed by the vendor.

TASK 5.3—DEVELOP TEST AND ROLLOUT PLANS

This task determines the methods to be used for system validation. These may include parallel or pilot testing. The task also determines the methods to be used for conversion and transition and develops a time-phased deployment plan. Finally, the task assesses the impacts of the new system and defines fallback and contingency plans.

TASK 5.4—EVALUATE PERSONNEL

This task assesses current personnel in terms of their skills, knowledge, orientation, the extent of their buy-in to the change, and their aptitude.

The assessment of aptitude is very important, because determination of the disposition of each person should be based on them and not on the job they hold. Some people are underqualified for their jobs, and other people are overqualified. And some people possess skills, knowledge, and orientation unrelated to their present job but very desirable in another job. The assessment of each person is then matched against the job requirements and staffing levels developed in Task 4B.4 in order to identify personnel shortages or excesses and training needs. The training needs from this task are then used to finalize the components of the education and training curriculum and to assign individuals to specific courses.

TASK 5.5—CONSTRUCT SYSTEM

This task produces an operations-ready version of the new process. It includes development and testing of databases, development and testing of systems and procedures, documentation, and data conversion.

TASK 5.6—TRAIN STAFF

This task provides training in the operation, administration, and maintenance of the new process, just in time for the staff to assume their new responsibilities. It also includes coaching as they assume those responsibilities.

TASK 5.7—PILOT NEW PROCESS

This task operates the new process in a limited area in order to identify any needed improvements or corrections without incurring the risk of a full deployment.

TASK 5.8—REFINE AND TRANSITION

This task corrects the flaws discovered during pilot operation and deploys the new process in a controlled manner in accordance with the rollout plan developed in Task 5.3.

TASK 5.9—CONTINUOUS IMPROVEMENT

In order that continuous process improvement take place, three requirements must be met:

1. Process personnel must be given clear performance goals, measures of goal attainment, and information on the current and past values of those measures.
2. Process personnel must be given the tools necessary to effect changes in performance.
3. Process personnel must be given the responsibility, authority, and incentives for improving performance.

The first two requirements were addressed by Task 4A.3—Instrument and Informate. The last two requirements were addressed by Task 4B.1—Empower Customer Contact Personnel. And the third requirement was also addressed by Task 4B.11—Design Incentives. In some cases, continuous improvement methods will be used to pursue the next subVision. Then performance gains will be continuous at those points. In other cases, some repetition of Stage 5 will be used to attain the next subVision, and discontinuous gains will be associated with the rollout. Then continuous improvement methods will be used *between* rollouts.

Appendix B

A Comparison of Reengineering Approaches

Since 1991, which marked the beginning of the Business Process Reengineering (BPR) approach and methodology called Rapid Re, there has been a broad rush to publication on many fronts. Business authors, consulting firms, and the academic sector have all been represented by a number of books based on a more-or-less common thought: Business must change radically to be competitive; changes must occur in core business processes; customer expectations determine the value-added character of these processes.

There has been a general acceptance of several terms of reference:

- ❏ *Business Process Reengineering,* which is the activity that analyzes the functioning and value of existing business processes and makes radical changes to dramatically improve their results, in the eye of the customer.
- ❏ *Breakthroughs* are radical changes in the way in which processes function. This is opposed to the incremental change represented by quality programs and other similar corporate initiatives.
- ❏ *Visioning* is the quasi-analytical process of describing the ideal state of a process, if all of the customers' expectations could be met.
- ❏ *Processes* are sequences of linked activities that take business inputs and produce business results (outputs).
- ❏ *Core Processes* are the fundamental processes of an organization

(developing new products/services, obtaining customer orders, fulfilling customer orders, etc.). These processes typically "cross" several organizational boundaries.

❑ *Value-Added Processes* are those processes whose results the customer considers important and which positively affect the buying decision.

While our approach is not based on the publications that are discussed here, these are important books by capable individuals. We find that there are both similarities (because we all tend to see the same problem) and dissimilarities (because the various authors have different ideas about how to solve the problem). This comparative analysis has been constructed to discuss the various approaches and the extent to which they coincide with our thinking.

Basis for Comparison

Our position with regard to BPR is quite straightforward:

❑ Contemporary corporate organizations and management structures have become obsolete: Business processes must radically change, along with the organization that structures their resources.
❑ Business objectives and goals, and thus strategies, must be driven by the needs of the customer.
❑ Employee empowerment is the key to improving decisions and the time they take, by moving the responsibility closer to the work itself.
❑ Information systems are not the reason for undertaking BPR but instead are the "enabler" of the changes that BPR designs.
❑ The primary concern of business management today is not simply understanding the need for change, but most important, how to make the changes in an economy of time, cost, and risk. We believe that a practical methodology is the essential complement to any present-day discussion of BPR.

We see as critical to any contemporary discussion of BPR the following points:

❑ Breakthroughs as opposed to incremental change
❑ A linkage of corporate (business) and process objectives

❑ A Change Plan to anticipate and neutralize resistance
❑ An Implementation Plan to put the "next steps" in concrete focus
❑ Clear roles and responsibilities for sponsors, reengineering teams, and consultants
❑ A Methodology that provides the missing "how to" that must follow the "why"

Now we will compare each of the listed publications to our position. This comparison is not meant to disparage the work of these authors in any way but rather to show how approaches vary. Our conclusions are also summarized in Figure B-1, Comparison of Reengineering Approaches, which appears at the end of this section.

1. Charlene B. Adair and Bruce A. Murray, *Breakthrough Process Redesign* (New York: AMACOM, 1994)

Adair and Murray discuss the Reengineering process, proposing BPR as two interlinked cycles: the first cycle determines which processes require reengineering, beginning with an understanding of the customer and market, and moving through a broad vision to determining business imperatives and strategies. The second cycle is the classic BPR approach. Both cycles are seen as being continuous, with BPR teams working on several projects in tandem. A six-step methodology is discussed in the course of the book, with a number of task sequences and documentation forms being specified. Several traditional management techniques appear in the methodology, including Work Flow Analysis, Cycle Time Analysis, and Benchmarking. Adair and Murray contend that most processes become obsolescent because they have been modified by changes and enhancements far beyond their original intent. The solutions produced by this methodology appear to be primarily redesigns of the processes. There is no analysis of the technologies being used or those necessary to implement the solution. In parallel to that, while teams of empowered employees are considered superior to current functional organizations, there is only a limited discussion about staff reorganization. Implementation of solutions is viewed as independent projects, and there is no integration of solutions or implementation plan.

Similarity to Rapid Re Approach

❑ Use of Steering Committee of "sponsors."
❑ BPR teams well organized and roles and responsibilities specified.

Figure B-1. Comparison of reengineering approaches.

Characteristic	Rapid Re™	Adair & Murray	Currid & Company	Davenport	Hammer & Champy	Hunt	Johansson, McHugh, Pendlebury, & Wheeler	Morris & Brandon	Nayak & Ketteringham	Tidy & Sherman	Tomasko
Reengineering Definition											
• Starting Point: Business Goals	Y	Y	Y	Y	Y	5	Y	Y	Y	Y	Y
• Focused on Process(es)	Y	Y	Y	Y	Y	Y	Y	Y	Y	Y	9
• Business/Process Goals Link	Y	Y	Y	Y	Y	Y	Y	Y	Y	Y	Y
• Value Added Priority	Y	Y	1	Y	Y	Y	Y	N	Y	Y	Y
• Customer Orientation	Y	Y	1	Y	Y	Y	Y	Y	Y	Y	Y
• Radical Change Proposed	Y	1	Y	Y	Y	N	Y	N	Y	Y	Y
• Extend BPR to Suppliers/Partners	Y	N	N	Y	Y	Y	Y	N	Y	Y	Y
Appropriate Application	Y	Y	N	Y	Y	5	Y	2	7	4	Y
Process(es) Addressed											
• Single	N	Y	8	N	N	Y	N	Y	N	Y	N
• Multiple	Y	Y	8	Y	Y	N	Y	Y	Y	Y	Y
• Value-Added	Y	Y	8	Y	Y	N	Y	3	Y	Y	Y
• Support	Y	Y	8	Y	Y	N	Y	Y	Y	Y	Y
Methodology			None	None	None	None			None		None
• Described	Y	Y	None	None	None	None	Y	Y	None	Y	None
• Adequate Detail	Y	Y	None	None	None	None	N	N	None	N	None
• Management Techniques Used	Y	Y	None	None	None	None	6	Y	None	11	None
• New Process Vision	Y	N	None	None	None	None	Y	N	None	Y	None
• New Process SubVisions	Y	N	None	None	None	None	N	N	None	Y	None
• Technical Design	Y	N	None	None	None	None	N	Y	None	11	None
• HR Design	Y	N	None	None	None	None	N	Y	None	11	None
• Addresses Barriers to Change	Y	Y	None	None	None	None	Y	Y	None	Y	None
• Implementation Plan	Y	N	None	None	None	None	N	N	None	11	None
Role of Automation											
• Starting Point	N	N	N	N	N	N	N	N	N	N	10
• Enabler	Y	N	Y	Y	Y	Y	Y	Y	Y	Y	10

Notes: 1. Not specifically stated; 2. Quality improvement is "given" objective; 3. Not always a determinant of priority; 4. Applicable to all aspects of the business; 5. Limited to quality improvement; 6. Limited to workflow and cycle time analysis; 7. Not a true BPR; 8. Not discussed; 9. Partially; 10. Technology not addressed; 11. Not specified.

❏ Very complete discussion of several analytic processes.
❏ Incorporation of appropriate management techniques for data gathering and analysis.
❏ Focus on customer "drivers" and value added processes.
❏ Identification of process inefficiencies.
❏ Measurement of results associated with solution implementation.

Important Differences

❏ On-going selection and reengineering of processes does not produce a cohesive Change Plan.
❏ Visioning is used only at the "executive" level and breakthroughs are the result of detailed reengineering, rather than from conceptualizing an "ideal" of how the process must meet customer expectations.
❏ Existing technology not identified.
❏ Technology plays no role as an enabler of the solution(s).
❏ Other than incorporating teams of empowered employees in the solution, there is no Social Solution.
❏ No Cost Benefit Analysis to allow the Steering Committee to make an informed decision.
❏ There is no Implementation Plan, only individual implementations.

2. Cheryl Currid & Company, *Computing Strategies for Reengineering Your Organization* (Rocklin, Calif.: Prima Publishing, 1994)

This well-organized and readable book is not about BPR. However, it can be of considerable value as an information resource for reengineering teams. Ms. Currid addresses three main topics: How business is changing, the role of information technology, and the state of the technology. This last topic is a constantly changing picture. The technological capabilities and availability that appear in this book will have undergone significant change themselves over the next very few years. However, the descriptions of the various technologies and their application will encourage reengineering teams in the visioning process to ignore technological constraints in their search for breakthroughs. The knowledge of what information technologies can accomplish will be a valuable adjunct when developing the Technical Solution.

In discussing change, the author proposes creating an environment for change. Directed at Information Systems professionals, she challenges them to "make the transition from being mainframe centered to being network centered, information centered, and, finally, people centered." This can be a necessary redirection in helping to reengineer the support process of application development.

Included in this book is a chapter on reengineering, which gives a brief, but complete overview of the BPR activity and its potential. There is the common focus on processes and the need for innovative thinking, based on questioning everything, including corporate assumptions and cultural constraints. Although the value-added aspect of customer-visible core process results is not mentioned specifically, a terse case history does illustrate the point. Within the context of reengineering, information technology is seen as an enabler of change, with expert systems given as an example of technology enabling a "nonexpert" employee to accomplish empowered tasks.

Similarity to Rapid Re Approach

❑ General agreement with definition of BPR and the team approach.
❑ Technology seen as the enabler.
❑ Radical changes needed to make imperative modifications to core processes.
❑ Inclusion of IS professionals on reengineering team.
❑ Impact of change on organization and staff is discussed.

Important Differences

❑ Not about BPR, but rather about technology as an enabler.
❑ No BPR methodology provided.

3. Thomas H. Davenport, *Process Innovation* (Boston: Harvard Business School Press, 1993)

Mr. Davenport's book is a discussion of virtually all aspects of BPR. Although the subtitle of the work is *Reengineering Work through Information Technology,* the author has not cast information technology in the role of the driver but rather as the primary enabler of change.

While there is no specific methodology included in the book, the chapter titles represent a sequence of activities, beginning with the identification and selection of processes with potential for innovation and continuing through an understanding of those processes and the information they utilize, the creation of a "vision" of possible innovation, to the improvement of the processes and the implementation of both the new processes and the organization now needed to manage and control the new work.

In addition to information technology as an enabler, Davenport makes the point that the human resource is equally important in effecting change. He contends that as information technology is critical to enabling change, the human resource and its organization is key to the implementation of change. The resulting job redesign and organization must motivate the employees and focus their capabilities on value-added work, and ongoing innovation. Innovation is not considered a project but rather a process.

Similarity to Rapid Re Approach

❏ Agreement with general definition.
❏ Focus on value-added processes.
❏ Senior management support is essential.
❏ Corporate and process objectives and goals must be synchronized.
❏ Visioning is the key technique to process innovation.
❏ Appropriate role of information technology.
❏ Technical and Social Solutions are equally important.
❏ Change management is necessary to anticipate and address resistance to change.

Important Differences

❏ No formal methodology.
❏ Reengineering team concept not explicitly addressed.

4. Michael Hammer and James Champy, *Reengineering the Corporation* (New York: Harper Business, 1993)

This very influential book has been instrumental in the development of a broad appetite for reengineering as a way to make the radical changes in business processes that can make the difference in corporate survival. The authors detail the obsolescence in contemporary organizational models which harken back to the emergence of the Industrial Revolution. Functional organizations, they contend, have little or no view of the processes that are actually what business does. Hammer and Champy propose reengineering (or, "starting over") as the direction to take rather than the incremental improvements in such current approaches as total quality or downsizing. Their solution (there is no methodology included in the book) is to establish reengineering teams that will develop "visions" of what must happen in order to produce the results that customers want. The visions, in turn, will determine how processes should function. The authors predict a "new world of work," where process teams will replace the traditional functional silos, and where the hand-offs and excessive controls will be reduced or eliminated, leading to greater process efficiency. Team members will be empowered to make more decisions and offer more complete service to customers.

Examples of reengineering are given (Hallmark, Taco Bell, Bell Atlantic, etc.) to show how reengineering has been successful and to point out many of its principles: achieving senior management acceptance, getting a clear set of goals, determining what the customer actually wants, focusing on processes, visioning the ideal, using technology as an enabler, and compressing organizations into process teams. The authors admit that too many reengineering efforts have not realized their potential. To counter this they identify and discuss a number of mistakes to avoid.

Similarity to Rapid Re *Approach*

❑ Makes the case for radical change to value-added business processes.
❑ Stresses the importance of customer expectations as the driving element.
❑ Gaining executive support is called critical to success.
❑ Uses visioning as a way of seeing what needs to be, rather than improving existing processes.
❑ Uses reengineering teams to address core processes.
❑ Uses technology as an enabler of solutions.
❑ Solution foundation includes process teams of empowered employees.

Important Differences

❑ No methodology provided.
❑ No explanation of how-to.
❑ Only limited direction as to what to do next.

5. V. Daniel Hunt, *Reengineering* (Essex Junction, Vt.: Oliver Wight Publications, Inc., 1993)

The author describes his reengineering process as Integrated Product Development (IPD). Although the primary focus of this redesign process is the optimizing of the Product Development Process, Mr. Hunt contends that IPD can be used to reengineer any of the processes within an organization, from financial to marketing. Taking somewhat of a different tack, this process is aimed at continuous change, rather than radical change. Radical change of processes is considered appropriate only when the company is under intense pressure and such draconian measures are the last resort. Radical change is portrayed as running counter to the culture of most organizations and one which the majority of senior managements will not accept. Hunt points out that many radical reengineering projects have failed or yielded indifferent results because the organizations could not tolerate large amounts of change, especially when a cultural change is required and the time frame is extensive.

IPD seeks to integrate the processes that begin at product conception and end with the completion of the design of the manufacturing process. While IPD acknowledges that the customer requirements are the primary driver, and senior management support is essential, the product and development process characteristic most prominent is quality. With quality in all phases of design, the author contends, customer needs will be met and the quality inherent in the activities and results of the reengineered process will positively affect cost, productivity, and profitability.

IPD is structured as a multidisciplinary team effort, with considerable attention paid to the current process, its flows, outputs, capacities and capabilities. The approach (no specific methodology is provided) makes extensive use of automated tools (CAD, CAE, CAM, CIM, and CALS) together with such quality tools and practices as statistical process control, benchmarking, and quality function deployment. A chart associates the various elements of IPD with major organizations that have reengineered the product development process, indicating the extent to which they utilized each tool and IPD principle. Case histories are discussed to support the data in the chart.

The IPD approach in its many phases is discussed at a relatively high level, with little or no emphasis on technical design, social design, or implementation.

Similarity to Rapid Re Approach

- ❑ Focuses on customer needs as a starting point (but considers quality as only dimension).
- ❑ Coordinates organization and process objectives and goals.
- ❑ Considers senior management support as essential.
- ❑ Utilizes multidisciplinary teams; augments teams as reengineering continues.
- ❑ Underscores importance of understanding the current process.
- ❑ Incorporates the use of management techniques and tools.

Important Differences

❏ Addresses only a single process.
❏ Includes no formal methodology.
❏ Has continuous, rather than radical change as an objective.
❏ Does not use visioning to develop breakthrough alternatives.
❏ Breakthrough changes would only be fortuitous, and incremental change is sought.
❏ Only partially specifies roles and responsibilities.
❏ Does not address Social and Technical designs.
❏ Does not discuss Change and Implementation Plans.

6. Henry J. Johansson, Patrick McHugh, A. John Pendleburg, and William A. Wheeler III, *Business Process Reengineering* (Chichester, England: John Wiley & Sons, 1993)

The four coauthors have conducted consulting assignments concerned with the improvement of the *functional* aspects of business. They have concluded that true meaningful change had to be liberated from the functional constraints of the existing paradigm and explore entirely new ground. Rather than settling for incremental change (no matter how continuous), they were now seeking breakthroughs, or what they call, "breaking the china." These would allow businesses to make the radical changes needed to leapfrog their competition in increasingly difficult markets—particularly those that were global in nature.

To "break the china" and then put it back together again, the authors have constructed an approach that focuses on core business processes, in particular those that provide value that is obvious to the customer. The approach, furthermore, aligns process goals with corporate goals, and incorporates measurable objectives. The approach has three distinct phases: Phase 1 Discover creates the strategic vision for either dominance or renewed competitiveness in the marketplace and determines what can be done to the core processes to help achieve that strategy; Phase 2 Redesign is directed to the detailing, planning, and engineering of the reengineering process; and Phase 3 Realize is concerned with the implementation of the redesign that will effect the strategy.

While each phase has several steps, these are discussed in a narrative format with brief examples of the work products associated with the steps. In a similar way, implementation and transitional organizations (moving toward a team-based, delayered organization) are examined and suggestions made as to how to proceed. The use of technology as an enabler of change and the empowerment of employees is acknowledged but is put beyond the scope of this book.

Similarity to **Rapid Re** *Approach*

❑ BPR is directed toward radical change of core processes.
❑ Customers are drivers of corporate and process goals.
❑ Senior management support is essential.
❑ Visioning is the activity that leads to breakthroughs.
❑ Organizational flattening through employee empowerment and elimination of unnecessary functional control layers is stressed.
❑ Role of technology is acknowledged, along with empowering employees.

Important Differences

❑ Approach is more of a structured discussion than a work plan.
❑ Reengineering teams are implied but not described in any detail.
❑ Reengineering roles and responsibilities are incompletely described.
❑ Lack of common example in discussion of approach.
❑ Technical and social (human resource) solutions are not included.
❑ Planning for change and implementation is not addressed here.

7. Daniel Morris and Joel Brandon, *Reengineering Your Business* (McGraw-Hill, Inc., New York, 1993)

The authors present a methodology for BPR called Dynamic Business Reengineering (DBR). The approach consists of two major subdivisions: Positioning and Reengineering. The Positioning activity addresses the development of corporate strategies with specific goals and quantified objectives. In addition, a model of the current business is produced using Business Activity Maps (BAM). These and other "change data" are maintained by a chief change officer (CCO). The intention here is to effect a shift to a Change Paradigm, within which context change can be continuous. Once the Positioning activity is established, the model can be analyzed and Reengineering projects identified. These are then the second activities of DBR. Reengineering is done by project teams, utilizing a nine-step methodology, which is a traditional project management approach, beginning with the identification of opportunities, the definition and evaluation of alternative solutions and the selection and implementation of the most appropriate course of action. Following completion of the Reengineering project, the Positioning baseline model and data are updated to set the stage for subsequent change.

The methodology, which incorporates a number of traditional management techniques (particularly for business and work flow modeling) is described in a narrative fashion, without specific tasks and work products.

In addition to providing a vehicle for continuous change, DBR, while focused on business processes, seeks improvements in quality and service, with resulting cost savings and revenue increases. Although significant changes are the subject of initial Reengineering projects, they are not characterized as being "radical" or "breakthrough" changes.

Similarity to Rapid Re Approach

❏ Customer value perception and orientation is the driver for change.
❏ Essential first step is the statement of corporate objectives and goals (Positioning) and developing senior management support.
❏ Require understanding of the primary elements for Reengineering success.
❏ Current business operations (processes) are mapped and analyzed.
❏ Acknowledges that changes in one process will affect others.
❏ Uses management techniques in the methodology.
❏ Insists on near-term results.
❏ Incorporates both technical and human resources design in the solutions.
❏ Considers information technology as prime "enabler."

Important Differences

❏ Does not target radical or breakthrough changes.
❏ Visioning is not included in methodology; processes are "improved" rather than dramatically changed.
❏ Methodology is in the form of a narrative discussion, without specific steps, tasks, and work products.
❏ Focuses on continuous change as the Reengineering process.
❏ Focuses on quality improvement as a given objective of Reengineering.
❏ Lacks a Change Plan.
❏ Lacks a formal Implementation Plan that integrates all projected changes; no subvisions for multiple year efforts.
❏ Does not specifically state roles and responsibilities of team members.

8. P. Raganath Nayak and John M. Keeteringham, *Breakthroughs!* (San Diego: Pfeiffer & Company, 1994)

This book does not propose a methodology for BPR. Rather, it is a collection of case studies of breakthrough thinking, aimed at encouraging the reader to emulate the creative process that led to these radical changes. Changes of this nature are considered absolutely essential to meeting and beating the competition. Catch-up is a game that is doomed to produce only "me-too" results, which simply will not be enough.

Although the case studies are almost all involved with conceptualizing and developing a commercial product or service, the analytical process is applicable to general BPR. This is particularly true when it comes to understanding the customer and the market, and "visioning" an ideal solution.

The stories of Federal Express are typical of most of the others. The idea of setting up a "hub and spoke" network to collect packages (in this case) and redistribute them was not new. The U.S. Postal Service had looked at it and discarded it as impractical. Others had developed a similar hesitation, faced with the large amounts of planes, trucks, distribution centers, and people that had to be in place on Day One. But Fred Smith was not dismayed. He had embraced the idea as a college student writing a business paper. From that day until Federal Express became a reality, Smith met continuous resistance and frequent temporary failures with an unmatchable spirit, born of his own convictions in his "vision" and people who shared his dream: people who became the "thinking and doing" resource of the company.

Similar studies explore the innovativeness and breakthrough thinking that led to the Sony Walkman, Club Med, 3M Post-It notepads, and the CAT Scanner. In almost all instances, one central figure stands out: the person with vision and perseverance who uses other "believing" people to get the job done and see the vision through to completion.

Similarity to Rapid Re *Approach*

- ❑ Radical change to business processes (notably new product/service development).
- ❑ Visioning as a way of breaking out of the existing paradigm.
- ❑ Use of people (teams) to expand and implement vision.
- ❑ Focusing on the needs of customers and markets (and, in some cases, inventing the market).
- ❑ Making process and corporate objectives and goals coincide.
- ❑ Technical and Social solutions inherent in the design of new products and services.

❑ Technology as an enabler is acknowledged, along with the empowerment of workers.
❑ Implementation plans thought through before committing to the new enterprise.

Important Differences

❑ No formal methodology (none intended); instead the use of case studies to show the approaches of the innovators.
❑ No formal Change Plan, but resistance is anticipated and met.

9. Noel M. Tichy and Stratford Sherman, *Control Your Destiny or Someone Else Will* (New York: Doubleday, 1993)

In 1980, Jack Welch was appointed CEO of General Electric. What he found was an organizational dinosaur, with eroding profits and market share, saddled with ailing businesses. Long the proponent of scientific management, GE had become an obsolete pyramid with layer upon layer of management, which effectively insulated senior management from market realities and workers from management directives. The new specter of global competition made the need for change imperative.

This book is an extended case study of how Jack Welch took on the monumental challenge of turning GE around and positioning it for not only survival, but for unparalleled success. His plan covered three distinct stages: the first stage awakened the organization to the need for change and featured staff reductions, deacquisitions, and the setting of immediate business goals (to be first or second in every market served); the second stage created a blueprint for the future based on a vision of a totally new organization dedicated to innovation and productivity. The last stage featured the creation of structures to institutionalize the organization's vision. No small task, the third phase is still in progress, ten years after Welch started. Incredible changes have been made—against broad-based resistance in GE. But the measures of success are there: revenues have nearly doubled, net income in dollars has almost tripled, and productivity has risen by over 400 percent.

Welch's approach to world-class innovation and productivity involved first accepting reality and acting accordingly (hence the deacquisitions and staff reductions), next removing all of the insulating layers of management and pushing responsibility deep into the pyramid, making employees more responsive to customers. Most important, with decision making at the operating level of the businesses, employees can then face reality and do what is necessary, without orders. Employees were encouraged to believe that they owned the business.

The author characterizes the entire change process as a "revolution" due to elimination of the "old way" paradigm and the impact of dramatic change. While Welch drove GE to change and was only interested in quantum changes, Tichy, who later headed the management training facility, institutionalized the approach in "Work Out" sessions, which used employee teams to envision solutions to problems, and which are now involved in continuous, incremental change.

Although the book contains no specific methodology, the principles of making change are shown through many examples of innovation and productivity improvements in the company. Tichy ends with a "Handbook for Revolutionaries," which coaches would-be revolutionaries and provides a challenging self-test to determine if change is needed.

Similarity to Rapid Re *Approach*

❏ Business objectives and goals are the starting point.
❏ Customer satisfaction is a primary goal.
❏ Productivity improvements lead to other benefits: cost reduction, price flexibility, etc.
❏ Value-added is a watch word ("if it isn't necessary, don't do it").
❏ Radical change is proposed to processes and organizations.
❏ Use of Transformation (reengineering) teams is addressed.
❏ Visioning process is used to project ideal operations that are free of the problem or that exploit the opportunity.
❏ Customers and suppliers are included in the problem analyses.
❏ Employee empowerment is key to making changes and maintaining productivity.
❏ Methodology is based on work experience.
❏ Information technology is seen as an "enabler."

Important Differences

❏ Methodology is based on energizing and motivating people to envision changes—not a specific step process with predetermined outputs.
❏ No specific technical or social designs, although implications are discussed.
❏ No formal implementation plans.
❏ No apparent integration of change efforts, although a high-level management council oversees the work.

10. Robert M. Tomasko, *Rethinking the Corporation* (New York: AMA-COM, 1993)

In considering the organization, its purpose, its construction, and its future, Tomasko borrows heavily from the field of architecture. This borrowing takes the form of applying architectural principles ("form follows function") to organizational design and also making the case for viewing organizational restructuring as more an art than engineering.

Although the main thrust of this book is in describing the process by which an organization can be structured to have the flexibility to meet the changing nature of markets and customer demands, the process, when viewed from this perspective, has a good deal to do with BPR. This is so because one of Tomasko's principles is to take a top-down look at the capabilities and competencies of the organization. Different from the strategic planners' "What business do we want to be in?" this introspection asks, "What are we good at?" And this discussion includes the capabilities and competencies that form the processes of a company. Part of the process in changing the organization's architecture is to "resize" or make more efficient those processes that matter to the customer (or, the processes that support the valued results).

The Resizing process, which concerns BPR most directly, takes both a top-down and a bottom-up view: top-down looks at the strategic use of capabilities, identifying those which are cutting edge, critical, core, or complementary. The strategies necessary to leverage such capabilities include acquisitions, spin-offs, deacquisitions, joint ventures, shutdowns, etc. The bottom-up view seeks to achieve simplicity, speed, and balance in business processes. Thus, the result is a focus on strategic capabilities that can be made as efficient as possible, improving capabilities and competencies.

Once the reengineering design is completed, the Reshaping process redefines jobs, working relationships, empowerment, and management control. Next, the rearchitected organization is defined, based on the true work (processes) of the organization. The processes now are focused on the customer.

Tomasko sees the resulting organization as much more horizontal, with "enterprise units" organized around customer needs, with process teams replacing functional departments, and overhead activities being bundled into "internal service centers" or outsourced.

Similarity to Rapid Re *Approach*

❑ Business and process objectives and goals are aligned (and focused on building and exploiting capabilities and competencies).

❏ Use of process teams as the building blocks of the organization.
❏ Delayering the organization by removing redundant control functions.
❏ Making breakthrough improvements in core processes.
❏ Social Solution is critical to implementation.

Important Differences

❏ The approach is essentially organizational restructuring, which depends to some extent on the optimizing of business processes.
❏ No reengineering methodology as such.
❏ The role of technology is not addressed.

Evaluative Characteristics of Reengineering Approaches Included in Figure B-1

Comparisons in this section have been made to the Rapid Re methodology. Thus, we consider that:

❏ *Reengineering definition* should encompass the development of radical changes in value-added business processes, where that value is determined by customer perception.
❏ *Appropriate application* means that the reengineering process should be directed at core business processes rather than their results (how new products are developed, not to develop a new product).
❏ *Process(es) addressed* means that the reengineering process should consider all strategic, value-added core processes. Concentration on a single process may well result in improvements in one place that compromise results in a process not considered.
❏ *Methodology* is the practical how-to that is an essential part of a reengineering approach. This satisfies senior management's need for a way to produce tangible results not just an interesting thought piece.
❏ *Role of automation* is important because information technology is the prime enabler of business process change, but it should not be used as the reason to do reengineering in the first place.

Appendix C

Examples

Many corporations have successfully employed reengineering to effect performance breakthroughs in their respective industries. Summary overviews of some of these cases are provided to illustrate how real companies have applied reengineering to address pressing business problems. The cases show several key features of reengineering projects, including:

❏ Reengineering focus on value-added processes and activities
❏ Achieving breakthrough performance measured in business results
❏ Reengineering's applicability to market leaders, as well as followers
❏ Reengineering as a vehicle for employee empowerment

First, reengineering focuses on enhancing the value offered to customers, something the customers care about and will pay for: the value-added. The most significant point of the U.S. Sprint and Connecticut Mutual Life Insurance case studies is that they directly impact key aspects of the provision of service to the customer. In the case of U.S. Sprint, customer turnover was directly reduced as an effect of the reengineering initiative. In both the U.S. Sprint and Connecticut Mutual Life cases, customers only have to call one source for information, where before they were aggravated at needing to make calls to several places for information.

Second, reengineering generates breakthrough productivity gains measured in terms of business results, i.e., enhanced profit or reduced costs. In the case of Corning Asahi Video CAV, the company was operating at a loss four years in a row. Through reengineering, the company reduced its cost-per-order by 75 percent and simultaneously cut order response time in half. The reduction in cost-per-order is a bottom-line business result. The improvement in the process measure "order response time" is important, but ultimately reengineering measures its net effect in terms of bottom-line results.

Third, just because a company is number one does not mean that they don't need to reengineer. Faced with increasing competition, the largest U.S. provider of standardized achievement testing for primary and secondary education (CTB Macmillan/McGraw-Hill) used reengineering to further secure its dominant position by cost-reduction and service turnaround times.

Fourth, reengineering is a powerful vehicle for employee empowerment. Both the NYNEX/New England and Pepsi case studies are examples in which reengineering empowered employees by eliminating non–value-added activity so that they could focus on their core work.

Of course, no reengineering project is one-dimensional. Each of the case studies demonstrates many other interesting aspects of reengineering in addition to the characterizations shown above.

Company:	**U.S. Sprint,** the third largest U.S. telecommunications company
Business Issues	• Rapid technology change and fierce competition • Customer service and billing processes failed to keep pace with rapid expansion of the business • A need to increase customer satisfaction and retention • Desire to better position Sprint for the future
BPR Goals	• Increase responsiveness to customers • Increase speed and flexibility of core processes • Control costs
BPR Scope	• Companywide, including product development, service delivery, sales and order processing, billing, and customer service processes
BPR Actions	• Focused reengineering efforts on processes that directly get customers, create value for customers, or have an impact on customer satisfaction • Entrusted each target process to a business unit executive, who headed up the effort and will maintain "ownership" of the process for three years • Removed functional barriers between departments to integrate target processes and established cross-functional teams

- Put in place cross-functional monthly, full-day meetings to track process performance
- Aligned information systems (IS) with the business to support companywide reengineering and involved IS in earliest product planning phases
- Used training and communication infrastructure from existing quality program to emphasize customer service, process orientation, and results to Sprint's 43,000 employees
- Used client/server architecture, customized applications on OS/2 based workstations, and computer-aided, software engineering tools and shared information warehouses to improve productivity and effectiveness
- Instituted an invoice-processing system wherein service agents review accounts every six months to ensure that customers are signed up for the most appropriate service that will meet their calling needs and save them money.

BPR Results
- One hundred percent on-time billing for the year
- Significant reduction in customer turnover rate
- Forty percent faster product development
- Billing inquiries handled in 45 seconds instead of 24 hours
- Less departmentalization

Company: **Connecticut Mutual Life Insurance,** the sixth oldest American life insurer with 1.3 million policyholders ($1.25 billion in premium income)

Business Issues
- S&P and Moodys downgraded the company's financial rating
- Three hundred employees out of 2,200—more than were expected—took advantage of an early retirement option, leaving remaining employees overburdened with the work of those who retired
- Fragmented operations and unconnected systems made it necessary for policyholders and agents to interact with several different departments of the company to meet their service needs
- Labor-intensive and paper-intensive legacy pro-

cesses and process flows marked by inconsistency, redundancy, serial processing, and hand-offs
- Rising costs
- Need to provide high-quality service

BPR Goals
- Present policyholders and agents with a uniform view of the company and one-stop service
- Speed response to customers and reliability
- Improve operating productivity
- Provide access to information and people
- Eliminate paper dependence
- Produce significant return on investment

BPR Scope
- Initially policyholder services and claims processes at its individual life insurance division

BPR Actions
- Secured senior management sponsorship and participation
- Assembled cross-functional teams and sought to convert employee ambivalence to commitment
- Conducted benchmarking outside the insurance industry and collected feedback from agents and customers
- Used large-scale retraining, team building, and user participation to create empowered work teams
- Went from host-based applications that were configured to meet vertical business needs and restricted information sharing, to client/server imaging, document management, and relational database tools that provide service representatives with a client's complete record

BPR Results
- Productivity is up 35 percent
- Twenty percent fewer people are involved
- Response time to queries improved from five days to a few hours
- When a policyholder calls, service personnel can access and print consolidated policy statements in seconds, instead of two to three weeks
- Death claims can be processed in four to six days, instead of twenty-one days
- Paperless operation in individual insurance division

Company: **Corning Asahi Video CAV,** one of Corning Inc.'s oldest and largest business units and one of two U.S. suppliers of television glass

Business Issues:
- Lost millions between 1987 and 1991
- Customers were dissatisfied with processing time and the difficulty of placing orders
- Corporate management mandated change to quickly restore the forty-seven-year-old troubled business unit to profitability
- Basic queries about inventory and order status often could not be answered

BPR Goals
- Restore profitability by meeting customer demands more efficiently
- Decrease error and cost overruns
- Improve communications and access to customer information

BPR Scope:
- Order fulfillment process was selected to be reengineered first as an important pilot for other reengineering projects and a major corporatewide reengineering initiative for the $3.7 billion maker of Corning glassware

BPR Actions:
- Appointed the customer service manager as head of the reengineering project and assembled a twelve-person cross-functional team to redesign the process and implement the new one
- Executed a seven-stage improvement method for process analysis of cost/time
- Conducted internal studies and customer interviews and provided three-day sessions for all 1,200 employees to discuss the business and hear customer complaints
- Used an existing Corning process for handling new technology and new product development to regularly communicate with top management and select the right technology to support the process
- Replaced multiple disjointed systems and pieces of paper with an integrated system and centralized database
- Purchased a commercial software package to support the new design to speed implementation and reduce cost
- Expanded the role of customer service and consolidated customer service operations in one location to simplify process flow

	• Provided all employees with updated and relevant information about the reengineering effort
BPR Results:	• Reengineered in fifteen months at a cost of $570,000
	• Eliminated more than $1.6 million a year in errors and cost overruns
	• Reduced per order costs by 75 percent
	• Reduced personnel costs by $400,000
	• Cut fulfillment time in half (from 180 to 90 days)
	• Reduced the number of tasks from 250 to as few as nine
	• Provided greater flexibility and real-time access to information
	• Eliminated data entry errors because customer information is only entered once

Company:	**CTB Macmillan/McGraw-Hill,** the largest U.S. provider of standardized achievement tests for children in grades kindergarten through 12
Business Issues:	• Previous streamlining and restructuring efforts only produced minimal results
	• Bureaucratic operations
	• Customer service is slow and unresponsive
	• To maintain its dominant market share, it needed dramatic change
BPR Goals:	• Decrease the turnaround time needed to score tests from twenty-one days to ten days
	• Slash $1 million in operating costs per year
	• Increase operational responsiveness and efficiency
BPR Scope:	• Cross-functional pilot program in CTB's Test Scoring Division
BPR Actions:	• Assembled a project team including an outside consultant and representatives from human resources, customer service, finance, information systems, computer operations and marketing
	• Redesigned the business processes with consideration of all employees involved
	• Documented and studied every step in the test scoring process
	• Determined major deficiencies
	• Designed cross-functional teams to work together to

eliminate unnecessary work and provided training for new technologies
- Implemented new performance measures driven by customer assessment instead of management-by-objective
- Provided continuing training for each team leader and team member and communicated new policies to the scoring division's 250 employees

BPR Results:
- Slashed $1 million in annual expenses
- Reduced the number of steps in the scoring process from 154 to 68 in just three months
- Expect profits to increase 120 percent
- Expect turnaround time for scoring tests to go from twenty-one days to five
- Will save $2.4 million during the next two years
- Expect reengineering to ripple through entire corporation because of the example that CTB set

Company:
NYNEX/New England Telephone—The Interexchange Service Center (ICSC). ICSC is the focal point for interexchange customers, for example, AT&T, MCI, US Sprint, cellular and mobile carriers, radio and television common carriers, and end-user access companies

Business Issues:
- Low morale and poor image
- No accountability for customer service
- No mechanism existed to coordinate and track service requests and results
- Few employees knew enough about the entire process to keep the customer satisfied
- Customer surveys brought about the grim realization that the way business was done needed to be changed

BPR Scope:
- Companywide

BPR Goals:
- To change the organization's strategy, structure, and processes so that all employees are interested and involved in the processes
- To establish a customer-focused service team structure responsible for all processing and service support for a specific customer base

- To train employees to handle responsibilities simultaneously to increase organizational effectiveness

BPR Actions:
- Jobs were redesigned to service all customer needs and handle diversified tasks
- Customer relationship management was assigned to managers, and supervisors began to coach, advise, and oversee the entire order provisioning and billing process
- End-to-end account responsibility was established for service representatives
- Mechanized Report System (MRS) was installed that provides monthly performance statistics and evaluations
- Extensive training programs to develop multiple skills were introduced to the entire organization
- Information tools were implemented to provide communication and education of new methods, procedures, and system changes that do not require formal training

BPR Results:
- NYNEX/New England has strengthened its ability to retain customers and minimize losses to competition
- A study found that NYNEX/New England Telephone was rated as providing the country's best service to valued customers and as the best competitive telephone company in the United States
- Instead of speaking to several different employees about different issues, diverse functions are handled by one person
- Not one person became unemployed because of the reengineering process
- Employee job satisfaction increased
- Billing claims adjustments decreased by 64 percent
- Expenses have fallen significantly
- Overtime was reduced 90 percent
- Order errors were down to 1.6 percent from 5.8 percent

Appendix D

Biographies

Raymond L. Manganelli
President and CEO
Gateway Management Consulting

Ray Manganelli is president and CEO of Gateway Management Consulting, a New York-based subsidiary of Swiss Reinsurance that specializes in reengineering training, facilitation, and consulting. His consulting experience has focused on problem-solving in the areas of productivity improvement, process optimization, and customer satisfaction.

A pioneer of business process reengineering programs, Dr. Manganelli is the originator of the Rapid Re approach to business transformation, a modular management tool designed to reengineer work processes rapidly and cost-effectively. He is featured in the AMA's corporate training videos on "Reengineering the Future" and "Business Process Reengineering." He has been quoted in more than one hundred periodicals; has spoken before numerous management audiences in the United States, Europe, and South America; and has contributed to business publications including:

Across the Board	*Forbes ASAP*
Boardroom Reports	*Industry Week*
Business Week	*Journal of Business Strategy*
Executive Excellence	*Management Review*
Executive Forum	*Planning Review*

Dr. Manganelli's writings and speeches challenge senior executives to question orthodox views on reengineering and to develop rapid, high-impact solutions to complex business problems. Dr. Manganelli is course leader for the American Management Association's North American seminars on Business Process Reengineering and Reengineering the Information Systems Organization. He is also a featured speaker on American Airlines' in-flight program, Executive Edition of the Air.

Among the many associations that he has addressed are:

AMA's Purchasing, Transportation, and Physical Distribution Council
American Society for Quality Control
Association for Services Management International (Netherlands)
Association for Systems Management
Decision Support Center Forum
Department of Defense Forum
IBM Guide Executive Forum
Institute of Electrical and Electronic Engineers
Instituto IMAM (Brazil)
Insurance Accounting and Systems Association
National Security Industrial Association
Society for Information Management

The winner of five teaching excellence awards, Dr. Manganelli has taught at Columbia University and Virginia Polytechnic Institute and has lectured at Rutgers University, the University of Maryland, and the University of Central Florida. He is also a visiting faculty member at Columbia Business School's Executive Program in Business Administration.

As a consultant, Dr. Manganelli has directed and conducted reengineering and organizational improvement programs for more than a dozen companies in the insurance, manufacturing, and utilities industries, as well as for numerous organizations in the transportation, retail, and technology sectors. His client assignments have included work for Agway, Bloomingdales, Canadian Pacific, Citibank, Liberty Mutual, McKesson, Merrill Lynch, Norfolk Southern, Prudential, Southern Pacific, Swiss Reinsurance, Texaco, U.S. Air, and W.R. Grace.

Before joining Gateway, Dr. Manganelli was a principal at the Diebold Group, an international management consulting firm, where he developed business plans, IT plans, market strategies, competitive strategies, productivity improvement programs, and business start-up plans for Fortune 500 companies. Earlier, he served as head of advanced information systems for the government support systems division of the Harris Corporation.

Dr. Manganelli holds a Ph.D. from Columbia University, an M.A. from Middlebury College, and a B.A. from Rutgers University. He is an alumnus of the Columbia Business School's Executive Program in Business Administration and is a member of the Columbia Executive Association and the Society of Columbia Scholars.

A member of Phi Beta Kappa, Dr. Manganelli is the recipient of numerous grants, awards, and commendations.

Mark M. Klein
Executive Vice President
Gateway Management Consulting

Mark Klein is the managing director of management consulting services at Gateway, a New York-based management consulting and professional services firm. He has more than eighteen years of management consulting experience and has held senior-level positions in industry.

A leader in the development of business process reengineering methodologies and the architect of Gateway's Rapid Re approach to business transformation, Mr. Klein has directed reengineering assignments in North America, South America, and Europe. He has been quoted widely in the business press and authored articles for numerous publications, including:

Bank Administration	*Industrial Engineering*
The Banker's Magazine	*Information Systems Management*
Best's Review	*Information Week*
Bottomline	*Informatique Canadien*
Chief Information Officer	*Information Strategy*
Executive Excellence	*Journal of Cash Management*
Financial Executive	*Management Review*

Mr. Klein has also spoken before numerous national management audiences. Among the organizations that he has addressed are:

American Bankers Association
American Gas Association/Edison Electric Institute
Association of American Railroads
Association of Field Service Managers International
Association for Manufacturing Excellence
Digital Consulting, Inc.
International Quality and Productivity Center

National Council of Savings Institutions
Society for Insurance Research

A provocative and informative speaker, Mr. Klein has taught courses at the University of Illinois.

As a consultant, Mr. Klein has directed reengineering and consulting studies for utilities companies, financial institutions, transportation companies, and information suppliers. A representative sample of his assignments includes:

- ❑ An assignment to streamline and reengineer a transportation company's business processes.
- ❑ A program to reengineer a leading business information supplier's information collection processes.
- ❑ A strategy to merge the telecommunications and systems capabilities of two large railroads.
- ❑ A program to improve the service, quality, cost, and performance of a global bank's international transaction services.

Mr. Klein's consulting clients include AT&T, Blue Cross, CBS, Chevron, Citibank, Con Edison, Dun & Bradstreet, Liberty Mutual, Norfolk Southern, PSE&G, Prudential, Seagram, Southern Pacific, Texaco, and US Air.

Before joining Gateway, Mr. Klein was senior vice president at the Diebold Group, an international consulting firm. Earlier, he was a consulting manager at a Big Six accounting firm.

A member of Phi Beta Kappa, Mr. Klein received a B.S. from Queens College where he graduated magna cum laude. He holds an M.S. in mathematics from New York University and is a certified management consultant.

Glossary

activities   The major components of the work done in a process. Each activity consists of input-process-output.

benchmarking   The process of finding relevant benchmarks for one's processes and understanding the process differences that account for the differences in results.

benchmarks   Comparisons of specific results achieved by different organizations.

BPR   Business process reengineering.

breakthrough performance   Performance gains that are unreasonable to expect from a continuation of current management methods. May range from 30 percent to 1,000 + percent.

business process reengineering (BPR)   The rapid and radical redesign of *strategic, value-added business processes*—and the systems, policies, and organizational structures that support them—to optimize the work flows and productivity in an organization.

entities   The "things" we are concerned about, e.g., customers, employees, machines, orders, and products. Each entity is an abstraction, realized in one or more instances, e.g., John Doe, Mary Smith. Entities have *relationships*, e.g., a customer *places* an order. Each entity is described in terms of its *attributes* (e.g., age, sex).

full-time equivalent (FTE)   The amount of work done by one person working full-time, two people working half-time, etc.

informate   (vt) To provide information on the performance and/or status of a process or part of a process on a continual basis. Requires instrumentation and feedback.

instrument   (vt) To implement measures of performance and/or status, i.e., to install instruments of measure.

modularize   (vt) To divide a design into modules.

modules   Major subdivisions of a design.

process   A series of interrelated activities that convert business inputs into business outputs (by changing the state of relevant business entities).

social design   The design of the social elements of a process: jobs, staffing, organization, reporting relationships, training, incentives, direction, etc.

stages   Major components of the Rapid Re methodology:

Preparation	How do we do the project?
Identification	Where do we focus our attention?
Vision	What results do we want to produce?
Solution	How do we produce those results?
Transformation	How do we implement the solution?

stakeholder   Anyone who has a vested interest in a process and in the outcome of reengineering the process.

state   The condition of an entity, described by the value of its attributes.

steps   Subdivisions of activities.

subVisions   A series of interim visions, intermediate between the present reality and the fully realized vision.

tasks   Subdivisions of stages.

technical design   The design of the technical elements of a process: technology, systems, procedures, policies, etc.

value-adding activities   Those activities that add value (from the customer's viewpoint) to the products or services produced by the process.

vision   A high-level conceptualization of a desired result. Generally described in terms of economic and noneconomic performance and the work "lifestyle."

Related Readings on Reengineering

Books

Balm, Gerald J. *Benchmarking: A Practitioner's Guide for Becoming and Staying Best of Best.* Schaumburg, Ill.: Quality & Productivity Management Association, 1992.

Batten, Joe D. *Tough-Minded Leadership.* New York: AMACOM, 1989.

Camp, Robert C. *Benchmarking: The Search for Industry Best Practices that Lead to Superior Performance.* Milwaukee: ASQC Quality Press, 1989.

Davenport, Thomas H. *Process Innovation: Reengineering Work Through Information Technology.* Boston: Harvard Business School Press, 1993.

Deming, Edwards W. *Out of the Crisis.* Cambridge, Mass.: Massachusetts Institute of Technology, 1986.

Fombrun, Charles J. *Turning Points: Creating Strategic Change in Corporations.* New York: McGraw-Hill, 1992.

Goldston, Mark R. *The Turnaround Prescription: Repositioning Troubled Companies.* New York: Maxwell Macmillan International, 1992.

Hammer, Michael, and James Champy. *Reengineering the Corporation.* New York: Harper Business, 1993.

Harrigan, Kathryn Rudie. *Managing Maturing Businesses: Restructuring Declining Industries and Revitalizing Troubled Operations.* Lexington, Mass.: Lexington Books, 1988.

Harrington, James H. *Business Process Improvement: The Breakthrough Strategy for Total Quality, Productivity, and Competitiveness.* New York: McGraw-Hill, 1991.

Herzberg, Frederick. *Work and the Nature of Man.* Cleveland: Cleveland World, 1966.

Laurence, Peter J. *The Peter Principle*. New York: Morrow, 1969.

Maslow, Abraham. *Motivation and Personality*. New York: Harper & Row, 1954.

Nadler, Gerald, and Shozo Hibino. *Breakthrough Thinking: Why We Must Change the Way We Solve Problems, and the Seven Principles To Achieve This*. Rocklin, Calif.: Prima Publishing, 1990.

Porter, Michael E. *Competitive Advantage*. New York: Free Press, 1985.

———. *Competitive Strategy*. New York: Free Press, 1984.

Spendolini, Michael J. *The Benchmarking Book*. New York: AMACOM, 1992.

Stalk, George, and Thomas M. Hout. *Competing Against Time: How Time-Based Competition Is Reshaping Global Markets*. New York: The Free Press, a division of Macmillan, Inc., 1990.

Strebel, Paul. *Breakpoints, How Managers Exploit Radical Business Change*. Boston, Mass.: Harvard Business School Press, 1992.

Tichy, Noel M., and Stratford Sherman. *Control Your Destiny or Someone Else Will*. New York: Currency Doubleday, 1993.

Tomasko, Robert M. *Rethinking the Corporation*. New York: AMACOM, 1993.

Tushman, Michael L., and William L. Moore. *Readings in the Management of Innovation*. New York: Ballinger, 1988.

Walton, Richard S. *Up and Running*. Boston: Harvard Business School Press, 1989.

Watson, Gregory. *The Benchmarking Workbook: Adapting Best Practices for Performance Improvement*. Cambridge, Mass.: Productivity Press, 1992.

Weiss, Alan. *Making It Work: Turning Strategy into Action Throughout Your Organization*. New York: Harper Collins Publishers, 1990.

Whitney, John O. *Taking Charge: Management Guide to Troubled Companies and Turnarounds*. Homewood, Ill.: Business One Irwin, 1987.

Zuboff, Shoshana. *In the Age of the Smart Machine: The Future of Work and Power*. New York: Basic Books, 1988.

Selected Articles and Special Magazine Report Issues

"Benchmarking: a Special Report." *Financial World*, September 17, 1991.

Biesada, Alexandra. "Tired of Getting Blindsided? Study How the Competition Plans for Tomorrow." *Financial World*, September 29, 1992, p. 30.

Byrne, John A. "Paradigms For Postmodern Managers." *Business Week: A Special Report on Reinventing America*, 1992, p. 62.

Cringely, Robert X. "Made in Japan." *Upside,* July 1992, p. 47.

Hall, Gene, Jim Rosenthal, and Judy Wade. "How to Make Reengineering Really Work." *Harvard Business Review,* November-December 1993, pp. 119–131.

Hammer, Michael. "Reengineering Work: Don't Automate, Obliterate." *Harvard Business Review,* July-August 1990, p. 104.

Harrigan, Kathryn Rudie, and Michael E. Porter. "End-Game Strategies for Declining Industries." *Harvard Business Review,* July-August 1993, p. 111.

Kaplan, Robert B. and Laura Murdock. "Core Process Redesign." *The McKinsey Quarterly,* 1991, no. 2, p. 27.

Klein, Mark M. "Quality and Business Process Reengineering in IS." *Canadian Information Processing,* November/December, 1992.

Klein, Mark M. "Don't Outsource . . . Reengineer!" *Quarterly DEC Journal,* Spring 1993, pp. 57–62.

Klein, Mark M. "Business Process Reengineering: Opportunity or Threat for the IE?" *Industrial Engineering,* September 1993.

Klein, Mark M. "Reengineering Methodologies and Tools." *Information Systems Management,* Spring 1994, pp. 30–35.

Klein, Mark M. "CIO's Advised to 'Embrace the Enemy'—or Die." *Quarterly DEC Journal,* Spring 1994, pp 48–50.

Klein, Mark M. "Ten Precepts for Reengineering." *Executive Excellence,* June 1994.

Klein, Mark M. "Most Fatal Reengineering Mistakes." *Information Strategy,* Summer 1994.

Klein, Mark M. "The Virtue of Virtuality." *Best's Review,* October 1994.

Krass, Peter. "Building A Better Mousetrap." *Information Week,* March 25, 1991, p. 24.

Main, Jeremy. "How to Steal the Best Ideas Around." *Fortune,* October 19, 1992, p. 102.

Manganelli, Raymond L. "Define Re-engineer." *Computerworld,* July 19, 1993.

Manganelli, Raymond L. and Mark M. Klein. "Business Process Reengineering," *Management Review,* June 1994.

Manganelli, Raymond L. and Mark M. Klein. "Methodology Versus a Clean Sheet of Paper." *Management Review,* July 1994.

Manganelli, Raymond L. and Mark M. Klein. "Automated Tools for Reengineering," *Management Review,* August 1994.

Marsh, David. " 'Keep It Simple' Is Key to German Story of Success." *Financial Times,* November 11, 1991, p. 5.

"Quality: A Special Report." *Business Week,* January 15, 1992.

"Quality: A Special Report." *Business Week,* November 30, 1992.

"Reinventing Companies." *The Economist,* October 12, 1991, p. 62.

Short, James E. "Beyond Business Process Redesign: Redefining Baxter's Business Network." *Sloan Management Review,* Fall 1992, p. 7.

Sirkin, Harold, and George Stalk. "Fix the Process,.Not the Problem." *Harvard Business Review,* July-August 1990, p. 26.

"Strategic Outlook On Reengineering the IS Group: Special Section." *CIO,* June 15, 1993, pp. 31–59.

Thompson, James G. "Benchmarking Rules of Thumb: Using Comparative Analysis of Other Warehousing Operations Inside Warehousing and Distribution." *Transportation & Distribution,* July 1992, vol. 33, no. 7, p. 46.

Verity, John W. and Gary McWilliams. "Is It Time To Junk the Way You Use Computers?" *Business Week,* July 22, 1991, p. 67.

Index